The Audubon Society
Field Guide to
North American Birds

P9-BYQ-455

A Chanticleer Press Edition

The Audubon Society Field Guide to North American Birds

Eastern Region

John Bull and John Farrand, Jr.,
The American Museum of Natural
History

Visual Key by Susan Rayfield

Alfred A. Knopf, New York

This is a Borzoi Book
Published by Alfred A. Knopf, Inc.

Prepared and produced by
Chanticleer Press, Inc., New York.

Color reproductions by Nievergelt
Repro AG, Zurich, Switzerland.
Type set in Garamond by
Dix Type Inc., Syracuse, New York.
Printed and bound in Japan.

Published July 26, 1977
Reprinted fifteen times
Seventeenth Printing, October 1988

Library of Congress Catalog Card
Number 76-47926
ISBN 0-394-41405-5

CONTENTS

THE AUDUBON SOCIETY

ACKNOWLEDGMENTS

The authors are very grateful to Dean
Amadon for reading and commenting
on the manuscript, to Davis W. Finch
for his great help with problems
of field identification, to Joseph M.
Cadbury, Miklos D. F. Udvardy, and
Edith Bull for numerous helpful
suggestions, and to Angus Cameron for
much practical advice.
They would especially like to thank
Paul Steiner and the staff at Chanticleer
Press for the creative contributions and
effort that made this guide possible:
Milton Rugoff, Gudrun Buettner,
Massimo Vignelli, Susan Rayfield,
Mary Suffudy, Kathy Ritchell, Helga
Lose, and Carol Nehring.
Range maps were researched by David
Ewert, John Dunn, and Kimball Garett
and coordinated by Jill Farmer.

THE AUTHORS

John Bull, a leading authority on birds of the Northeast, has been on the staff of the Ornithology Department of the American Museum of Natural History since 1962. He is the author of two classics on Eastern birds, *Birds of the New York City Area* (1964) and *Birds of New York State* (1974), and has contributed articles on birds to various books and magazines. He has also served as a nature guide on tours around the world as well as in the United States, the Caribbean, and Australia. He has been a delegate to many meetings of the International Ornithological Congress and received a National Science Foundation grant in 1973.

John Farrand, Jr., has been on the staff of the Ornithology Department of the American Museum of Natural History since 1973. After studying birds at Cornell University, the University of Oklahoma, and Louisiana State University, he served in the Division of Birds at the Smithsonian Institution. He has published papers on birds in *The Wilson Bulletin* and other journals and made field trips throughout the United States and in South America, Europe, and Africa.

INTRODUCTION

Each year thousands of people take up the absorbing hobby of bird-watching or "birding." Regardless of their motives, their first goal is learning to identify the hundreds of species in their own region.

It is to make this step as simple—and pleasurable—as possible that this book has been prepared. Its pocket size and its format make it easy to carry into the field and consult on the spot. Take it with you. And welcome to the hobby, or sport, or science, of birding.

Geographical Scope
A number of American bird guides divide North America into eastern and western regions at the 100th meridian. This is an arbitrary line that bears no relationship to natural habitats. We have chosen a line (see map) that follows the 100th meridian from the Edwards Plateau in Texas and cuts northward through the Oklahoma panhandle but then curves west and runs along the Rockies through eastern Colorado, Wyoming, and Montana, and, in Canada, along the eastern foothills of the Rocky Mountains. Thus our line for the most part follows the Rockies, a natural barrier in the range of many eastern and western birds. Of course, many birds can and do pass over this barrier in both directions.

Slowly but surely the number of identical species found on both sides is increasing. Indeed, one ornithologist has predicted that by the year 2000 all the species in the United States will have reached California.

Photographs as a Visual Guide

There are two major ways of illustrating bird guides, each with its advantages and disadvantages: One is the traditional way, by means of paintings, and the other is a newer way, by means of photographs. We have chosen to use color photographs because it has become possible in recent years to get superb portrait photographs of almost every bird seen regularly in America. In using the work of America's leading bird photographers, we believe we are adding an exciting new dimension to what generally appears in guides illustrated by an artist. Every artist's rendering of a bird is his interpretation, whereas a good photograph captures the natural color and stance of birds as you will usually see them. In most instances it also shows birds in their habitat or natural setting, making identification that much easier. Finally there is the beauty itself of pictures made by outstanding photographers: this guide is meant to be a delight to look at as well as use.

How the Guide Works

Most field guides to birds are arranged according to families, that is, according to the bird's structural features. But these are often invisible or not evident to a novice. What a beginner or even an experienced watcher first notes when he glimpses a bird is its size, shape, and color. But if he then consults a standard field guide, organized by families, he must know what family the bird belongs to—whether it is a warbler, a vireo, a finch, or such—before he can locate it in the guide. What he generally does is page laboriously through the book until he comes on a drawing that resembles the bird he has seen. He must go through this trial-and-error procedure each time he uses the guide.

To avoid this hit-or-miss approach the photographs in this guide have been organized on visual principles, that is, by what you see. Thus the 584 photographs are arranged (in the first half of the book) according to a bird's shape and, in most cases, its color. Captions under each pictured species include the plate number (which refers to the photograph), the size of the bird, and the number of the page on which the species is described. If the photograph is not of a breeding male, that is also indicated.

Since you may be afforded only a brief glimpse of a bird, you must learn to note essential details quickly. Such essentials include the following:

Field Marks When you see a new bird, make note of such points as the size and shape of the bill (whether long or short, slender or stout, curved or straight), the tail (long or short, rounded, squared, wedge-shaped, notched, or forked) and the wings (long or short, rounded or pointed). Note any distinctive features such as a crest, or eye-rings, or wing bars, or a flashing white patch in the wings, tail, or rump. Many species have color patterns that identify them at a glance; by studying the pictures in this book in advance, you may be able to identify many species at first sight.

Relative Size It is useful to keep in mind the sizes of a few common species like the House Sparrow, Blue Jay, American Robin, and Common Crow so that you can quickly estimate the relative size of an unfamiliar bird.

Behavior Note what the bird is doing. Is it alone or in a flock? Is it foraging on the ground like a thrasher or is it walking like a starling or hopping like a sparrow? Is it foraging on high or feeding in foliage, like a warbler or vireo? Is it creeping about on the trunk of a tree; if so, is it hitching up the tree like a woodpecker or a creeper, or is it working its way headfirst down the trunk like a nuthatch? If the bird is in flight, is it flapping or soaring? If soaring, are the wings held horizontally, as in gulls and most hawks, or in a shallow V, as in the Turkey Vulture, Rough-legged Hawk, and Marsh Hawk? If in the water, is it feeding at the surface or diving? Make note also of the bird's voice or call.

What the Photographs Show
Most of the photographs show adult males, since these are characteristic of a species, but pictures of females, immatures (imm.), and males in winter plumage are also included when they differ significantly from the breeding male.

The photographs are grouped according to (*a*) obvious similarities in appearance, such as "Long-legged Waders" or "Duck-like Birds," or (*b*) a visible similarity in behavior or habitat, as in "Tree-clinging Birds." Sometimes (*a*) and (*b*) will coincide, as in "Chicken-like Marsh Birds," many of which not only look like each other but have much the same "life-style" and live in the same kind of habitat.

Groups
The groups are as follows:

Long-legged Waders
Gull-like Birds
Upright-perching Waterbirds
Duck-like Birds
Sandpiper-like Birds
Chicken-like Marsh Birds
Upland Ground Birds
Owls
Hawk-like Birds
Pigeon-like Birds
Swallow-like Birds

Tree-clinging Birds
Perching Birds

These broad categories are of course not
foolproof and are intended to serve only
as a starting point.
Within each of these major categories
the birds are grouped according to
other similarities. Thus, among the
Duck-like Birds the photographs of the
Canvasback and Redhead, or of the
American Goldeneye and Barrow's
Goldeneye, are shown together so that
they can be compared at a glance.
Similarly, among the Tree-clinging
Birds all the woodpeckers with barred
backs are placed together for easy
comparison.

Silhouette and   Preceding the photographs is a section
Thumbprint   showing silhouettes of birds typical of
Guides   their groups. For example, the group
Long-legged Waders is represented by a
silhouette of an ibis; and each type of
bird within the group, such as spoonbills
and bitterns, is also represented by a
typical silhouette. To make it easy to
locate each group a silhouette typical
of the group has been inset as a
"thumbprint" on the left of all the
picture spreads in that section.

Perching (Song)   The perching birds are by far the
Birds Grouped   largest category, but the term is now
by Color   technically restricted to the small
songbirds that make up the group
known as the passerines. But we have
included additional species that we
thought belonged best in this section,
such as cuckoos and kingfishers. Because
songbirds are so numerous these birds
are arranged according to their most
prominent color (whether overall color
or only a distinctive patch) in the
following eight groups:

Yellow
Orange/Rust
Red

Gray
Blue
Olive/Green
Brown
Black

This color arrangement of the perching birds depends, of course, on such factors as the light in which a bird is seen or even on individual judgment as to color, and a few birds, such as the multicolored Painted Bunting, do not fit into any simple color category. We have placed each species in the color category where it seemed to fit best. Since most birds the average birder will see are perching birds, this color key will help you make a more rapid initial identification.

Females are usually much duller in coloring and can sometimes be identified only when one knows the male. But after a little practice the reader will surely find our inclusion of distinctive females helpful.

We have also included the different plumages or color phases of some species. For a few birds that are uncommon or of very restricted range no satisfactory color photographs were available. These birds are fully described in the text and each is shown in a drawing next to the description.

Finally, following this Introduction, under the title "How to Use the Keys" is a sample of how to use this book to identify a particular bird.

Text Descriptions Arranged by Habitat   In the text, birds have been grouped according to their primary habitats, giving the reader an additional check on the identification that began in the picture section. The habitat groups are as follows:

Open Ocean
Seashore
Salt Marshes
Freshwater Marshes

Lakes, Ponds, Rivers
Florida Swamps and Keys
Grasslands
City Parks and Suburban Areas
Thickets and Second Growth
Texas Thickets and Second Growth
Deciduous Forests
Coniferous Forests

Note that two of the above categories are partly geographical as well as ecological: "Texas Thickets" and "Florida Swamps and Keys." Both Texas and Florida have a number of species found nowhere else in the eastern United States and grouping these together makes identification in those states much easier.

Before setting out on a field trip to a particular habitat, the reader should glance through the section in the text describing the birds in that habitat in order to get some idea of the species likely to be encountered. Thus in a coniferous forest the birder knows that the owl seen will be one of five species and not a dozen others.

Species Descriptions English and Scientific Names The English, or common, names of birds are those accepted in the 1957 edition of the American Ornithologists' Union's *Check-list of North American Birds,* as revised in the 32nd supplement in 1973, and in the 33rd supplement in 1976. Where a bird's name has been changed recently by the A.O.U. we have included its former name in quotation marks.

Every bird has a scientific name consisting of two Greek or Latin words. The first word is the genus and the second is the species. The genus, which is always capitalized, includes a number of species. Thus, the scientific name of the Mallard, *Anas platyrhynchos,* tells us that it is a member of the genus *Anas,* which includes most of the surface-feeding or dabbling ducks in North America and elsewhere. The species name, *platyrhynchos,* describes the Mallard duck specifically. Since a bird's common name varies not only from country to country but often from region to region, its scientific names identify it everywhere and provide ornithologists with an international language. These scientific names also tell us what species are in the same genus, family, and so forth. Often the Latin or Greek names reveal an interesting fact about the history or biology of a species or they honor an ornithologist or bird artist; we have included such information wherever it seems particularly interesting.

Under the species name we have given the family name in Latin and its English equivalent, or where there are several large groups in a family, the names of each group.

The description of each species covers all or almost all of the following:

Size   Measurements of average overall length (from tip of bill to tip of tail) of each species are given in inches, along with the metric equivalent. Since measurements of either living birds or museum specimens depend on the way they are measured as well as the individual bird, such measurements are approximate.

Wingspread measurement (W.) is given for many of the larger birds.

Description: This opening paragraph covers physical
Color and   characteristics and plumage. In general,
Plumage   the most striking or distinctive features or field marks are italicized. While a few species like the Blue Jay and the Common Crow look much the same throughout the year and at every age, in many birds the plumage varies with age, sex, or season. In the Starling, for example, adults of both sexes look alike, but young birds, instead of being glossy black like the adults, are grayish-brown; adults have white spots,

and in summer a yellow bill. Breeding plumage is usually the brightest plumage in both sexes and is generally worn in spring and summer.

The young of some species, such as the Herring Gull, pass through a number of distinct plumages before they acquire the final adult plumage. In many species the male and female differ in appearance, but the young bird looks like the female; in the Cardinal, for example, the adult male is bright red, while the female and young are duller and browner. Many species show seasonal variation: male Scarlet Tanagers are bright red during the breeding season but in the fall acquire an olive-green plumage not unlike that of the female. These variations in plumage may be puzzling at first, but one soon learns to recognize the major variations in each species.

Where several species resemble each other closely, we have described the features that distinguish them. Certain birds such as some of the hawks, ducks, swallows, and gulls are likely to be glimpsed in flight. To help in recognizing them on the wing many drawings of birds in flight have been added.

Voice   Since most species have distinctive call notes and songs, a brief description or a simple phonetic transcription is given for all species. Indeed, a few birds are more readily identified by voice than by appearance. Although one can now obtain recordings of voices of many species, a knowledge of calls is best gained by experience with birds in the field.

Habitat   We next describe the habitat or habitats that this species prefers—beach, lake, deciduous forest, grassland, city park, suburb, and so forth—as well as the type of area preferred within the habitat. When a species has a different habitat during the winter from that occupied during the breeding season, that, too, is indicated. All the major habitats in eastern America are described in the pages preceding the species descriptions.

Nesting   The eggs, nests, and breeding habits of each species are described. The number of eggs given is that normally found in a nest; sometimes a larger clutch may be found, perhaps due to the fact that a second female has laid eggs in a nest.

Range   The geographic range is given for all species, even where the range extends beyond the area covered by the book. The breeding range is described first, followed by information on the North American portion of the winter range. Following a common practice, we have generally given the range of each species in clockwise fashion, that is, from west to east and then from north to south. In most instances we have named enough localities for the reader to be able to draw a usable line between the various points. Thus, when we say that the Nashville Warbler breeds from Saskatchewan, Quebec, and Newfoundland south to Connecticut, Pennsylvania, and Nebraska, a line drawn through the first three localities gives the northern limits of the species and another line drawn through the last three localities gives the southern limits in the East.
Range statements may be given in more detail in the West because there the mountains or local differences in rainfall create irregularities in the distribution of a species.

Range Maps   In addition to a statement of the geographic range, a range map is provided for species of more than irregular or casual occurrence within the area covered by this book. No range maps are provided for exclusively oceanic species. On these maps the following designations are used:

Breeding rage

Winter range

Areas in which a species occurs in both winter and summer are indicated by cross-hatching.

Permanent range

Notes At the end of each species descripion notes have been added on such subjects as behavior and feeding habits, population status, and lore.

How to Find Although it is almost impossible to go
Birds outdoors without seeing at least a few birds, some advance planning will enable you to increase the number of species you see on a field trip. Many birds tend to confine their activity to one particular habitat, so you should plan to visit as many different habitats as possible during a day of birding. A good system is to begin your field trip at dawn, going first to a freshwater marsh. Rails, bitterns, and other marsh birds are most active and vocal at that hour, and a few minutes in a marsh at sunrise can be more productive than several hours later in the day. From the marsh you can go on to woodlands, fields, or thickets. Until the middle of the morning most songbirds are busily searching for food and singing and are relatively easy to see. From midmorning until late in the afternoon land birds are quiet, while the birds of the beaches, lakes, and other aquatic or marine habitats are active all day. This, then, is the time to search for herons, cormorants, ducks, and sandpipers. Late in the day land birds start singing and foraging again, so you can return to woods and other inland habitats to spot

the species you may have missed in the morning. To round out a full day of birding, make an after-dark visit to a forest or wooded swamp to listen for owls.

The greatest variety of birds can be seen during the migration seasons. It is, therefore, a good idea to plan several field trips during the spring and fall. In spring the best time to search is during the latter half of April and the first half of May, when most of the songbirds migrate north through eastern North America. Most migrating birds fly at night, breaking their journey during the day, when they rest and feed. They tend to gather in quiet places where food is easy to find. In a light woodland along a stream, where there are newly opened leaves and an abundance of small insects, it is possible to see as many as two dozen species of warblers in a single spring morning. Migrating songbirds also concentrate in isolated groves of trees along the coast or in the prairie, and in well-planted city parks. When the land bird migration tapers off in late May, sandpipers and plovers are still flying through. Now is the time to visit beaches, lakes, and marshes. The fall migration is under way by August, when the first of the sandpipers and plovers reappear. In September and October most of the song birds pass through. The migration of ducks, geese, and other water birds continues into November; visits to lakes and bays will pay dividends then. While many species are rather tame, others are shy or secretive. Learn to move slowly and quietly and to avoid wearing brightly colored clothing. Some of these elusive birds can be lured into view by an imitation of the sound of a bird in distress, or by a whistled imitation of a Screech Owl. Rails and certain other secretive species can be attracted by playing tape recordings of their calls.

PARTS OF A BIRD

The generalized drawing of a bird on the following two pages shows the external parts of a bird that are mentioned frequently in the species descriptions in this book. Definitions of terms that are not in everyday use may also be found in the Glossary, on pp. 749–754.

Crown

Eye-stripe / Forehead

Nares

Auriculars / Upper mandible / Lower mandible

Nape

Chin

Side of neck

Throat

Mantle

Back

Breast

Scapulars / Bend of wing

Shoulder

Wing coverts

Side

Secondaries

Rump

Flank

Abdomen or Belly

Upper tail coverts

Primaries

Under tail coverts

Tail feathers or Rectrices

Tarsus

HOW TO USE THE KEYS

Example
A Bird Clinging
to a Tree Trunk
You have seen a streamlined, sparrow-sized bird with a longish bill creeping down the trunk of a maple or other deciduous tree. It was grayish blue, with a white face, black cap and light-colored breast.

1. To make sure it is one of the Tree-clinging Birds, check the typical silhouettes preceding the entire color section.
2. Turn to the photographs in the group labeled Tree-clinging Birds.
3. Among the 20 photographs in this color group, all showing birds clinging to the trunks of trees, some have red on cap or body, several have black, and one is brown. Only two, the White-breasted Nuthatch and the Red-breasted Nuthatch, have grayish blue backs and a black cap.
4. Under the photographs you find the numbers of the pages on which the two nuthatches are described. The Red-breasted Nuthatch is described in the habitat section labeled Coniferous Forest, while the White-breasted Nuthatch is described among the Deciduous Forest birds and, like the bird you saw, it has white underparts. Although both habitually creep downward on tree trunks, your bird was plainly the White-breasted Nuthatch.

Example
Birds Flying
Over a Beach

You have seen several birds flying overhead that have white bodies with gray backs, white tails, yellow feet, and yellow and black bills.

1. You turn to the bird silhouettes at the opening of the color section and find that your birds look most like the gulls found on Plates 31–39 and 41–57.
2. After glancing at the color plates, you find that the Herring Gull, Ring-billed Gull, and Glaucous Gull all resemble the birds you saw. But the Glaucous Gull has no black on its wingtips or bill, and the Herring Gull has pinkish legs and no black on its bill. Only the Ring-billed Gull seems to fit.
3. In the captions under the plates you find the page numbers on which these three birds are described. The descriptions confirm that the birds you saw were Ring-billed Gulls.

Part I
Color Key

Keys to the Color Plates

The color plates in the following pages
are divided into thirteen groups:

Long-legged Waders
Gull-like Birds
Upright-perching Water Birds
Duck-like Birds
Sandpiper-like Birds
Chicken-like Marsh Birds
Upland Ground Birds
Owls
Hawk-like Birds
Pigeon-like Birds
Swallow-like Birds
Tree-clinging Birds
Perching Birds

Thumb Prints To make it easy to locate a group, a
typical outline of a bird from that
group is inset as a thumb print at the
left edge of each double-page of plates.
Thus you can find the Long-legged
Waders by flipping through the color
pages until you come to a series of
thumb prints showing the outline of a
typical wading bird.

Silhouettes of To help you recognize birds by their
the Families in general shape, the color plates are
Each Group preceded by pages showing you
silhouettes of the families in each
group. If the bird you saw looks like
one of these silhouettes, you will find
the bird in that group.

Captions The caption under each photograph
gives the common name of the bird, its
size, and the page number on which it is
described. The color plate number is
repeated in front of each description as
a cross reference.
Most of the photographs show birds in
typical breeding plumage. Certain birds,
as indicated in the caption, are also
shown in distinctive immature or winter
plumage.

Symbol	Category
	Long-legged Waders

Family Symbols		Plate Numbers
	herons, egrets	1–8, 10, 13–16, 18–22
	storks	9
	spoonbills	11
	flamingos	12
	bitterns	17, 24
	limpkins	23
	ibises	25–28
	cranes	29–30

Symbol	Category
	Gull-like Birds

Family Symbols		Plate Numbers
	gulls	31–39, 41–57
	shearwaters	40, 79–81
	terns	58–69, 71–75
	skimmers	70
	gannets, boobies	76–78
	storm-petrels	82–83
	frigatebirds	85–86

Symbol	Category

Gull-like Birds

Upright-perching Waterbirds

Duck-like Birds

Family Symbols		Plate Numbers
	skuas, jaegers	84, 87–89
	tropicbirds	90
	auks, murres, puffins	91–98
	cormorants	99, 101–103
	anhingas	100, 104
	surface-feeding ducks	105–108, 112, 115, 119, 133, 135–144, 164
	diving ducks	109–110, 116–118, 120–127, 129–132, 145–158, 160

Symbol	Category
	Duck-like Birds

Family Symbols		Plate Numbers
	stiff-tailed ducks	111, 159
	mergansers	113–114, 128, 161–163
	coots	134
	whistling-ducks	165–168
	geese	169–172
	swans	173–174
	pelicans	175–176
	grebes	177–185
	loons	186–190

Symbol	Category
	Sandpiper-like Birds
	Chicken-like Marsh Birds

Family Symbols		Plate Numbers
	sandpipers	191–193, 197–202, 209–232, 245–246
	plovers, turnstones	194–196, 233–241
	phalaropes	203–208
	oystercatchers	242
	avocets, stilts	243–244
	gallinules	247–248
	rails	249, 251–254
	jaçanas	250

Symbol	Category
	Upland Ground Birds
	Owls

Family Symbols		Plate Numbers
	snipes, woodcocks	255–256
	quails, partridges, pheasants	257–258, 267, 274
	grouse	259–266, 268, 270
	turkeys	269, 273
	roadrunners	271
	chachalacas	272
	nightjars	275–278
	true owls	279–290, 292
	barn owls	291

Symbol	Category
	Hawk-like Birds

Family Symbols		Plate Numbers
	hawks	293–301, 311, 319
	kites	302–304, 320
	eagles	305, 307–308
	ospreys	306
	harriers	309–310
	caracaras	312
	falcons	313–316
	vultures	317–318

Symbol	Category
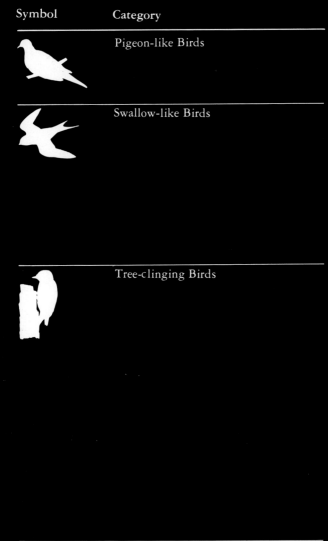	Pigeon-like Birds
	Swallow-like Birds
	Tree-clinging Birds
	Perching Birds

Family Symbols		Plate Numbers
	pigeons, doves	321–328
	swallows	329–334, 336
	swifts	335
	woodpeckers	337–352
	nuthatches	353–354, 356
	creepers	355
	wood warblers	357–361, 363–380, 382, 402–404, 444–448, 455–457, 460, 503–505, 509, 514, 563–564
	vireos	362, 383, 449–454

Symbol	Category
	Perching Birds

Family Symbols		Plate Numbers
	titmice	381, 427–428, 431–432, 511
	cardinals, grosbeaks	384, 399, 405–408, 414, 424, 439, 561–562
	buntings, finches, sparrows	385–386, 401, 409–413, 429, 437–438, 476–478, 513, 520, 527–545, 547–554, 557–559, 566
	orioles, blackbirds	387–388, 393–398, 515–519, 555, 560, 567–576, 583
	tanagers	389, 416–417, 442, 473–475
	flycatchers	390, 415, 418, 423, 426, 461–472, 512
	meadowlarks	391–392
	thrushes	400, 440–441, 498–502, 510

Symbol	Category
	Perching Birds

Family Symbols		Plate Numbers
	mockingbirds, thrashers	419–420, 494–497
	shrikes	421–422
	jays, magpies	425, 435–436, 483, 584
	becards	430
	kingfishers	433–434, 482
	gnatcatchers, kinglets	443, 458–459
	hummingbirds	479–481
	parrots	484

Symbol	Category
	Perching Birds

Family Symbols		Plate Numbers
	wrens	485–493
	waxwings	506–507
	bulbuls	508
	cuckoos	521–523, 577 578
	weaver finches	524–526
	pipits	546
	larks	556
	starlings	565
	crows	579–582

The color plates on the following pages are numbered to correspond with the number preceding each species description in the text. Most of the birds shown are adult males but also shown are some distinctive females and immatures and a few instances of seasonal changes in plumage.

7   Little Blue Heron imm., 25–30″, p. 406

8   Cattle Egret non-breeding plumage, 20″, p. 490

9 Wood Stork, 40–44", p. 478

10 "Great White Heron", 39–52", p. 478

11 Roseate Spoonbill, 30–32″, p. 380

13 Louisiana Heron, 25–30″, p. 381

15 Reddish Egret dark phase, 30″, p. 330

16 Little Blue Heron, 25–30″, p. 406

17   Least Bittern, 11–14″, p. 407

18   Green Heron, 15–22″, p. 444

19   Yellow-crowned Night Heron, 22–27″, p. 408

20   Black-crowned Night Heron, 23–28″, p. 409

21   Yellow-crowned Night Heron imm., p. 408

22   Black-crowned Night Heron imm., p. 409

23 Limpkin, 25–28″, p. 480

24 American Bittern, 23–34″, p. 410

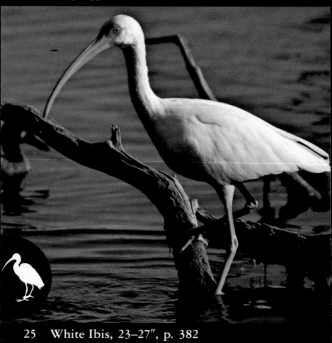

25 White Ibis, 23–27″, p. 382

26 White Ibis imm., 23–27″, p. 382

27 Glossy Ibis, 22–25″, p. 382

28 White-faced Ibis, 22–25″, p. 383

29   Whooping Crane, 45–50″, p. 384

30 Sandhill Crane 34–48" p. 410

Gull-like Birds

These waterbirds spend much of their time in flight. All have long, pointed wings. Gulls, terns, gannets, and boobies are predominantly white, while frigatebirds are black. Most of these birds occur along seacoasts or on the ocean, but some of the gulls and terns are found on inland waters.

31 Iceland Gull imm., 23", p. 330

32 Ivory Gull, 17", p. 331

33 Glaucous Gull imm., 28", p. 332

34   Iceland Gull, 23", p. 330

35   Thayer's Gull, 24", p. 333

36   Glaucous Gull, 28", p. 332

37   Herring Gull, 23–26″, p. 445

38   Ring-billed Gull, 18–20″, p. 446

39   Black-legged Kittiwake, 16–18″, p. 333

40 Northern Fulmar, 18″, p. 314

41 Lesser Black-backed Gull, 23″, p. 334

43 Laughing Gull, 15–17″, p. 385

44 Sabine's Gull, 13–14″, p. 314

46 Black-headed Gull, 15″, p. 447

47 Little Gull, 11″, p. 448

49 Ivory Gull imm., 17", p. 331

50 Herring Gull imm., 23–26", p. 445

52 Ring-billed Gull imm., 18–20", p. 446

53 Bonaparte's Gull imm., 12–14", p. 449

55   Bonaparte's Gull winter plumage, 12–14″, p. 449

56   Laughing Gull winter plumage, 15–17″, p. 385

70 Black Skimmer, 18″, p. 340

71 Sooty Tern, 16″, p. 341

73   Brown Noddy, 15″, p. 342

74   Black Noddy, 12″, p. 343

76 Gannet, 35–40″, p. 344

77 Brown Booby, 30″, p. 316

78 Blue-faced Booby, 32″, p. 317

79   Cory's Shearwater, 20–22″, p. 317

80   Greater Shearwater, 18–20″, p. 318

81   Sooty Shearwater, 16–18″, p. 320

82 Wilson's Storm-Petrel, 7″, p. 321

83 Leach's Storm-Petrel, 8–9″, p. 322

84 Skua, 21″, p. 323

85 Magnificent Frigatebird, 38–40″, p. 345

86 Magnificent Frigatebird ♀, 38–40″, p. 345

87 Long-tailed Jaeger, 21″, p. 324

88 Pomarine Jaeger, 22″, p. 325

89 Parasitic Jaeger, 17″, p. 326

90 White-tailed Tropicbird, 32″, p. 480

Upright-perching Waterbirds

These birds are usually seen perching
on rocks or trees at the edge of the
water. In most cases, their feet are
located far back on the body, which
gives the birds a distinctive upright
posture when perching. The auks,
murres, and puffins are patterned in
black-and-white, while the cormorants
and anhingas are largely or entirely
black.

91   Razorbill, 17″, p. 346

93 Thick-billed Murre, 18″, p. 347

94 Common Murre, 17″, p. 348

95   Common Puffin, 12″, p. 349

96   Dovekie, 8″, p. 349

97 Common Puffin, 12″, p. 349

99 Double-crested Cormorant, 30–35″, p. 451

101 Olivaceous Cormorant, 25", p. 453

103   Double-crested Cormorant, 30–35″, p. 45

Duck-like Birds

Included here are the many ducks, geese, and swans, as well as other birds that, like the ducks, are usually seen swimming. Many of the male ducks, and breeding-plumaged loons and grebes, are boldly patterned, while female ducks and winter-plumaged loons and grebes are clad in modest browns and grays.

105 Green-winged Teal, 12–16″, p. 413

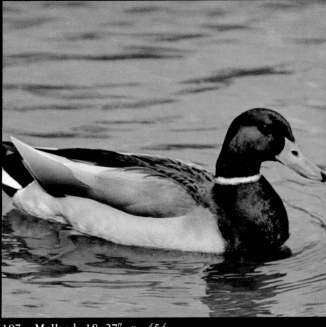

107 Mallard, 18–27″, p. 454

108 Northern Shoveler, 17–20″, p. 416

109   Redhead, 18–22″, p. 455

110   Canvasback, 19–24″, p. 455

11 Ruddy Duck, 14–16″, p. 416

113 Red-breasted Merganser, 19–26″, p. 351

15   Pintail, 25–30″, p. 418

117 Common Eider, 23–27″, p. 353

119   Wood Duck, 17–20″, p. 457

120   Harlequin Duck, 14–20″, p. 354

121   Ring-necked Duck, 14–18″, p. 458

122   Tufted Duck, 17″, p. 459

123 Lesser Scaup, 15–18″, p. 460

124 Greater Scaup, 15–20″, p. 461

125   Barrow's Goldeneye, 20–23″, p. 355

126   Common Goldeneye, 16–20″, p. 356

127 Bufflehead, 13–15″, p. 357

129   Surf Scoter, 17–21″, p. 358

131 Black Scoter, 17–21″, p. 359

132 European Wigeon, 18–20″, p. 415

133   Black Duck, 19–22″, p. 387

134   American Coot, 15″, p. 419

35 Gadwall, 18–21", p. 420

137   Mallard ♀, 18–27″, p. 454

239 Gadwall ♀, 18–21″, p. 420

141   Cinnamon Teal ♀, 14–17″, p. 417

143   Northern Shoveler ♀, 17–20″, p. 416

144   Green-winged Teal ♀, 12–16″, p. 413

145   Common Eider ♀, 23–27″, p. 353

146   King Eider ♀, 18–25″, p. 353

47 White-winged Scoter ♀, 19–24″, p. 359

149 Barrow's Goldeneye ♀, 16–20″, p. 355

51 Bufflehead ♀, 13–15", p. 357

153 Redhead ♀, 18–22″, p. 455

155   Tufted Duck ♀, 17″, p. 459

156   Ring-necked Duck ♀, 14–18″, p. 458

157   Lesser Scaup ♀, 15–18″, p. 460

158   Greater Scaup ♀, 15–20″, p. 461

159 Ruddy Duck ♀, 14–16″, p. 416

161 Common Merganser ♀, 22–27″, p. 456

63 Hooded Merganser ♀, 16–19", p. 461

165 Fulvous Whistling-Duck, 18–21″, p. 422

167 Black-bellied Whistling-Duck, 20–22″, p. 422

168 Black-bellied Whistling-Duck, 20–22″, p. 422

169   White-fronted Goose, 27–30″, p. 423

170   Canada Goose, 22–45″, p. 462

71 Snow Goose blue and white phases, p. 388

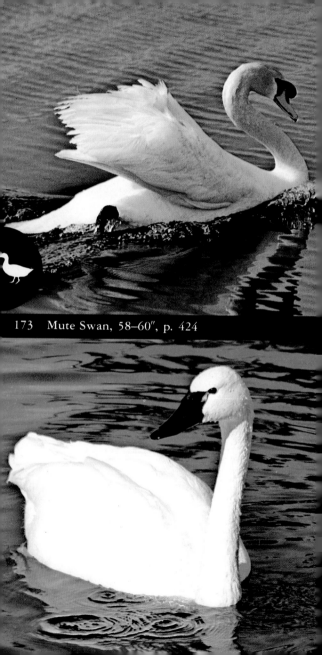

173 Mute Swan, 58–60″, p. 424

75 White Pelican, 55–70″, p. 425

177 Least Grebe winter plumage, 8–10″, p. 464

79 Least Grebe, 8-10", p. 464

181 Eared Grebe winter plumage, 12–14″, p. 361

3   Eared Grebe, 12–14″, p. 361

185 Red-necked Grebe, 18–20″, p. 465

187   Arctic Loon, 24″, p. 363

189   Red-throated Loon winter plumage, p. 363

Sandpiper-like Birds

This is a large group of small to medium-sized birds that have long legs and slender bills and are usually seen foraging on the beach or along the margins of lakes, ponds, marshes, or streams. Although these birds are collectively called "shorebirds," a few, such as the Killdeer, are often found on bare ground, far from water. Many of these birds are cryptically colored, but some, like the American Oystercatcher and the avocets and stilts, are boldly patterned in black-and-white.

191 Red Knot winter plumage, 10½″, p. 364

192 Dunlin winter plumage, 8½″, p. 365

193 Sanderling winter plumage, 8″, p. 365

94   American Golden Plover winter plumage, p. 366

95   Black-bellied Plover winter plumage, p. 367

197 Spotted Sandpiper winter plumage, 7½", p. 467

198 Purple Sandpiper winter plumage, 9", p. 369

00 Stilt Sandpiper winter plumage, 8½″, p. 391

201 Short-billed Dowitcher winter plumage, p. 391

203   Northern Phalarope winter plumage, 7″, p. 326

204   Wilson's Phalarope winter plumage, 9″, p. 427

206 **Northern Phalarope** ♀ summer plumage, p. 326

207 **Wilson's Phalarope** ♀ summer plumage, p. 427

208 **Red Phalarope** ♀ summer plumage, p. 327

209   Dunlin, 8½″, p. 365

210   Curlew Sandpiper winter plumage, 8″, p. 370

211   Red Knot, 10½″, p. 364

212 Short-billed Dowitcher, 12", p. 391

213 Long-billed Dowitcher, 12½", p. 393

215   Spotted Sandpiper, 7½″, p. 467

216   Solitary Sandpiper, 8½″, p. 428

217   Purple Sandpiper, 9″, p. 369

218 Upland Sandpiper, 12″, p. 490

219 Pectoral Sandpiper, 9″, p. 429

220 Sanderling, 8″, p. 365

221   Semipalmated Sandpiper, 6½″, p. 371

222   Western Sandpiper, 6½″, p. 371

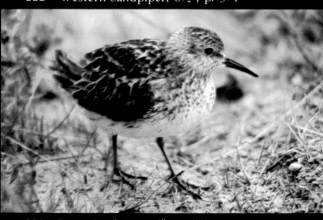

223   Least Sandpiper, 6″, p. 426

224   Buff-breasted Sandpiper, 8″, p. 491

225   Baird's Sandpiper, 7½″, p. 372

226   White-rumped Sandpiper, 7½″, p. 373

227   Lesser Yellowlegs, 10½″, p. 394

228   Greater Yellowlegs, 14″, p. 395

229   Willet, 15″, p. 392

230   Stilt Sandpiper, 8½", p. 391

231   Marbled Godwit, 18", p. 396

233   Snowy Plover, 5–7", p. 373

234   Piping Plover, 6–7", p. 374

236 Semipalmated Plover, 6–8″, p. 375

237 Wilson's Plover, 7–8″, p. 376

238 Killdeer, 9–11″, p. 492

239 American Golden Plover, 9–11″, p. 366

240 Black-bellied Plover, 10–13″, p. 367

241 Ruddy Turnstone, 8–10″, p. 368

242 American Oystercatcher, 17–21″, p. 376

243 Black-necked Stilt, 13–16″, p. 397

245   Whimbrel, 17″, p. 398

Chicken-like Marsh Birds

These are small to medium-sized marsh
birds, most of which keep themselves
well concealed in the reeds or marsh
grasses. The bill may be long and
slender, as in the Clapper Rail or
Virginia Rail, or stubby and chicken-
like, as in the Sora. The two gallinules,
allied to the modestly plumaged rails
that make up the rest of this group, are
more often seen in the open and are
more brightly colored.

247   Common Gallinule, 13″, p. 430

249   Sora, 8–10″, p. 432

251 Yellow Rail, 6–8", p. 433

253   Clapper Rail, 14–16″, p. 399

Upland Ground Birds

This group contains the familiar game
birds—grouse, quails and pheasants—
as well as certain other cryptically
colored birds of woodlands, such as the
woodcocks, snipe, and the nightjars.
Many of these birds are difficult to
detect against a background of dead
leaves or grass until they flush
unexpectedly into the air.

255 Common Snipe, 10½–11½″, p. 435

57 Bobwhite, 8–11″, p. 493

259   Sharp-tailed Grouse, 16–18″, p. 493

261 Greater Prairie Chicken, 16–18″, p. 494

263   Willow Ptarmigan, 15", p. 674

265   Willow Ptarmigan winter plumage, 15″, p. 674

267 Gray Partridge, 12–14″, p. 496

269   Turkey displaying, 48″, p. 631

270   Spruce Grouse displaying, 15–17″, p. 675

271   Roadrunner, 24″, p. 497

272   Chachalaca, 18–21″, p. 599

273   Turkey, 48″, p. 631

274   Ring-necked Pheasant, 30–36″, p. 497

275 Common Nighthawk, 10″, p. 498

276 Pauraque, 12″, p. 600

277 Whip-poor-will, 10″, p. 632

278 Chuck-will's-widow, 12″, p. 633

Owls

This well-known group of birds scarcely needs a description. They are small to large birds with large round heads, loose, fluffy plumage and disk-like faces. Many are nocturnal, and are usually seen roosting quietly in trees during the day, but a few, such as the all-white Snowy Owl or the Short-eared Owl, often hunt by day and may be seen in open country.

279   Screech Owl red phase, 10″, p. 634

280   Screech Owl gray phase, 10″, p. 634

281 Long-eared Owl, 15″, p. 676

282 Great Horned Owl, 25″, p. 677

283   Burrowing Owl, 9″, p. 499

284   Short-eared Owl, 16″, p. 436

85 Barred Owl, 20″, p. 634

86 Great Gray Owl, 24–33″, p. 678

287 Elf Owl, 5½″, p. 600

288 Hawk-Owl, 15–17″, p. 678

89　Saw-whet Owl, 7″, p. 635

291　Barn Owl, 18″, p. 500

Hawk-like Birds

The hawks and their allies range in size from the American Kestrel, scarcely larger than a Blue Jay, to the huge eagles and vultures. All have sharply hooked bills for tearing their prey, and many are often seen soaring high in the air. The wings may be rounded, as in the Red-tailed and Sharp-shinned Hawks, or pointed, as in the falcons and some of the kites.

293 Cooper's Hawk, 14–20″, p. 636

294 Sharp-shinned Hawk, 10–14″, p. 680

95 Rough-legged Hawk light phase, 19–24″, p. 501

297   Broad-winged Hawk, 13–15″, p. 637

299 Swainson's Hawk, 18–22″, p. 502

301 White-tailed Hawk, 21–23″, p. 503

303 White-tailed Kite, 15–16″, p. 504

304 Mississippi Kite, 12–14″, p. 639

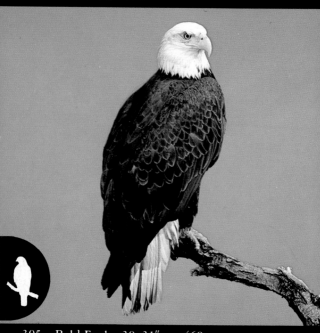

305 Bald Eagle, 30–31″, p. 468

306 Osprey, 21–24″, p. 469

307 Bald Eagle imm., 30–31″, p. 468

308 Golden Eagle, 30–41″, p. 640

309 Marsh Hawk, 16–24″, p. 437

310 Marsh Hawk ♀, 16–24″, p. 437

311 Harris' Hawk, 18–30″, p. 601

312 Caracara, 20–22″, p. 505

313   Merlin, 10–14″, p. 682

314   American Kestrel, 9–12″, p. 505

15 Peregrine Falcon, 15–21″, p. 470

317 Turkey Vulture, 25–32", p. 641

319   Short-tailed Hawk, 13–14″, p. 481

Pigeon-like Birds

This group includes the familiar Rock
Dove or city pigeon and its allies.
These are small to medium-sized birds,
small-headed, and clad in soft browns
and grays. On the ground they walk
with a characteristic mincing gait.

321 White-winged Dove, 12″, p. 602

322 Mourning Dove, 12″, p. 542

Swallow-like Birds

Included here are the swallows and
martins and the similar but unrelated
swifts. These are small birds that spend
most of their time in the air, flying
gracefully about in pursuit of their
insect prey. They have pointed wings
and often gather in large flocks.

329   Barn Swallow, 5¾–7¾″, p. 507

330   Cliff Swallow, 5–6″, p. 508

331 Tree Swallow, 5–6¼″, p. 471

333 Rough-winged Swallow, 5–5¾″, p. 472

35   Chimney Swift, 5½", p. 545

Tree-clinging Birds

The woodpeckers, nuthatches, and creepers are usually seen climbing about on the trunks of trees, in search of insects hidden in the bark. Most of the woodpeckers are clad in black-and-white, although a few, like the Common Flicker, are mainly brown. The nuthatches are soft gray above and whitish or rusty below, and the creepers are brown and streaked.

337   Downy Woodpecker ♀, 6″, p. 643

339   Downy Woodpecker, 6″, p. 643

340   Hairy Woodpecker, 9″, p. 643

341 Black-backed Three-toed Woodpecker ♀, 9″, p.

342 Northern Three-toed Woodpecker ♀, 8½″, p. 68

343   Black-backed Three-toed Woodpecker, 9″, p. 683

344   Northern Three-toed Woodpecker, 8½″, p. 683

345 Ladder-backed Woodpecker, 7″, p. 605

346 Yellow-bellied Sapsucker, 8½″, p. 644

347   Red-cockaded Woodpecker, 8″, p. 684

349 Red-bellied Woodpecker, 10″, p. 645

351 Red-headed Woodpecker, 10″, p. 508

353   Red-breasted Nuthatch, 4½–4¾", p. 685

55 Brown Creeper, 5–5¾″, p. 647

Perching Birds

This very large group includes nearly
all of the songbirds, as well as cuckoos,
kingfishers and hummingbirds, which,
while unrelated, resemble songbirds
rather closely. They range in size from
the three- or four-inch hummingbirds
and kinglets, to the large crows and
ravens. They occur in a great variety of
habitats and show an even greater
variety of patterns and colors.

357   Yellow Warbler, 4½–5″, p. 568

358   Wilson's Warbler, 4½–5″, p. 568

359   Yellow-breasted Chat, 6½–7½″, p. 569

60 Prothonotary Warbler, 5½", p. 648

61 Blue-winged Warbler, 4½", p. 570

363   **Prairie Warbler,** 5″, p. 571

364   **Pine Warbler,** 5½″, p. 686

366   Magnolia Warbler, 5″, p. 687

367   Canada Warbler, 5″, p. 688

368   Cape May Warbler, 5″, p. 688

369   Hooded Warbler, 5½″, p. 649

370   Kentucky Warbler, 5½″, p. 650

371   Common Yellowthroat, 4½–6″, p. 572

372 Mourning Warbler, 5½″, p. 651

373 Nashville Warbler, 4–5″, p. 573

375 Black-throated Green Warbler, 5″, p. 690

376 Yellow-throated Warbler, 5″, p. 691

378 Golden-winged Warbler, 4½", p. 574

379 Yellow-rumped Warbler, 5–6", p. 691

380 Blackburnian Warbler ♀, 5", p. 692

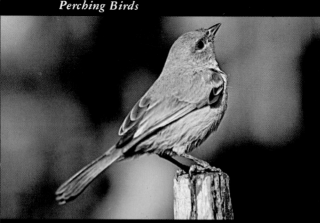

381   Verdin, 4–4½″, p. 606

382   American Redstart ♀, 4½–5½″, p. 575

383   White-eyed Vireo, 5″, p. 576

384   Evening Grosbeak, 7½–8½″, p. 693

85   American Goldfinch, 4½–5½″, p. 510

387 Black-headed Oriole, 9″, p. 606

388 Orchard Oriole ♀, 7″, p. 652

393   Northern ("Baltimore") Oriole, 7–8½″, p. 546

394   Northern ("Bullock's") Oriole, 7–8½″, p. 546

396   Orchard Oriole, 7″, p. 652

397   Lichtenstein's Oriole, 9″, p. 609

399   **Black-headed Grosbeak, 7½″, p. 653**

400   **American Robin, 9–11″, p. 548**

402 American Redstart, 4½–5½″, p. 575

403 Bay-breasted Warbler, 5½″, p. 695

404 Blackburnian Warbler, 5″, p. 692

405 Pyrrhuloxia, 7½–8½″, p. 610

406 Cardinal ♀, 8–9″, p. 578

07 Cardinal, 8–9″, p. 578

08 Rose-breasted Grosbeak, 8″, p. 654

409   Purple Finch, 5½–6½″, p. 696

410   House Finch, 5–6″, p. 549

411   Common Redpoll, 5–5½″, p. 578

12　Red Crossbill, 5¼–6½″, p. 696

13　White-winged Crossbill, 6–6½″, p. 697

415 Vermilion Flycatcher, 6″, p. 611

416 Scarlet Tanager, 7½″, p. 655

18 Scissor-tailed Flycatcher, 14″, p. 513

19 Mockingbird, 9–11″, p. 549

421 Northern Shrike, 9–10½″, p. 514

422 Loggerhead Shrike, 8–10″, p. 514

427 Carolina Chickadee, 4–5″, p. 656

428 Black-capped Chickadee, 4¾–5¾″, p. 657

430 Rose-throated Becard, 6½", p. 612

431 "Black-crested Titmouse," 5–6", p. 613

432 Tufted Titmouse, 6", p. 658

433   Belted Kingfisher, 13″, p. 473

434   Ringed Kingfisher, 13″, p. 474

435 Blue Jay, 12", p. 552

437   Lazuli Bunting, 5–5½″, p. 580

438   Indigo Bunting, 5½″, p. 581

440 Eastern Bluebird, 7″, p. 516

441 Mountain Bluebird, 7″, p. 517

443 Blue-gray Gnatcatcher, 4½–5″, p. 659

444 Cerulean Warbler, 4½″, p. 660

446 Black-throated Blue Warbler, 5″, p. 700

447 Northern Parula, 4½″, p. 701

449   Bell's Vireo, 4¾", p. 582

450   Solitary Vireo, 5–6", p. 701

52 Black-whiskered Vireo, 5½″, p. 486

53 Red-eyed Vireo, 5½–6½″, p. 660

455   Bay-breasted Warbler ♀, 5½", p. 695

456   Orange-crowned Warbler, 4½–5½", p. 584

58   Golden-crowned Kinglet, 3½–4″, p. 704

59   Ruby-crowned Kinglet, 3¾–4½″, p. 705

460   Connecticut Warbler 5½″, p. 706

461   Acadian Flycatcher, 6″, p. 662

462   Willow Flycatcher, 6″, p. 584

463   Yellow-bellied Flycatcher, 5½″, p. 707

464   Least Flycatcher, 5¼", p. 663

465   Eastern Wood Pewee, 6½", p. 664

467 Western Kingbird, 9″, p. 518

468 Tropical Kingbird, 8½″, p. 615

470 Olive-sided Flycatcher, 7½″, p. 706

471 Wied's Crested Flycatcher, 9½″, p. 615

473   Summer Tanager ♀, 7–8″, p. 655

474   Scarlet Tanager ♀, 7½″, p. 655

476 Painted Bunting, 5½", p. 586

477 Painted Bunting ♀, 5½", p. 586

478 Olive Sparrow, 5¾", p. 617

479 Ruby-throated Hummingbird, 3½″, p. 554

480 Rufous Hummingbird, 3½–4″, p. 555

481 Buff-bellied Hummingbird, 4½″, p. 618

482   Green Kingfisher, 8″, p. 475

483   Green Jay, 12″, p. 619

484   Monk Parakeet, 11″, p. 555

485   Short-billed Marsh Wren, 4–4½″, p. 437

486   House Wren, 4½–5¼″, p. 556

487   Winter Wren, 4–4½″, p. 708

488   Long-billed Marsh Wren, 4–5½″, p. 438

489   Carolina Wren, 5½″, p. 587

490   Bewick's Wren, 5½″, p. 588

491   Canyon Wren, 5½–6″, p. 619

492   Rock Wren, 5–6½″, p. 620

493   Cactus Wren, 7–8¼″, p. 621

494 Brown Thrasher, 11½″, p. 557

495 Long-billed Thrasher, 11″, p. 621

497   Sage Thrasher, 8½″, p. 623

498   Gray-cheeked Thrush, 6½–8″, p. 709

500   Wood Thrush, 8″, p. 666

501   Hermit Thrush, 6½–7½″, p. 709

502   Swainson's Thrush, 6½–7¾″, p. 710

503 Ovenbird, 6″, p. 667

504 Louisiana Waterthrush, 6½″, p. 668

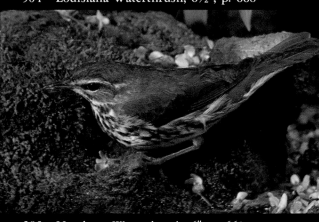

505 Northern Waterthrush, 6″, p. 669

506 Cedar Waxwing, 6½–8″, p. 558

507 Bohemian Waxwing, 7½–8½″, p. 711

509 Worm-eating Warbler, 5½″, p. 670

510 Wheatear, 5½–6″, p. 518

512 Vermilion Flycatcher ♀, 6″, p. 611

513 Indigo Bunting ♀, 5½″, p. 581

514 Black-throated Blue Warbler ♀, 5″, p. 700

515 Brewer's Blackbird ♀, 8–10″, p. 519

516 Brown-headed Cowbird ♀, 6–8″, p. 559

517 Bronzed Cowbird ♀, 8½″, p. 520

18 Yellow-headed Blackbird ♀, 8–11″, p. 439

19 Boat-tailed Grackle ♀, 12–13″, p. 402

521   **Black-billed Cuckoo,** 12″, p. 589

522   **Yellow-billed Cuckoo,** 10½–12½″, p. 590

324 Eurasian Tree Sparrow, 6″, p. 560

525 House Sparrow, 5–6½″, p. 560

527   Lark Sparrow, 5½–6½″, p. 521

528   Black-throated Sparrow, 5¼″, p. 624

530   Chipping Sparrow, 5–5½", p. 561

531   Tree Sparrow, 5½–6½", p. 522

532   Field Sparrow, 5¼", p. 522

533 Sharp-tailed Sparrow, 5½″, p. 440

534 Seaside Sparrow, 6″, p. 402

535 Clay-colored Sparrow, 5–5½″, p. 523

36 Grasshopper Sparrow, 4½–5″, p. 524

37 Henslow's Sparrow, 5″, p. 525

539   White-throated Sparrow, 6–7″, p. 591

540   White-crowned Sparrow, 6–7½″, p. 592

42   Song Sparrow, 5–7", p. 562

43   Fox Sparrow, 6½–7½", p. 593

44   Lincoln's Sparrow, 5–6", p. 712

545   Dickcissel, 6″, p. 528

546   Water Pipit, 6–7″, p. 528

547   Snow Bunting, 6–7¼″, p. 530

48   Savannah Sparrow, 4½–6″, p. 531

49   Lark Bunting ♀, 6–7½″, p. 532

551   Lapland Longspur, 6–7″, p. 533

552   Chestnut-collared Longspur, 5½–6½″, p. 534

554　Smith's Longspur, 5¾–6½″, p. 536

555　Bobolink ♀, 6–8″, p. 537

556　Horned Lark, 7–8″, p. 538

557   Pine Siskin, 4½–5″, p. 713

558   Purple Finch ♀, 5½–6½″, p. 696

559   House Finch ♀, 5–6″, p. 549

560 Red-winged Blackbird ♀, 7–9½″, p. 441

561 Rose-breasted Grosbeak ♀, 8″, p. 654

563 Blackpoll Warbler, 5½", p. 714

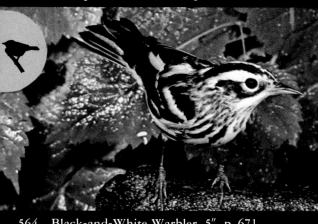

564 Black-and-White Warbler, 5", p. 671

66 Lark Bunting, 6–7½″, p. 532

67 Bobolink, 6–8″, p. 537

569   Rusty Blackbird, 9″, p. 715

570   Brewer's Blackbird, 8–10″, p. 519

572 Common Grackle (Bronzed), 12″, p. 564

573 Common Grackle (Purple), 12″, p. 564

575   Boat-tailed Grackle, 16–17", p. 402

377   Smooth-billed Ani, 14″, p. 539

579   Common Crow, 17–21″, p. 565

581　Common Raven, 21–27", p. 716

583 Yellow-headed Blackbird, 8–11″, p. 439

Part II
Habitat Key

The number preceding each species description in the following pages corresponds to the number of the illustration in the color plates section. If the description has no number there is no color plate but in that case a drawing accompanies the description.

Open Ocean

Pelagic waters, mostly out of sight of land. Much of this water overlies the continental shelf and so is rich in plankton, the microscopic marine organisms that provide food for fish and seabirds.

In addition to the birds treated in this section, one will occasionally see flocks of migrating waterfowl, shorebirds, and songbirds.

40 Northern Fulmar
"Fulmar"
(*Fulmarus glacialis*)
Shearwaters, Fulmars (Procellariidae)

Description: 18" (46 cm). A stocky, gull-like seabird; typical birds are pale gray on back and wings, white elsewhere, but uniformly dark gray individuals occur, as well as intermediates between pale and dark gray. Yellow bill. Easily distinguished from gulls by its flight: several fast wingbeats followed by a stiff-winged glide.

Voice: Chuckling and grunting notes when feeding; various guttural calls during the breeding season.

Habitat: Rocky cliffs; open seas.

Nesting: 1 white egg on a bare rock or in a shallow depression lined with plant material.

Range: Arctic Ocean south to Newfoundland wintering at sea south to New Jersey; also in northern Eurasia.

The Fulmar feeds on fish, squids, and shrimp and the refuse of the whaling industry. The expansion of the fishing industry in this century has caused an increase in the North Atlantic population of this species, especially noticeable in the British Isles. Fulmars have been reported in greater numbers on the east coast of America in the last few years, but this may be due to the increasing number of observers going out to sea to look for them.

44 Sabine's Gull
(*Xema sabini*)
Gulls, Terns (Laridae)

Description: 13–14" (33–36 cm). A small, *fork-tailed* gull with black primaries and *triangular white patch on rear edge of wing.* Hood dark in breeding plumage. Bill black with yellow tip. Immature lacks dark hood but can be told by forked tail.

Voice: High-pitched grating or squeaking notes.

Habitat: Tundra ponds in summer; open ocean in migration and winter.

Nesting: 3 or 4 olive-brown eggs, spotted with darker brown, placed in a grass-lined depression on the ground. In small colonies.

Range: Coastal tundra around the shores of the Arctic Ocean, farther inland in Alaska. Migrates mainly at sea. Winter range not fully known; some birds winter off the Pacific coast of northern South America.

This delicate gull is seldom seen outside of the breeding season as it is almost exclusively oceanic. On the tundra it gracefully plucks small crustaceans and insects from the surface of the water like a tern. It also takes eggs from nesting colonies of Arctic Terns.

72 Bridled Tern
(*Sterna anaethetus*)
Gulls, Terns (Laridae)

Description: 14–15" (35–38 cm). A stocky oceanic tern, dark gray above, white below, with a black cap; white forehead and eyebrow, and a conspicuous white collar or "bridle" on hindneck. Sooty Tern similar, but lacks collar and is blacker on upperparts.

Voice: Usually silent; various high-pitched barking notes on the breeding grounds.

Habitat: Open ocean; breeds on rocky or sandy islands.

Nesting: 1 white egg, spotted with brown, placed in a shallow depression among rocks on an island. In colonies.

Range: Breeds in tropical Atlantic, Indian, and Pacific oceans; ranges in nonbreeding season to offshore waters from the Carolinas to Florida.

This bird was long thought to be a casual visitor to the North American coast, but as more birders travel out to the Gulf Stream, it is becoming evident that the species is fairly common twenty or thirty miles offshore.

77 Brown Booby
(*Sula leucogaster*)
Gannets, Boobies (Sulidae)

Description: 30″ (76 cm). Adult has dark brown head and upperparts, with a sharply contrasting white breast and belly and white underwing coverts; immature is gray-brown, darker on head, wings, and tail.

Voice: Usually silent, but a variety of quacking, grunting, and screeching calls have been described.

Habitat: Tropical and subtropical seas, breeding on coastal islands.

Nesting: 2 pale blue eggs on the ground in a slight mound of broken shells and scattered vegetation.

Range: Pantropical waters; in America, breeds on islands north to the Gulf of Mexico and the Caribbean Sea; wanders occasionally to the coasts of Florida, Louisiana, and Texas; perhaps occurs regularly on the Dry Tortugas, Florida.

Of the three boobies seen off the beaches of the Gulf of Mexico, the Brown is by far the most plentiful. Related to the larger Gannet, boobies also dive for fish by plunging into the sea. They also skim the surface, catching flying fish that leap clear of the surf. These birds are dependent on a strong wind for takeoff from a tree or other elevated perch. On a calm day they rest in the vegetation or on the ground.

78 Blue-faced Booby
(*Sula dactylatra*)
Gannets, Boobies (Sulidae)

Description: 32″ (80 cm). A stocky white seabird
with black tail, black tips and trailing
edges to the wings, and a stout pinkish
or orange bill. In the breeding season,
birds have a patch of bare, bluish skin
at the base of the bill. The Gannet is
similar but larger, with only the wing
tips black.

Voice: Usually silent; a variety of hissing
and quacking notes on the breeding
grounds.

Habitat: Tropical seas.

Nesting: 2 chalky, pale blue eggs in a shallow
depression on the ground. In colonies.

Range: The Bahamas and West Indies, and on
other islands in the tropical Atlantic,
Indian, and Pacific oceans. A casual on
the coasts of Florida, Louisiana, and
Texas.

Like many birds that nest on remote
oceanic islands, these birds have little
fear of man and because of their
tameness, they were easily killed for
food by early mariners, who gave them
the name "Booby" for this reason.
Boobies obtain their food in spectacular
plunges into the sea from the air. A
principal food of this species is flying
fish; These birds are therefore seldom
found in areas where flying fish are
not plentiful.

79 Cory's Shearwater
(*Puffinus diomedea*)
Shearwaters, Fulmars (Procellariidae)

Description: 20–22″ (51–56 cm). Dull gray above,
white below; *pale bill (usually yellow)*.
Similar to the Greater Shearwater, but
the dull gray crown of Cory's Shearwater
blends evenly with the white sides of the
face, without the abrupt contrast seen

in the Greater Shearwater.

Voice: Howling, gurgling calls heard only on breeding grounds.

Habitat: Open oceans.

Nesting: 1 white egg laid in a rock crevice or on open ground on an island, less often in caves or burrows. In colonies.

Range: Breeds in eastern Atlantic and Mediterranean, and occurs in summer and fall off the east coast of North America.

This is the only one of our large shearwaters that breeds in the Northern Hemisphere. After the breeding season the birds move westward into American waters, usually becoming common in July and remaining until late in the fall. A powerful bird, it does not resort to burrows for protection from predators during the breeding season. Like the Sooty and Greater Shearwater, it often follows ships in search of food.

80 Greater Shearwater
(*Puffinus gravis*)
Shearwaters, Fulmars (Procellariidae)

Description: 18–20" (46–51 cm). Narrow-winged gull-sized seabird usually seen skimming over the waves in the wake of ships. Dull brown above, white below; *dark cap contrasting sharply with white side of face;* may show white at base of tail; *black bill.* Cory's Shearwater is paler, lacks the contrast between crown and face, and has a pale bill.

Voice: Usually silent in our area; a snarling *eeyah,* given by birds resting in flocks on the water.

Habitat: Open ocean.

Nesting: 1 white egg laid in a burrow on a grassy slope. In very large colonies.

Range: Islands of the Tristan da Cunha group, South Atlantic. Spends the northern summer as a nonbreeding visitor to the North Atlantic.

It is incredible that the millions of
Greater Shearwaters that appear in the
North Atlantic each summer have bred
on one small group of islands in the
Southern Hemisphere. Like the Sooty
Shearwaters, these birds follow a "Great
Circle" route around the Atlantic,
appearing in North American waters in
May, then moving on to the eastern
Atlantic in late summer. Expert divers,
they feed mainly on small fish and
squid.

Audubon's Shearwater
(*Puffinus lherminieri*)
Shearwaters, Fulmars (Procellariidae)

Description: 11–12" (28–30 cm). A small shearwater
with white cheeks, throat, breast, and
abdomen; black crown, upperparts, and
black undertail coverts. Half the size of the
Greater Shearwater. The rarer Manx
Shearwater has white undertail coverts.
Voice: Twittering calls and mewing notes
heard at night in the breeding colonies.
Habitat: Open oceans.
Nesting: 1 white egg laid in a burrow or rock
crevice on an island. In colonies.
Range: Islands in tropical seas around the
world. Wanders northward, as far north
as New York City in the U.S.

Very similar to the Manx Shearwater,
this tropical species appears regularly
on the Gulf Stream during the summer.
There is no evidence that this bird
undertakes the great migrations of the
other shearwaters. Like the Manx, it
is not a ship-follower, and so is often
difficult to see closeup.

Manx Shearwater
(*Puffinus puffinus*)
Shearwaters, Fulmars (Procellariidae)

Description: 12½–15″ (32–38 cm). A small
shearwater, *black above and white below.*
Greater Shearwater is nearly twice as
large, and usually shows white at the
base of the tail. Audubon's Shearwater
is almost identical but has *dark
undertail coverts.*

Voice: Cooing and clucking notes heard at
night at breeding colonies.

Habitat: Open oceans.

Nesting: 1 white egg laid in a burrow or rock
crevice on an island. In colonies.

Range: Breeds in the eastern Atlantic. Occurs
as an uncommon visitor (and very rare
breeder) off the east coast of North
America. Allied forms breed in Pacific
and Indian oceans.

Unlike the larger Sooty, Greater, and
Cory's Shearwaters, this species does
not follow ships and is usually seen
skimming past at some distance. Manx
Shearwaters are known to have bred
once in Massachusetts, but because they
are entirely nocturnal on the breeding
grounds, they may have bred more
frequently on our shores and have
simply gone unnoticed. These birds are
great travelers whose movements are
poorly understood; a bird that was
banded in Great Britain was later
recovered in Australian waters.

81 ## Sooty Shearwater
(*Puffinus griseus*)
Shearwaters, Fulmars (Procellariidae)

Description: 16–18″ (41–46 cm). Gull-sized. The
only Atlantic shearwater that appears
all dark sooty brown, paler on the wing
linings. This slender, narrow-winged
seabird skims on stiff wings over the
waves, alternately gliding and flapping.

Voice: Silent except for a variety of cooing and croaking notes heard on breeding grounds.

Habitat: Open ocean.

Nesting: 1 white egg in a burrow lined with plant material. In colonies.

Range: Islands in subantarctic seas. Spends the northern summer in the North Atlantic and North Pacific oceans.

One of the most abundant birds in the world, this species nests in millions on islands off New Zealand. Most that appear off the east coast breed around Tierra del Fuego off the southern tip of South America. After breeding, they begin a great circular migration around the Atlantic Ocean, arriving off the east coast of North America in May, continuing on to Europe, then down the west coast of Africa, returning to their nesting islands in November.

82 Wilson's Storm-Petrel
"Wilson's Petrel"
(*Oceanites oceanicus*)
Storm-Petrels (Hydrobatidae)

Description: 7″ (18 cm). A small seabird that skims over the surface like a swallow. Black with a white rump; *tail not forked*. Leach's Petrel is similar, but has a forked tail and butterfly-like flight.

Voice: A soft peeping, heard at close range when the birds are feeding.

Habitat: Open ocean; breeds on rocky cliffs and offshore islands.

Nesting: 1 white egg in a crevice among rocks or in a burrow in soft earth.

Range: Breeds in Antarctic and subantarctic seas; in nonbreeding season ranges over Atlantic, Pacific, and Indian oceans, in the western Atlantic north to Labrador.

One of the most abundant birds in the world, this species, formerly called

"Wilson's Petrel," nests in countless millions on islands in the Southern Hemisphere, and visits the Northern Hemisphere during our summer months. It often hovers at the surface of the water, its wings held over its back and its feet gently touching the water. Although normally a bird of the open ocean, it may occasionally enter bays and estuaries. It is named after the early American ornithologist Alexander Wilson (1766–1813).

---

83 Leach's Storm-Petrel
"Leach's Petrel"
(*Oceanodroma leucorhoa*)
Storm-Petrels (Hydrobatidae)

Description: 8–9″ (20–23 cm). Small, swallow-like seabird, all black with a white rump. Differs from Wilson's Storm-Petrel in having the tail somewhat forked, dark feet, and a flight that is more erratic. Unlike Wilson's, this species seldom follows boats.

Voice: A variety of trills, screams, and cooing notes.

Habitat: Open seas, resorting to rocky islands and coasts to breed.

Nesting: One white egg, often with a faint ring of spots at the large end, placed in a shallow burrow in the ground or under a log or board, often well-concealed. In colonies.

Range: Coasts and offshore islands from Labrador south to Maine, rarely to Massachusetts. Winters on the open ocean. Also breeds in the eastern Atlantic and on both sides of the Pacific Ocean.

Although not uncommon, Leach's Storm-Petrel, until recently called "Leach's Petrel," is seldom seen because it feeds far out at sea, and visits its breeding grounds under cover of darkness.

The presence of the birds is not difficult to detect, however: the nesting burrows have an unmistakable musky odor, caused by an oily orange liquid that the birds emit when disturbed, and the air is filled with their nocturnal calls.
These birds are vulnerable to many predators, but their nocturnal habits no doubt save them from heavy predation by their principal enemies, gulls. Like other storm-petrels, they feed mainly on small shrimp and other planktonic animals, which they pluck deftly from the surface of the ocean.
It has been reported that, because of their high oil content, these birds were at one time used as lamps. A cotton wick was inserted in the throat of a dead bird, which when lighted would burn for a considerable length of time.

84 Skua

(*Catharacta skua*)
Jaegers, Skuas (Stercorariidae)

Description: 21″ (53 cm). A large, dark, heavy-bodied, gull-like bird, grayish brown with conspicuous white patches in the outer wing. Tail short and blunt. Immatures of the larger gulls lack the white wing patches.

Voice: A harsh *hah-hah-hah-hah;* various quacking and croaking notes.

Habitat: Breeds on open bare ground near the sea; at other times ranges over the open sea.

Nesting: 2 olive-brown eggs with dark brown spots, in a grass-lined nest on the ground. Often in loose colonies.

Range: Nests on Iceland and islands north of Britain, ranging widely over the North Atlantic. Also breeds on islands in the Southern Hemisphere.

Skuas occur off the shores of the Northern Hemisphere most often in late summer and early fall, where they

are abundant on the fishing banks off
Newfoundland. They feed on a variety
of shrimp, fish, rodents, and the eggs
and young of colonial seabirds. They
are vigorous in the defense of their
nests, diving boldly at intruders.

---

87 Long-tailed Jaeger
(*Stercorarius longicaudus*)
Jaegers, Skuas (Stercorariidae)

Description: 21″ (53 cm). Adults similar to light-
phase Parasitic Jaegers, but smaller,
more graceful, and with *very long central
tail feathers.* Upperparts paler than in
other jaegers, and blackish cap smaller
and more sharply defined. Flight more
buoyant.

Voice: A harsh *kreeah;* other yelping and
rattling notes on the breeding grounds.

Habitat: Breeds on tundra and stony hillsides; a
other times ranges over open ocean.

Nesting: 2 olive-brown eggs with brown spots
in a grass-lined nest placed either on
bare ground or among rocks.

Range: North of the Arctic Circle, wintering
far offshore in both Atlantic and Pacific
oceans.

Smallest of the three jaegers, the Long-
tailed is the rarest in eastern North
America, presumably because it
migrates chiefly in mid-ocean.
Although occasionally, like other
jaegers, it harries terns and gulls, it
feeds mainly by catching its own fish,
taking flying insects in the air, and
sometimes preying on small birds. On
the breeding grounds its staple food is
lemmings.

88 Pomarine Jaeger
(*Stercorarius pomarinus*)
Jaegers, Skuas (Stercorariidae)

Description: 22" (56 cm). Larger and stockier than
the Parasitic Jaeger, with a more
extensive white flash in the outer wing
and with central tail feathers twisted
and blunt, not pointed; breast band
often darker and wider; bill heavier;
flight more direct. Dark-phase and
light-phase individuals occur.

Voice: Harsh chattering calls; a harsh *which-yew*.

Habitat: Swampy tundra; on migration and in
winter on the ocean.

Nesting: 2 olive-brown eggs with darker brown
spots, in a grass-lined depression on the
ground.

Range: Above the Arctic Circle in Alaska,
northern Canada, and Greenland; in
eastern United States winters mainly
south of Cape Hatteras, North
Carolina. Also in Eurasia.

Largest of our jaegers, it preys on
birds up to the size of terns and small
gulls, as well as lemmings, carrion, and
the eggs and young of colonial seabirds.
Like the Parasitic Jaeger it also pursues
gulls and terns, forcing them to disgorge
their food, which it catches in mid-air.
Although it can be seen from land at
times, it is much more often seen far
off shore.

89 Parasitic Jaeger
(*Stercorarius parasiticus*)
Jaegers, Skuas (Stercorariidae)

Description: 21″ (53 cm). A fast-flying, gull-like
seabird. Typical adults are brown
above, white or light dusky below,
with a *gray-brown band across the breast*
and a dark, almost black crown. Dark-
phase birds are uniform dusky brown
with pale cheeks. Intermediates between
the two color phases occur.
Distinguished from other jaegers by
*pointed central tail feathers extending up
to three inches beyond rest of tail* and
moderate white flash in outer wing.
Often seen harrying gulls and terns.

Voice: Usually silent; a variety of mewing and
wailing notes on the breeding grounds.

Habitat: Grassy tundra and stony ground near
inland lakes in summer; at other times
on the ocean.

Nesting: 2 olive-brown eggs with darker brown
spots, in a grass-lined depression on the
ground or among rocks.

Range: Aleutians, northern Alaska, Canada,
and Greenland south to central Canada;
winters in warm waters south to
Argentina. Also in northern Eurasia.

This is the most familiar of our jaegers
since it comes more readily into bays
and estuaries and feeds more often close
to shore. Like the other jaegers, it
usually obtains food by pursuing gulls
and terns and forcing them to drop
food.

203, 206 Northern Phalarope
(*Phalaropus lobatus*)
Sandpipers (Scolopacidae)

Description: 7″ (18 cm). Sparrow-sized. In summer,
head and back dark, chin and belly
white separated by *chestnut throat and
upper breast*. In winter, much paler and
grayer above, entirely white below. *Bill*

thin. Conspicuous wing stripe.

Voice: Sharp *whit* or *twit.*

Habitat: Open ocean, beaches, flats, lake and river shores.

Nesting: 4 brown-spotted olive eggs in a slight hollow on the ground in marshy tundra.

Range: Arctic and subarctic zones of both hemispheres; in America south to central Canada. Winters at sea in the Southern Hemisphere.

The Northern or "Red-necked Phalarope" belongs to a group in which the female is brighter than the male and the male incubates the eggs. It has fully lobed toes and swims buoyantly. In effect an oceangoing sandpiper, it spends nearly all of its nonbreeding life at sea, although on occasion it wades in pools and feeds in mud like many other shorebirds. Phalaropes often feed by spinning around in the water. The motion of their feet stirs up plankton, which they gather from the surface by rapid jabs of the bill.

205, 208 Red Phalarope
(*Phalaropus fulicarius*)
Sandpipers (Scolopacidae)

Description: 8" (20 cm). In summer, *rich chestnut, dark crown, white face; short, stout, yellow bill* with a black tip. In winter, gray above and white below, bill darker. Paler than the Northern Phalarope with an *unstreaked back* and a less contrasting wing stripe. Like other phalaropes, the female is more brightly colored than the male.

Voice: Sharp metallic *beek.*

Habitat: The most pelagic of all shorebirds, mostly ocean-inhabiting in the nonbreeding season; otherwise it is found in bays, inlets, inland lakes, shores, coasts, and on the tundra in the breeding season.

Nesting: 4 brown-speckled olive eggs placed on
the ground in a grass-lined nest on an
elevated spot in low marshy areas.

Range: Islands and coasts along the Arctic
Ocean of both hemispheres; in America
south to northern Canada. Winters at
sea, chiefly in the Southern
Hemisphere.

Hundreds of these shorebirds may be
seen from a fishing boat far at sea,
where they look like bobbing corks or
miniature gulls riding the waves. The
greater part of their diet while they are
at sea is made up of tiny marine
animals known as plankton. On land
they forage around the tundra pools for
aquatic larvae of mosquitoes, midges,
and beetles. After egg-laying the male
takes over the duties of hatching and
rearing the young.

Seashore

Open sandy beaches, mudflats, and dunes, the latter covered with beach grass. This section includes the birds most likely to be seen on the water from shore.

3, 15   Reddish Egret
(*Egretta rufescens*)
Herons, Bitterns (Ardeidae)

Description: 30″ (76 cm). W. 46″ (1 m). Medium-sized heron. Slaty with shaggy rufous head and neck; *black legs; pink bill with black tip.* Also a white phase.

Voice: Squawks and croaks.

Habitat: Salt and brackish waters, breeding in shallow bays and lagoons; in mangroves (Florida); among cacti, willows, and other shrubs (Texas).

Nesting: 3 or 4 bluish-green eggs in a grass and stick nest in mangroves, low bushes, or on the ground.

Range: Local in extreme southern Florida and along the Texas coasts, south to the West Indies and Mexico.

This egret feeds on fish, frogs, and crabs, pursuing its prey with rapid rushes and upraised wings as it twists and turns. It is uncommon and rather local throughout its range. Both color phases may be seen on the Gulf Coast, the dark one predominating in Florida waters, the white in Texas, but this varies according to locality; sometimes both occur together. During the nuptial display the plumes on its head, neck, and back stand out in a bristly ruff.

31, 34   Iceland Gull
(*Larus glaucoides*)
Gulls, Terns (Laridae)

Description: 23″ (58 cm). A smaller version of the Glaucous Gull, with a relatively smaller bill. Adults are pearl-gray to white; pinkish bill and feet. Immatures creamy buff.

Voice: Like the Herring Gull, a variety of croaks, squeaks, and screams.

Habitat: Lake and river shores, ocean beaches, sewer outlets, and refuse dumps.

Nesting: 2 or 3 light brown eggs with darker blotches in a nest lined with grass, moss, and seaweed placed either on a cliff or a sandy shore.

Range: Breeds in Greenland and south to Baffin Island. Winters in eastern North America south to New Jersey and the Great Lakes. Also in northern and temperate Europe.

The habits of the two "white-winged" gulls are similar, but the smaller Iceland Gull is more buoyant and graceful on the wing. It is also more of a scavenger and much less predatory. In addition to garbage dumps and sewage outlets, this species frequents places where fish are being cleaned. Both of these pale gulls, being relatively rare, are avidly sought by bird-watchers.

32, 49 **Ivory Gull**
(*Pagophila eburnea*)
Gulls, Terns (Laridae)

Description: 17" (43 cm). A rather small, *short-legged* gull; adults are pure white with yellowish bill and legs; immatures similar but with *black bars and spots* in varying numbers.

Voice: A harsh *eeeer*.

Habitat: Rocky cliffs or stony ground; winters at the edge of the pack ice in Arctic seas.

Nesting: 2 buff-olive eggs marked with dark blotches, in a nest lined with moss, lichens, and seaweed, on bare ground among rocks or on gravel-covered polar ice.

Range: Known to breed in the New World only on Somerset and Ellesmere Islands in the Canadian Arctic; more widespread in Eastern Hemisphere. Winters in the Arctic Ocean, appearing rarely farther south.

With the Eskimos and the polar bear, the Ivory Gull shares the realm of icebergs and ice floes. Indeed, it follows these hunters in quest of food, for it is largely a scavenger, feeding on the remains of their kills—mainly seals. It also eats wolf and fox dung, whale blubber, lemmings, crustaceans, and insects.

33, 36 **Glaucous Gull**
(*Larus hyperboreus*)
Gulls, Terns (Laridae)

Description: 28″ (71 cm). Large gull. Adults pearl gray to white; yellowish bill and pinkish feet. Immatures creamy-buff. *No black in wing tips.*

Voice: Hoarse croaks and screams.

Habitat: Shores of lakes, rivers, and the seacoast; also refuse dumps and sewage outflow.

Nesting: 3 light brown eggs with dark chocolate blotches placed in a cliff nest lined with moss and grass.

Range: Arctic and subarctic portions of Alaska and Canada. Winters in the northern United States. Also in the arctic, subarctic, and north temperate areas of Eurasia.

The great white Glaucous Gull is ordinarily rare south of Canada; usually found with flocks of the abundant Herring Gulls when it visits the United States. This is one of the most predatory gulls, capturing and eating alcids, plovers, small ducks, ptarmigan, and songbirds as well as lemmings and fish. It is also a scavenger, feeding on garbage, dead animal matter, and even bird droppings.

35 Thayer's Gull
(*Larus thayeri*)
Gulls, Terns (Laridae)

Description: 24" (61 cm). In all plumages, very
similar to the Herring Gull, gray
above, white below, but *eye of adult
dark* instead of yellow.

Voice: Mewing and squealing notes.

Habitat: Arctic coasts and islands, usually on
rocky cliffs.

Nesting: 3 bluish or greenish eggs spotted with
brown, in a nest lined with grass,
moss, or lichens placed on high rocky
cliffs.

Range: Greenland and northeastern Canada;
winters chiefly on the Pacific Coast of
North America south to Baja
California. Very rare winter visitor to
southeastern Canada and northeastern
United States.

Until recently this bird was thought to
be a subspecies of the Herring Gull, or
of the Iceland Gull, or even a hybrid
between the two. Experiments with
color-dyed individuals have now
demonstrated that differences in eye
and eye-ring color of Herring, Iceland,
and Thayer's gulls are sufficient to
prevent them from interbreeding.

39, 54, 57 Black-legged Kittiwake
(*Rissa tridactyla*)
Gulls, Terns (Laridae)

Description: 16–18" (40–46 cm). Small, seagoing
gull. Adult white with pale gray back
and wings; *sharply defined black wing tip,*
as if dipped in black ink; black feet;
yellow bill; slightly forked tail. Winter
adult has dusky gray patch on nape.
Young bird has dusky band on nape,
dark diagonal wing band, and black-
tipped tail.

Voice: Variety of loud, harsh notes. Very noisy
on the breeding ground. With a little

imagination, its common call can be said to resemble its name, *kittiwake*.

Habitat: Cliffs and seacoasts in the Arctic; winters at sea.

Nesting: 2 pinkish-buff spotted eggs in a well made cup of mosses and seaweed at the top of a cliff or on a ledge. In colonies.

Range: North Pacific and Arctic Ocean to the Gulf of St. Lawrence. Winters from the edge of the sea ice south to the Sargasso Sea. Also in Eurasia.

This abundant gull is not commonly seen from shore, for it generally spends the entire winter on the open ocean, where it feeds on small fish and plankton. Most young gulls flee from the nest if disturbed, but the young of this cliff-nesting species stay put no matter how close a human observer gets; to leave a nest on a high, narrow ledge could result in a fatal plunge to the rocks below. This is the only gull that dives and swims underwater to capture food.

41 **Lesser Black-backed Gull**
(*Larus fuscus*)
Gulls, Terns (Laridae)

Description: 23″ (58 cm). Slightly smaller than the Herring Gull. Adult has *yellow legs;* dark slate-gray back and wings. Immatures of this species and the Herring Gull are virtually indistinguishable.

Voice: A strident *kyow,* deeper than that of the Herring Gull.

Habitat: Nearly all types of open country—coasts, islands, fields, lakes, airports, refuse dumps, etc.

Nesting: 3 pale blue-green eggs spotted with brown in a nest sparsely lined with grass or laden with debris, placed on open ground or on rocky islets. Usually in colonies.

Range: Northern Europe south to France; winters from central Europe south to central Africa. Rare but regular visitor to eastern North America.

Although this Old World species is still rare on the American side of the Atlantic, it is being seen in and around larger cities, not only along the coast but also in the Great Lakes region. During the colder months it may be found at garbage dumps, sewer outlets, and reservoirs.

42, 51 Great Black-backed Gull
(*Larus marinus*)
Gulls, Terns (Laridae)

Description: 30" (76 cm). Very large gull. Adult has black back and wings, rest of plumage white. Bill yellow and legs pinkish. Immature mottled with brown, has a black tip to its tail, and a dark bill.

Voice: Similar to that of the Herring Gull but deeper and more guttural. A deep *keeow*.

Habitat: Coastal beaches, estuaries, and lagoons; also at refuse dumps. Less commonly on inland lakes and rivers.

Nesting: 3 olive eggs with dark brown blotches placed in a ground nest, lined with grass.

Range: Coasts on both sides of the North Atlantic, south to southern United States and the Mediterranean.

Our largest gull, this conspicuous bird accompanies the ever-present Herring Gull at all times of the year, even during the summer when they nest together in mixed colonies. However, the Black-backed always asserts dominance over its smaller relative. It preys on almost anything smaller than itself, including Dovekies, small ducks, petrels, fish, and shellfish as well as the eggs and young of other gulls. It has extended its breeding range south in recent years and nests in a number of places on the shores of Long Island, New York, and New Jersey. Although found close to man's habitations, it is a shyer bird than the Herring Gull.

59, 67   Sandwich Tern
(*Sterna sandvicensis*)
Gulls, Terns (Laridae)

Description: 16″ (40 cm). Robin-sized. White with gray mantle, black cap, short crest, and *long, black, yellow-tipped bill.* Formerly called Cabot's Tern.
Voice: Loud, harsh *curr-it.*
Habitat: Coastal beaches and islands.
Nesting: 2 greenish, black-marked eggs on bare sand, usually with Royal Terns.
Range: Locally on the Atlantic and Gulf coasts from Virginia to Florida and Texas; also in the Caribbean and from Scandinavia and the British Isles to the Mediterranean. Winters south to Panama, Brazil, Africa, and India.

The Sandwich Tern is one of three crested terns occurring along our coasts. Its range is most unusual. It breeds much farther north in Europe than it does in America because of the warming influence of the Gulf Stream. Sandwich Terns feed offshore diving for fish, shrimp, and squid; inshore they have been reported to eat marine worms as well.

---

62   Roseate Tern
(*Sterna dougallii*)
Gulls, Terns (Laridae)

Description: 14–17″ (35–43 cm). Robin-sized. White with a black cap and *very pale gray back and wings.* Similar to Common, Arctic, and Forster's Terns, but bill usually solid black, upper parts

paler, tail longer and more deeply
forked.

Voice: Loud, harsh *zaap,* likened to the sound
of tearing cloth. Also a softer *cue-lick.*

Habitat: Coastal beaches, islands, and inshore
waters.

Nesting: 2 or 3 spotted buff or olive eggs in a
hollow in the ground, sometimes lined
with dead grass; may be placed in the
open but more often concealed in
vegetation or among rocks. Colonial,
often nesting with other species of
terns.

Range: Along the coast from Gulf of St.
Lawrence south to Venezuela; winters
from Gulf Coast to Brazil. Also breeds
in eastern Atlantic, western Indian
Ocean, and southwest Pacific.

The Roseate Tern is much less
numerous than other terns of similar
size, and its patchy distribution around
the world suggests that it is an old
species, perhaps more abundant and
widespread ages ago. It probably suffers
from competition for nesting sites with
the Common Tern, at least in American
waters, and like that species is sensitive
to disturbance by human beings. For
these reasons our breeding population is
small, and the location of known
colonies is often kept secret by those
eager to protect the birds. It frequently
nests in colonies of Common Terns,
occupying the less favorable, marginal
sites.

63 Arctic Tern
(*Sterna paradisaea*)
Gulls, Terns (Laridae)

Description: 14–17″ (35–43 cm). Whitish, with
white streak below the black cap and
pale gray upperparts. Deeply forked
tail. Similar to Common Tern but
underparts grayer, bill blood-red, legs
shorter, tail longer.

Voice: Harsh *TEE-ar* or *kip-kip-kip-TEE-ar,*
       higher in pitch than the Common Tern
Habitat: Coastal islands and beaches; also on
       tundra in summer.
Nesting: 2 spotted olive-buff eggs in a shallow
       depression in ground, sometimes lined
       with grass or shells. Usually nests on
       islands or protected sand spits. In
       colonies.
Range: Aleutians, northern Alaska, Ellesmere
       Island east to Newfoundland,
       Massachusetts, Quebec, northern
       Manitoba and British Columbia.
       Winters at sea in the Southern
       Hemisphere. Also breeds in northern
       Eurasia.

Seldom seen south of its breeding
grounds in the East, these terns
annually perform spectacular
migrations, every fall heading eastward
across the Atlantic and down the west
coasts of Europe and Africa to winter in
the Antarctic Ocean. In spring they
retrace the same route, a round trip
totaling as much as 22,000 miles. They
see more daylight than any other living
creature since they are in both the
Arctic and Antarctic during the periods
of longest days. During the northern
winter this species is more truly oceanic
than its close relatives, feeding chiefly
on small seagoing shrimp and other
planktonic animals. Like most other
terns, it vigorously defends its nest,
often making painful attacks on the
heads of human intruders.

64 **Royal Tern**
    (*Sterna maxima*)
    Gulls, Terns (Laridae)

Description: 18–21″ (46–53 cm). Crow-sized. A
       large tern with a heavy *yellow-orange* to
       orange-red bill. Black cap, pale gray
       back and wings, white forehead, black
       crest. Tail moderately forked. Similar

Caspian Tern has blood-red bill, darker underwing, and shorter tail.

Voice: Harsh *Kak,* like the Caspian Tern but higher-pitched.

Habitat: Sandy beaches.

Nesting: Usually a single buff, spotted egg in a sand scrape on an island or a sheltered peninsula.

Range: Breeds along the coast from Virginia to Texas and Mexico, wandering regularly farther north in summer. Winters from the Gulf Coast southward. Also breeds in West Africa.

It nests in large, dense colonies. Nests are sometimes washed away by storm tides but the birds usually make a second attempt, often at a new location. It has fewer young than other terns but maintains its numbers wherever it has protection from disturbance. It feeds almost entirely on small fish, rather than crustaceans and insects taken by most other terns.

69 Least Tern
(Sterna albifrons)
Gulls, Terns (Laridae)

Description: 8–10″ (20–25 cm). Size of a large sparrow. *Very small* tern with a *yellow bill* and a fast, shallow wingbeat. White with black cap, pale gray back and wings, and forked tail; *forehead white.*

Voice: Sharp *killick* or *kip-kip-kip-killick.*

Habitat: Sandy and pebbly beaches along the coast; sandbars in large rivers. Often on land fills.

Nesting: 2 or 3 buff, lightly spotted eggs in an unlined scrape on a sand spit or gravel beach. In colonies.

Range: Maine south to Venezuela; occasionally along rivers in the Mississippi Valley; coastal California. Winters from Gulf Coast southward. Also breeds in Eurasia, Africa, and Australia.

This tern, despite its small size, is more tolerant of human disturbance than its larger relatives, often breeding close to heavily populated areas. It suffered greatly in the days when terns were shot for the millinery trade, and long after the shooting stopped it seemed unable to recover its former numbers. Finally, within the last few decades, it began to increase again and has become a familiar sight along the coast. Because of its habit of nesting on low sandbars, whole colonies are sometimes destroyed by extra high tides. It is most often seen hovering over the water, peering downward in search of small minnows and other marine or freshwater organisms.

70 Black Skimmer
(*Rynchops niger*)
Skimmers (Rynchopidae)

Description: 18″ (46 cm). Crow-sized. Black above, white below; red legs. *Bill red with black tip; laterally compressed, bladelike;* unique among birds in having *lower mandible much longer (about one-third) than the upper.*

Voice: In addition to their barking call they have softer cooing notes on the nesting site.

Habitat: Breeds chiefly on sandbars and beaches; feeds in shallow bays, inlets, and estuaries.

Nesting: 3 or 4 brown-blotched buff eggs on bare sand, usually among shell fragments and scattered grass clumps.

Range: Atlantic and Gulf coasts from Massachusetts and Long Island to Florida and Texas and from Mexico to southern South America. Winters regularly north to the Carolinas.

This extraordinary bird can hardly fail to attract attention from even the most blasé observer, especially when in flight. Usually only one or two individuals are seen as they skim the surface (hence their name) for fish, with the tip of the lower mandible cutting through the water. They also wade in shallow water jabbing at the fish scattering before them. At other times compact flocks may be seen flying in unison, wheeling in one direction and then another—showing first the jet black of the wings, then the gleaming white of the underparts. Black Skimmers have extended their breeding range northward within the past forty years and today nest on the less disturbed sand beaches and dunes of Long Island. They are especially attracted to the sand fill of newly dredged areas; such places contain colonies of up to 200 pairs. These sites are usually temporary, being abandoned as soon as too much grass appears.

71 Sooty Tern
(*Sterna fuscata*)
Gulls, Terns (Laridae)

Description: 16″ (40 cm). Robin-sized. *Adult black above with white forehead; white below.* Deeply forked tail; thin, black bill. Immature birds are dark brown.

Voice: Harsh, squeaky notes and croaks.

Habitat: Coastal and oceanic islands during the breeding season; pelagic at other times.

Nesting: 1 white egg with reddish-brown blotches in a hollow in the sand; occasionally on rocks or ledges. Almost always in large colonies. Has an unusual nine-month breeding cycle.

Range: Tropical seas; in North America breeds only on the Dry Tortugas, Florida.

Sooty Terns are notorious wanderers, and when not nesting they range far and wide over the seas. Perhaps this is why they are so often blown inland, sometimes many hundreds of miles, by

hurricanes and tropical storms. These
birds have a remarkable homing ability
when individuals marked with a dye
were taken from their breeding ground
on the Dry Tortugas, and released along
the coasts of North Carolina and Texas,
all returned to their breeding grounds
in one to seven days. Sooty Terns feed
largely at dusk and at night. Unlike
most other terns they do not dive, but
pluck small fish and squid from the
surface of the water. They spend most
of their time in the air, rarely perching
or alighting on the water.

---

73 Brown Noddy
(*Anous stolidus*)
Gulls, Terns (Laridae)

Description: 15″ (38 cm). Robin-sized. Dark sooty
brown with pale grayish-white crown;
wedge-shaped tail; slender, black bill.

Voice: Low *cah,* similar to call of a young
crow.

Habitat: Coastal and oceanic islands during the
breeding season; pelagic at other times.

Nesting: 1 buff egg, spotted with lilac and
brown, in a stick nest lined with
seaweed and often bits of shell and
coral, placed on rocks, in trees, bushes,
or on exposed coral reefs.

Range: Breeds on the Dry Tortugas, Florida.
Found nearly throughout the warmer
regions of the world.

These dark brown terns with light caps
associate commonly with Sooty Terns,
at least at breeding colonies. Unlike
them, however, the Noddy does not
wander northward after the nesting
season and, as a result, few are reported
in our area north of southern Florida.
Noddies get their name from their
habit of nodding and bowing to each
other during courtship. They catch
their food—primarily small fish—by
pouncing on it when it comes to the

surface rather than diving after it as most terns do. These oceangoing terns are fond of perching on floating pieces of driftwood and occasionally alight on the water and float.

74 Black Noddy
(*Anous tenuirostris*)
Gulls, Terns (Laridae)

Description: 12″ (30 cm). Bill black, top of head white, rest of plumage dark sooty-brown, feet brownish-black. Bill long, thin, and straight; tail wedge-shaped.

Habitat: Small oceanic and coastal islands in the breeding season; otherwise wanders at sea.

Nesting: One egg, whitish spotted with brown, laid in a stick nest lined with grass or seaweed in a tree or bush.

Range: Tropical portions of the Atlantic, Pacific, and Indian oceans. In the East found only in the Dry Tortugas, off southern Florida.

This pantropical tern is of extremely local occurrence in North America, but each year since 1960 one or two individuals have been found among nesting Brown Noddies in the Dry Tortugas. Although occurring there regularly, the Black Noddy has not yet been known to nest there. This species may easily be told from the Brown Noddy by its smaller size, blacker color, and white rather than gray cap; it is sometimes called the White-capped Noddy.

76 Gannet
(*Morus bassanus*)
Gannets, Boobies (Sulidae)

Description: 35–40" (89–102 cm). Goose-sized.
Adult white with black wing tips; head
tinged with rich orange-buff in breeding
season. Long, pointed tail and wings.
Immature bird is dark gray speckled
with white. Alternately flaps and glides
in flight—shaped like a flying
cross.

Voice: Guttural croak or grunt, heard only on
the breeding islands.

Habitat: Large colonies on rocky cliffs of coastal
islands.

Nesting: 1 bluish-white egg that soon changes to
brown is placed in a shallow nest of
dried seaweed high on a precipitous
cliff or along the top of a bluff. Nests
are close together.

Range: Breeds on a few islands off
Newfoundland, in the Gulf of St.
Lawrence, and off Nova Scotia. Winters
in coastal waters south to Florida. Also
the west coast of Europe.

This strictly maritime species, the only
northern member of the Booby family,
is one of the most spectacular birds.
During migrations they may be observed
offshore, either gliding above the water
or diving into the sea after fish,
sometimes plunging headlong from
heights as great as 50 feet or more. A
remarkable system of interconnected air
sacs under the skin of the breast serves
as a cushion to protect the bird from
the shock of striking the water.
A trip to the breeding colony on
Bonaventure Island, off the Gaspé
Peninsula, Quebec, yields one of the
great sights in the bird world: over
15,000 pairs of gannets incubating,
brooding their young, or searching for
food. Gannets, like other members of
the family, take part in an elaborate
series of displays. When one bird
returns to the nest site it is greeted by

its mate. Both birds raise their heads
and cross bills, which they clash
together like fencers, then bow to each
other with wings and tails raised. This
is followed by mutual preening of the
head and neck. Usually the bird who
has been relieved at the nest will pick
up sticks or seaweed to present to its
mate. Finally, the departing bird stands
with head and neck extended straight
up and wings raised over the back, then
launches itself into the air with an
upward leap.

85, 86 Magnificent Frigatebird
(*Fregata magnificens*)
Frigatebirds (Fregatidae)

Description: 38–40″ (96–102 cm). W. 90″ (2.5 m).
Black with very long, pointed wings,
deeply forked tail, and long hooked
bill. Male has a brilliant red throat
pouch in breeding season and inflates it
to huge size during courtship; female
has a white breast. Young have white
head and underparts.

Voice: Usually silent; harsh, guttural notes
during courtship.

Habitat: Mangrove islets in shallow waters.

Nesting: 1 white or greenish-white egg in a stick
nest in mangrove clumps.

Range: Local on islets in Florida Bay. In the
nonbreeding season, ranges to the
coasts of Florida, Louisiana, and Texas.
Also south to Peru and Brazil.

Frigatebirds, also known as Man-o'-
War-birds, are masters of flight—
whether soaring on outstretched wings,
circling in the sky, swooping down on
flying fish, or giving chase to boobies
and other seabirds. They have the
largest wingspread in proportion to
weight of any bird. A frigatebird will
harass a booby until the latter drops its
catch, which the frigatebird deftly
snatches in midair. These birds have

been known to eat squid, jellyfish, young sea turtles, and nestling seabirds. They never alight on land or water because their short legs and broa wings make it difficult for them to tak off except from a height, such as the limb of a tree or a rock.

91 **Razorbill**
(*Alca torda*)
Auks (Alcidae)

Description: 17″ (43 cm). A crow-sized diving bird Black above, white below. Very deep bill, laterally compressed.

Voice: Low croaks and growls.

Habitat: Coastal waters.

Nesting: 1 brown-spotted bluish egg placed on or under rocks.

Range: Greenland south to Maine and from northern Europe to France. Winters south as far as New Jersey and the Mediterranean.

These birds can often be recognized at distance on the water by their large heads, stout bills, and upward-pointed tails. As with many alcids, Razorbills migrate southward after severe cold spells and visit our shores in the midst of winter. They are hardy birds, spending most of their time at sea and approaching land only after strong easterly gales. During the breeding season they prefer rocky coasts, where they lay their eggs and raise their young. Razorbills feed mostly on fish, shrimp, and squid. They are very adep at diving and have been caught in gill nets as deep as sixty feet.

92 Black Guillemot
(Cepphus grylle)
Auks (Alcidae)

Description: 13" (33 cm). Pigeon-sized. In summer, *all black with a large white wing patch; bright red feet;* pointed bill. In winter the black is largely replaced by white. Locally called Sea Pigeon.

Voice: Shrill mouselike squeaks.

Habitat: Rocky coasts, even in winter.

Nesting: 2 whitish eggs with dark brown blotches placed under rocks, either on a bare surface or on loose pebbles.

Range: Circumpolar, breeding south to Maine, the British Isles, Scandinavia, and Alaska. Winters south to Long Island (rarely), France, and Alaska.

In summer plumage these jet-black seabirds with their large white wing patches and bright red feet are conspicuous, especially when in flight. A characteristic field mark is their habit of dipping their bills into the water. Guillemots are hardy birds, rarely migrating even in subzero weather. Their food consists primarily of small fish, crustaceans, mollusks, and marine worms.

93 Thick-billed Murre
(Uria lomvia)
Auks (Alcidae)

Description: 18" (46 cm). Crow-sized. Black above, white below; throat white in winter.

Voice: Purring or murmuring, hence the name "murre." Also a guttural croak and higher pitched bleat.

Habitat: Rocky coasts.

Nesting: 1 large bluish-green egg with brown scrawls. They nest in dense colonies of countless thousands on sheer sea cliffs. The single egg, laid on a narrow ledge, is pear-shaped, so that instead of rolling off the cliff it merely rolls around on its own axis.

Range: High Arctic and subarctic coasts of both hemispheres; in America it breeds south to islands in the Gulf of St. Lawrence. Winters on the Pacific Coast south to southern Alaska, on the Atlantic south to New Jersey.

Unlike the other alcids, which are exclusively oceanic, this species occurs very rarely on the Great Lakes and other large inland bodies of water. Murre eggs are a rich source of food for both Eskimos and Indians, while the birds themselves are among the chief prey of Gyrfalcons, Peregrines, and Skuas. In turn the murres feed on fish, squid, and various crustaceans.

94 Common Murre
(*Uria aalge*)
Auks (Alcidae)

Description: 17″ (43 cm). Crow-sized. An almost exact counterpart of the previous species, but *bill thin and pointed;* face with more white in winter; dark line above eye projects backward.

Voice: Similar to the Thick-billed Murre.

Habitat: Rocky coasts.

Nesting: 1 blue-green egg with black marks on bare rock ledge.

Range: Arctic and subarctic shores; breeds in America south to California on the Pacific side but only to islands in the Gulf of St. Lawrence on the Atlantic. Winters south to California and Massachusetts.

On the Pacific Coast this species breeds much farther south than the Thick-billed Murre, but curiously enough not on the Atlantic coast. Much more abundant on the Pacific side. The murres, like all alcids, use their wings for swimming and diving, and seem to fly through the water.

95, 97 Common Puffin
(Fratercula arctica)
Auks (Alcidae)

Description: 12" (30 cm). Short, stocky bird. Black
above and white below, with a white
face and red legs; its remarkable
*triangular bill is brilliant red and
yellow.* In fall the horny outer covering
of the bill peels off, leaving the bill
smaller and duller in appearance.

Voice: Deep, throaty purrs and croaks. One
call sounds like *Hey, Al.*

Habitat: Chiefly rocky coasts.

Nesting: 1 white egg in a burrow in soft soil
or a rock crevice. Nest cavity is lined
with grass.

Range: Greenland and arctic Europe south to
Maine and Portugal. It is essentially
nonmigratory and winters chiefly
offshore in the breeding range.

This clown of the sea is a comical-
looking bird with a short dumpy
figure, red-rimmed gleaming yellow
eyes, gaudy triangular bill, and a habit
of waddling around, jumping from rock
to rock. It nests in much smaller
colonies than do most of the other
alcids. Puffins hunt their food in rocky
coastal waters and also at sea. Their
food consists of small fish, shellfish, and
shrimp. They are excellent swimmers
and divers. An attempt is being made
to reintroduce the puffin into a former
breeding area on the Maine coast.
Nestlings from Newfoundland have
been hand-reared on islands with
the hope that they will return to this
area as adults.

96, 98 Dovekie
(Alle alle)
Auks (Alcidae)

Description: 8" (20 cm). Starling-sized. Very small,
chunky, black-and-white seabird. Black

above, white below. Bill very short.

Voice: Lively chattering.

Habitat: Breeds on rocky cliffs and winters chiefly at sea.

Nesting: 1 bluish-white egg in a rock crevice.

Range: High Arctic south to Greenland. Winters south to New Jersey.

The little Dovekie, smallest of Atlantic Alcidae, exists in countless thousands in the cold Arctic regions and is considered by some to be the most abundant bird in the world. Greenland Eskimos catch large numbers of them in long-handled nets, eating the birds raw and making shirts from their skins. Great flocks move southward during severe cold spells, but the vast majority winter far out at sea. On occasion, during migration in November, powerful easterly gales may blow them great distances inland, where they usually succumb to the elements or die of starvation. Dovekies feed on phytoplankton, krill, small fish, and crustaceans.

102 Great Cormorant
(Phalacrocorax carbo)
Cormorants (Phalacrocoracidae)

Description: 35–40″ (89–102 cm). Goose-sized. Adult black with white throat and yellow chin pouch; in breeding plumage it has white flank patches. Immatures are dull brown, paler below often white on belly.

Voice: Deep, guttural grunts.

Habitat: Cliffs, rocks, and trees of coastal inlands.

Nesting: 3 or 4 pale blue-green eggs overlaid with a chalky coating, placed in seaweed-lined stick nests.

Range: Greenland and locally in Atlantic Canada south to southwestern Nova Scotia. Winters south to New Jersey. Also in the Old World.

Largest of all cormorants, in the Orient this species is trained to catch fish. Cormorants dive from the surface of the water and are excellent swimmers. They feed largely on fish but also take crustaceans and mollusks. The Great Cormorant has increased in numbers within the past quarter century, and dozens may now be observed in winter on offshore rocks in the northeast.

113, 162 Red-breasted Merganser
(*Mergus serrator*)
Swans, Geese, Ducks (Anatidae)

Description: 19–26" (48–66 cm). Male has a green head, *gray sides, white neck-ring, and rusty breast*. Female grayish, with brown head shading gradually into white of breast. Both sexes are crested and have red bills.

Voice: Usually silent; various croaking and rasping notes during courtship.

Habitat: Northern lakes and tundra ponds; in winter, principally on the ocean and in salt bays.

Nesting: 8–10 olive-buff eggs in a down-lined depression on the ground concealed under a bush or in a brush pile.

Range: Alaska, Baffin Island, and Labrador south to Maine, Michigan, and British Columbia. Winters chiefly along the coast south to the Gulf Coast and northern Mexico. Also breeds in northern Eurasia.

This is the only one of our three mergansers commonly found on salt water. Like the others it lives mainly on fish, which it captures in swift underwater pursuit, aided by its long, pointed bill lined with sharp toothlike projections.

116, 152 Oldsquaw
(*Clangula hyemalis*)
Swans, Geese, Ducks (Anatidae)

Description: Males 19–22″ (48–56 cm); females 15–
17″ (38–43 cm). Male boldly patterned
in black and white (chiefly white in
winter, chiefly black in summer), with
very long, slender central tail feathers.
Females are duller and lack the long tail
feathers. In all plumages has *all-dark,
unpatterned wings.*

Voice. Various clucking and growling notes;
musical *ow-owdle-oo,* frequently
repeated, during courtship.

Habitat: Tundra; in winter on open bays and
inshore waters.

Nesting: 6–9 pale buff eggs, in a down-lined
cup of grass and twigs, concealed under
a bush or in a hollow on the tundra.

Range: Aleutian Islands, northern Alaska
eastward along the arctic coast of
Canada and the islands to Greenland,
south to southern Hudson Bay and
northern British Columbia. Winters
along the coast south to Oregon and the
Carolinas. Also in Eurasia.

The Oldsquaw is one of the very few of
our diving ducks that travels under
water by using its wings; other species
propel themselves with their feet. This
fact may explain the birds' ability to
dive to such great depths—as deep as
80 fathoms. Their food consists of
shrimps, small fish, and mollusks.
These very noisy birds are noisiest in
early spring, when males gather and
utter their mellow, barking courtship
calls; this pleasing sound is audible
for a mile or two on a still, spring
morning.

117, 145 **Common Eider**
(*Somateria mollissima*)
Swans, Geese, Ducks (Anatidae)

Description: 23–27″ (58–68 cm). Our largest duck.
Male has *black underparts; white back,*
breast, and head; dark crown; back of
head has greenish tinge. Female is
mottled brown. Long, sloping bill
gives the bird a distinctive profile.

Voice: During courtship the male gives a
human-like moan. Female quacks.

Habitat: Rocky coasts and coastal tundra.

Nesting: 4–7 olive or buff eggs in a substantial
mass of grass thickly lined with down.
Often several pairs form a loose colony.

Range: Alaska across the Arctic to Greenland
and south to Maine. Winters along the
coast south to Alaska and Long Island.
Also breeds in northern Eurasia.

Eiders are best known for their down—
very soft feathers plucked from the
breast of the female. For hundreds of
years down has been gathered from
nests in northern Europe and used to
make pillows and quilts. Only eiders in
the Arctic are strongly migratory; in
the warmer parts of their range they
may remain near the breeding grounds
all year. Their principal foods are
mussels and other shellfish, which are
swallowed whole and crushed by
muscles in the bird's stomach. Since the
persecution of eiders was ended after
the turn of the century, there has been
a spectacular increase along the Maine
coast and they are once again nesting in
large numbers.

118, 146 **King Eider**
(*Somateria spectabilis*)
Swans, Geese, Ducks (Anatidae)

Description: 18–25″ (46–63 cm). A large duck.
Similar to the Common Eider, but male
has a *black back* and a conspicuous

orange-yellow bill and "shield" on forehead. Female similar to female Common Eider but bill is shorter, not extending as far back toward eye, and lacks the distinctive sloping profile.

Voice: A guttural croaking.

Habitat: Rocky coasts and islands.

Nesting: 4–7 buff-olive eggs in a down-lined depression on rocky tundra, often some distance from the edge of the water.

Range: Usually in freshwater ponds and lakes in Alaska and Arctic islands east to Greenland, south locally to Hudson Bay. Winters along coasts south to southern Alaska and New Jersey; rarely farther south and on the Great Lakes. Also breeds on Arctic coasts of Eurasia.

Although the world population of the King Eider is large, the birds are seldom seen in the United States; most winter farther north and favor deeper water than the Common Eider. They often dive far for food, and have been caught in nets as much as 150 feet below the surface. Like the Common Eider, they take large numbers of mussels and other shellfish, but vary their diet with small fish, squids, sand dollars, and sea urchins. Their breeding grounds are so remote that their down is not collected as extensively as that of the Common Eider.

120, 160 **Harlequin Duck**
(*Histrionicus histrionicus*)
Swans, Geese, Ducks (Anatidae)

Description: 14–20″ (35–51 cm). A small, dark duck. Male is blue-gray, appearing black at a distance, with chestnut flank and distinctive white patches on the head and body. Female is dusky brown with three whitish patches on sides of face. In flight, this species lacks white patches on the wings.

Voice: Call has been described as a mouse-like squeak; hence the local name "Sea mouse."

Habitat: Swift-moving streams in summer; rocky, wave-lashed coasts and jetties in winter.

Nesting: 5 or 6 pale buff eggs in a mass of down concealed in a crevice in rocks along a stream.

Range: Alaska, Baffin Island, and northern Quebec south to Labrador and California. Winters along the coast south to Long Island and central California. Also breeds in Asia and Iceland.

In the Northeast these ducks are known locally as "Lords and Ladies." They spend most of their lives on salt water, visiting inland streams only during the breeding season. As soon as the female begins incubating, her mate returns to the ocean and undergoes the annual molt. The preferred habitat—rugged seacoasts—offers food that few other species can exploit. The birds are adept at riding a wave up against the rocks and quickly tearing loose snails, limpets, and barnacles. They also feed on small shrimp, crabs, and small fish, which they catch by diving. In their stay on freshwater streams, they feed mainly on larvae of aquatic insects.

125, 149 **Barrow's Goldeneye**
(*Bucephala islandica*)
Swans, Geese, Ducks (Anatidae)

Description: 16½–20" (42–51 cm). Male has a white body, black back, and black-appearing (actually glossed with purple) head. Similar to male Common Goldeneye, but has more black on sides, a stubbier bill, and a *crescent-shaped—instead of round—white spot in front of eye.* Female gray with white collar and brown head; differs from female Common Goldeneye

in having steeper forehead, duller (less
warm brown) head, and smaller white
wing patches.

Voice: A harsh croak.

Habitat: Forested lakes and rivers; in winter on
open bays and estuaries along coast.

Nesting: 9 or 10 pale green eggs on a bed of
down in a hollow tree or, in treeless
areas, under a rock.

Range: Alaska south in mountains to central
California and Colorado, and along the
coast of Labrador; winters along Pacific
coast and in smaller numbers from
Maritime Provinces south to Long
Island. Also breeds in western
Greenland and Iceland.

Barrow's Goldeneye favors alpine lakes,
often breeding at elevations of 10,000
feet or more. Its patchy distribution
suggests that it is an ancient species,
perhaps now in decline. In the East it is
outnumbered by the Common
Goldeneye, but may occur in flocks of
hundreds in the Maritimes.

126, 150 **Common Goldeneye**
(*Bucephala clangula*)
Swans, Geese, Ducks (Anatidae)

Description: 16–20″ (40–51 cm). Male has a white
body; black back; black-appearing
(actually glossy greenish) head; and a
*large, round, white spot in front of the
bright yellow eye.* Female is grayish with
white neck ring and warm brown head.
Both sexes have a distinctive puffy head
shape and a large white wing patch in
flight.

Voice: In February and March, one can often
hear the nasal, rasping calls of courting
males even when the birds themselves
cannot be seen.

Habitat: Nests on lakes and ponds in the North;
in migration and winter mainly along
the coast in bays and inlets.

Nesting: 8–15 pale green eggs in a mass of down

in a natural tree cavity, sometimes as high as 60 feet aboveground.

Range: Alaska and Labrador south to northern New England, Minnesota, and British Columbia. Winters south to northern Mexico, the Gulf Coast, and Florida.

Called the "Whistler" because the loud sound produced by the wings identifies it even at night, when the birds fly overhead from one feeding ground to another. In the courtship display, which begins in late winter, the male stretches his head forward along the water, then throws it rapidly upward over his back, bill pointed skyward, while uttering a loud rasping note. Then he swings his orange feet forward, sending up a spray in front of him. In winter these ducks feed mainly on mollusks; in summer, mostly on aquatic plants and insects.

127, 151 Bufflehead
(*Bucephala albeola*)
Swans, Geese, Ducks (Anatidae)

Description: 13–15″ (33–38 cm). Small, chubby duck. Male largely white, with black back, black head with greenish- and purplish gloss, and a *large white patch from eye to top and back of head.* Female all dark with a single whitish patch on cheek. It is a fast flier and has a rapid wingbeat.

Voice: A squeaky whistle (male); a soft, hoarse quack (female).

Habitat: Northern lakes and ponds; in winter, mainly on salt bays and estuaries.

Nesting: 8–12 pale buff eggs in a mass of down placed in a woodpecker hole up to 20 feet aboveground.

Range: Alaska, Mackenzie, and Ontario south to Manitoba and the mountains of California. Winters on both coasts south to Mexico, the Gulf Coast, and Florida.

The Bufflehead, or "Butterball" as it is known to hunters, is a smaller relative of the goldeneyes and like them breeds in tree cavities. Its courtship is similar to that of the Common Goldeneye. It is one of the most familiar ducks along the coast in winter. Usually in small parties, it does not form great rafts as do scaups, Redheads, and Canvasbacks.

129, 148 Surf Scoter
(*Melanitta perspicillata*)
Swans, Geese, Ducks (Anatidae)

Description: 17–21" (43–53 cm). Male black with white patches on the crown and nape; hence the local name "Skunk-head." Bill swollen at the base and bearing a large black spot. Female brownish-black with two whitish patches on cheek. Both sexes lack white wing patch.

Voice: A low, guttural croaking.

Habitat: Northern lakes; winters almost entirely on the ocean and in large coastal bays.

Nesting: 7–9 pale buff eggs in a down-lined depression concealed under bushes or in marshy vegetation.

Range: Aleutians, Alaska and northern Canada south to northern Quebec, Saskatchewan and British Columbia. Winters on Atlantic, Pacific, and Gulf coasts.

The Surf Scoter is the only one of the three scoters confined to the New World. These birds are similar in habits to White-winged Scoters but are more likely to be seen diving for mollusks and crustaceans along the line of breaking surf. When alighting on the water they have a distinctive habit of holding their wings up over their backs while coasting to a stop. Because they consume little plant food, hunters do not consider their flesh good to eat; nevertheless, many thousands are shot annually for sport.

130, 147 White-winged Scoter
(*Melanitta fusca*)
Swans, Geese, Ducks (Anatidae)

Description: 19–24" (48–61 cm). Male black with *bold white wing patches* and yellow bill with a large black knob at the base. Females are dull brown with two whitish facial spots and white wing patches.
Voice: A hoarse croak.
Habitat: Large lakes; in winter most birds move to the ocean or coastal bays, but a few remain on big lakes in the interior.
Nesting: 8–12 buff-pink eggs in a hollow under bushes or crevice near water.
Range: Aleutians, Alaska and Manitoba south to North Dakota and Washington. Winters regularly south to British Columbia, Colorado, Louisiana, and South Carolina. Also in Eurasia.

During the height of migration, in October and November, the long, irregular lines of thousands of scoters migrating southward just offshore provide a most impressive sight. This scoter, known in Europe as the Velvet Scoter, is the most widespread of the three species. It feeds chiefly on mollusks, which it collects from mussel beds at depths of 15 to 25 feet. Unlike most diving ducks, which propel themselves underwater with their feet, scoters may also use their wings.

131 Black Scoter
"Common Scoter"
(*Melanitta nigra*)
Swans, Geese, Ducks (Anatidae)

Description: 17–21" (43–53 cm). Male black; black bill with large yellow knob at base, hence the local name "Butterbill." Female duller, with pale cheeks and all-dark bill.

Voice: In spring a musical, whistled *cour-coo*.

Habitat: Ponds in boreal forest; winters on the ocean and in large salt bays.

Nesting: 6–8 pale buff eggs in a down-lined cup of grass hidden in a rock crevice or clump of grass near the edge of water.

Range: Western Alaska, Labrador, and Newfoundland. Winters along the coast south to California and South Carolina, more rarely in the interior. Also found in Eurasia.

The Black Scoter, formerly called Common Scoter, is actually the least common of three species, being more abundant in the Old World than in North America. Like the others it preys heavily on mussels and other mollusks, but also spends much time tearing barnacles and limpets from submerged rocks and reefs. Newly hatched young remain on fresh water for several days, feeding on freshwater mussels and the larvae of aquatic insects, but then move to salt water.

176 Brown Pelican
(*Pelecanus occidentalis*)
Pelicans (Pelecanidae)

Description: 45–54″ (114–137 cm). W. 90″ (2.5 m). Very large, stocky bird with a dark brown body and a massive bill and throat pouch. Head whitish in adults, dark brown in young. Usually rests its bill on its breast.

Voice: Adults are silent but young birds in nesting colonies are very noisy, emitting loud grunts and screams.

Habitat: Sandy coastal beaches and lagoons.

Nesting: 2 or 3 whitish eggs in a mass of sticks and grass placed in a tree or low bush, or on the ground on an island. In colonies.

Range: Atlantic Coast from North Carolina south to Venezuela; on the Pacific Coast from British Columbia to Chile.

186, 189 Red-throated Loon
(*Gavia stellata*)
Loons (Gaviidae)

Description: 24–27" (61–68 cm). Goose-sized.
Large, long-bodied bird seldom seen
away from salt water. In breeding
plumage, *gray head and neck, rusty
throat,* black back spotted with white.
In winter, similar to the Common Loon
but smaller, paler, with bill thinner
and *seemingly upturned.*

Voice: Its call, more rarely heard than that of
the Common Loon, is a high-pitched
wail. More often heard is a low,
goose-like growl.

Habitat: Salt bays and tundra ponds during the
summer; bays and estuaries and ocean
in winter.

Nesting: 2 olive-buff, spotted eggs in
vegetation, at the edge of or in water.

Range: Aleutian Islands and coastal tundra
south to Newfoundland and northern
Manitoba. In winter, south to Florida
and the Gulf Coast. Also breeds in
northern Eurasia.

The attractive breeding plumage of this
loon is seldom seen in southern
latitudes, for it is acquired just before
the birds depart for their nesting
grounds. Loons have difficulty walking
on land because their legs are located at
the extreme rear of their bodies, so they
are seldom seen away from the water.
They are extremely vulnerable to oil
pollution; many have been killed along
both coasts as a result of recent spills.

187 Arctic Loon
(*Gavia arctica*)
Loons (Gaviidae)

Description: 24" (60 cm). A *small* loon with a *slender
straight bill.* In breeding plumage, head
pale gray, neck and back black with
white stripes, throat black with purple

reflections. In winter plumage blackish above, white below. Red-throated Loon in winter has paler, brownish upperparts and an upturned bill; Common Loon is larger, with a stouter bill.

Voice: A harsh *kok-kok-kok-kok*.

Habitat: Tundra, lakes, ponds, and sloughs; in winter, coastal bays and inlets but also on the ocean.

Nesting: 2 spotted olive-brown eggs laid directly on the bare ground or in a slight depression lined with stems and roots, never far from water.

Range: High Arctic regions of both hemispheres; in America, south and east to Hudson Bay. Winters chiefly on the Pacific Coast, but ranges east in migration to the northern portions of Manitoba, Ontario, and Quebec. Very rare in northeastern United States.

This little-known species is the rarest of the three loons in the East. Its diet consists mainly of fish, but on the breeding grounds it also takes crustaceans.

191, 211 Red Knot
(*Calidris canutus*)
Sandpipers (Scolopacidae)

Description: 10½″ (26 cm). Robin-sized. In spring, *rufous underparts and gray upperparts;* in fall, whitish below; short, almost plover-like bill. In flight it shows a whitish rump.

Voice: Soft *quer-wer.* Also a soft rolling trill.

Habitat: Tundra; in migration on tidal flats and rocky shores, and on beaches in inland areas.

Nesting: 4 olive-buff, brown-spotted eggs in a lichen-lined slight depression on dry ground, often among rocks.

Range: Arctic coasts of both hemispheres. Winters from southern United States to southern South America.

Knots in breeding plumage, with their rich rufous underparts set off by marbled gray backs, are among the handsomest of shorebirds. They make a nearly 20,000-mile round trip between the Arctic and Antarctic oceans each year.

192, 209 Dunlin
(*Calidris alpina*)
Sandpipers (Scolopacidae)

Description: 8½″ (21 cm). Starling-sized. *Fairly long bill with a distinct droop at the tip.* In summer, *reddish back;* white below with a *conspicuous black belly.* In winter, dull gray; paler below.

Voice: *Cheerp* or *chit-lit.*

Habitat: Beaches, extensive mud and sand flats, tidal inlets and lagoons; also inland lake and river shores.

Nesting: 4 brown-splotched olive eggs in a grass clump on a dry hummock on the open tundra.

Range: Arctic coasts on both hemispheres. In America, south to southern Alaska and Hudson Bay. Winters on the Pacific Coast from British Columbia and on the Atlantic Coast from New England south to Mexico and Florida.

These handsome birds, also known as Red-backed Sandpipers, are very tame and thus easy to approach and study. Among the hardiest of shorebirds, thousands sometimes spend the winter months on sandbars or inlets along the coast as far north as Long Island.

193, 220 Sanderling
(*Calidris alba*)
Sandpipers (Scolopacidae)

Description: 8″ (20 cm). Starling-sized. In summer, rufous head and breast and white belly;

in winter the rufous areas are replaced by pale gray; *black bill and legs; conspicuous white wing stripe.*

Voice: Sharp *kip.* Conversational chatter while feeding.

Habitat: Ocean beaches, sandbars, occasionally mud flats; inland lake and river shores.

Nesting: 4 brown-spotted olive eggs in a hollow on the ground lined with grasses and lichens.

Range: Worldwide. In the Americas it breeds along the coasts of the Arctic Ocean south to Hudson Bay. Winters from the United States (both coasts) to southern South America.

Practically every day of the year these birds may be found on any ocean beach. As a wave comes roaring in, the birds run up on the beach just ahead of the breaker, then rush after the retreating surf to feed on the tiny crustaceans and mollusks stranded by the outgoing water.

194, 239   American Golden Plover
(*Pluvialis dominica*)
Plovers (Charadriidae)

Description: 9–11″ (23–28 cm). Quail-sized. Dark brown above, with black throat, breast, and belly; bold white stripe from forehead, over the eye, and down the side of the neck. In winter, underparts dusky whitish. Lacks the white wing stripe and the black patch under the wing of the larger and paler Black-bellied Plover.

Voice: A mellow *quee-lee-lee.*

Habitat: Tundra; in migration, on coastal beaches and mudflats and inland on prairies and plowed fields.

Nesting: 3 or 4 spotted buff eggs in a shallow depression lined with reindeer moss, usually on a ridge or other elevated spot in the tundra.

Range: Eastern Siberia, northern Alaska, and

Devon Island south to southern Alaska and Baffin Island. Winters to southern South America and in India, Australia, and the South Pacific.

The American Golden Plover annually performs one of the longest migrations of any American bird. In late summer, birds from the eastern Arctic gather in Labrador and Newfoundland, where they fatten on crowberries and other small fruits before beginning their nonstop flight to the northern coast of South America, a journey of some 2500 miles. Smaller numbers move southward in the fall across the Great Plains. Relatively few of these birds are found along the east coast of the United States. Once in South America, they make another long flight across the vast Amazon Basin, finally arriving at their principal wintering grounds on the pampas of Argentina, Patagonia, and Tierra del Fuego. Here in former times they gathered in enormous numbers, but heavy shooting in both North and South America took a serious toll from which the species has not fully recovered. In the spring the birds return to the Arctic, but at that time they move north by way of the Great Plains.

195, 240 **Black-bellied Plover**
(*Pluvialis squatarola*)
Plovers (Charadriidae)

Description: 10–13" (25–33 cm). Quail-sized. Similar to the American Golden Plover but larger, grayer, with a bold white stripe on the wing visible when the bird flies. In flight it always shows a *black patch under the wing*. At any season it has a *white rump;* the rump is dark in the American Golden Plover.

Voice: Clear, whistled *pee-a-weee* reminiscent of the Wood Pewee.

Habitat: Tundra; in migration and in winter it occurs on beaches and coastal marshes, less commonly on inland marshes, lakeshores, and plowed fields.

Nesting: 3 or 4 spotted buff eggs in a shallow hollow lined with moss, lichens, and grass in tundra.

Range: Northern Alaska and Arctic islands to southern Alaska, Southampton Island, and southern Baffin Island. Winters to northern South America. Also breeds in northern Eurasia.

It seldom travels in large flocks like the American Golden Plover; it is usually found singly or in small groups. Our largest plover, it is conspicuous among its usual companions, the smaller plovers, turnstones, and sandpipers. It is wary and is usually the first to fly off when approached, commonly flying out over water, circling, and landing again behind the observer. It is one of the familiar winter shorebirds along the Atlantic Coast, and a few—mostly fledged the previous summer—spend the summer south of the breeding range. Its principal foods are small crabs and sandworms.

196, 241 Ruddy Turnstone
(*Arenaria interpres*)
Sandpipers (Scolopacidae)

Description: 8–10" (20–25 cm). A stocky shorebird with orange legs. Upperparts rusty red in summer, duller in winter; white below. Face and breast have conspicuous black markings, duller but still visible in winter. Because of their striking flight pattern they are sometimes called "Calico-backs."

Voice: A metallic but musical *netticut* or *kek-kek*.

Habitat: Coastal tundra; in winter on rocky, pebbly, and sandy coasts and beaches.

Nesting: 4 buff-olive spotted eggs in a shallow

hollow sparsely lined with grass and dead leaves and concealed under low bushes.

Range: Islands and coasts in the Arctic. Winters regularly from California and the Carolinas south to South America, in smaller numbers farther north. Also breeds in Arctic Eurasia and in the interior of central Asia.

Turnstones are named from their method of feeding, in which they walk along the beach, deftly rolling small stones and pebbles and seizing the animals hiding underneath. They also dig holes in the sand, often larger than themselves, in pursuit of burrowing crustaceans. Although turnstones are usually encountered in small groups, they are very abundant; during the winter they scatter over a huge area, regularly occurring as far south as Australia, New Zealand, southern Africa, and South America as well as on remote islands in the South Pacific, where they sometimes prey on nesting terns' eggs.

198, 217 Purple Sandpiper
(*Calidris maritima*)
Sandpipers (Scolopacidae)

Description: 9″ (23 cm). *Dark slate* with *orange-yellow legs;* bill dull orange with black tip. Paler and more streaked in winter.
Voice: Single or double *twit*.
Habitat: Rocky coasts and promontories.
Nesting: 4 brown-spotted buff eggs in a depression lined with grass and leaves on the ground.
Range: Arctic and subarctic Canada. Winters on the Atlantic Coast south to South Carolina. Also in arctic, subarctic, and temperate regions of Europe.

These hardy birds remain through the coldest winters on wave-washed rocks along the ocean front. Sometimes flocks of as many as fifty or more may be found on stone jetties. Purple Sandpipers are among the tamest of shorebirds and can be approached closely. In recent years these birds have been found lingering later in spring, and a few nonbreeders have been reported even in summer as far south as Long Island. Their food consists of small crustaceans and mollusks such as periwinkles and snails.

210 Curlew Sandpiper
(*Calidris ferruginea*)
Sandpipers (Scolopacidae)

Description: 8″ (20 cm). In summer, rich cinnamon or chestnut; in winter, gray above and white below. Curved bill. White rump is visible in flight.

Voice: A soft, dry *chirrip*.

Habitat: Tundra; chiefly coastal mud flats on migration.

Nesting: 4 pale yellow eggs with dark brown spots, in a depression on the ground in the tundra.

Range: Northern Siberia; winters in Africa, Asia, and Australia. In America, a rare but regular migrant on the Atlantic Coast.

Except for a small area on the arctic coast of Alaska, this Old World species breeds solely in northern Siberia. During spring migration the adults are in their bright chestnut breeding plumage and, with their curved bills and white rumps, are easily distinguished in the field from their usual associates, the Knots and Dunlins. However, on fall migration in their dull winter plumage they are much more difficult to spot among the hordes of other shorebirds.

221 Semipalmated Sandpiper
(*Calidris pusilla*)
Sandpipers (Scolopacidae)

Description: 6½″ (16 cm). Brownish-gray above,
white below; short, straight bill; *black
legs.*

Voice: A soft *krip.* Also a conversational
chatter while feeding.

Habitat: Coastal beaches, lake and river shores,
flats, and pools in salt marshes.

Nesting: 4 brown-marked buff eggs in a
depression on the ground.

Range: Northern Alaska and Canada south to
Hudson Bay. Winters from the
southeastern U.S. and Mexico to South
America.

These small sandpipers are perhaps the
most numerous shorebirds in North
America, sometimes occurring by the
thousands on migration. Often they are
found on flats feeding together with
their close relatives, the Least and
Western sandpipers. The name
"Semipalmated," referring to the birds'
toes, means "partially webbed."
Actually the toes are only slightly lobed
at their bases, but they do enable the
birds to walk on mud without sinking.

222 Western Sandpiper
(*Calidris mauri*)
Sandpipers (Scolopacidae)

Description: 6½″ (16 cm). Sparrow-sized. Similar to
the Semipalmated Sandpiper, but *bill
longer with a droop at the tip.* In summer,
crown and upper back rusty; in winter,
dull gray.

Voice: *Cheep* or *kreep,* higher and thinner than
the Semipalmated.

Habitat: Shores, mud flats, grassy pools, and wet
meadows.

Nesting: 4 creamy eggs with red-brown spots in
a grass-lined depression on either wet or
dry tundra.

Range: Coasts of Alaska and eastern Siberia. Winters from the coasts of southern United States to South America. Migrates both on the coasts and less commonly in the interior.

This species often associates with the slightly smaller Semipalmated Sandpipers. Western Sandpipers usually feed in deeper water than the other small "peeps" and sometimes immerse their bills completely. In all other respects these sandpipers are much alike in their behavior and are difficult to separate in the field.

225 Baird's Sandpiper
(*Calidris bairdii*)
Sandpipers (Scolopacidae)

Description: 7½" (19 cm). Bluebird-sized. Buff-brown with dark greenish legs; when the bird is at rest, the *wings project beyond the tail.* Back appears scaly because of the pale edges of its feathers.

Voice: *Kreep,* also a loud trill similar to that of other "peeps."

Habitat: Chiefly inland areas with grassy pools, wet meadows, and lake and river shores; in summer on the tundra.

Nesting: 4 dark-spotted, tawny eggs in a dry depression on the ground, often among rocks.

Range: Arctic coasts of northeastern Siberia, Alaska, Mackenzie, the islands in the Canadian Arctic, and Greenland. Winters at high elevations in the Andes in South America. Migrates chiefly through the center of the continent.

Baird's Sandpiper is the least common of the sandpiper group known as "peeps;" and is often overlooked because of its similarity to other small sandpipers. It was named in honor of Spencer Fullerton Baird, an early American ornithologist (1823–1887).

226 White-rumped Sandpiper
(*Calidris fuscicollis*)
Sandpipers (Scolopacidae)

Description: 7½" (19 cm). Small sandpiper with a
short, straight bill and a *white rump.* In
summer, rufous above; in winter, gray
with *conspicuous white eye-stripe.* About
the same size as Baird's Sandpiper;
larger than Least, Semipalmated, and
Western sandpipers; distinctly smaller
than Pectoral Sandpiper.

Voice: Mouselike *jeet-jeet* or swallow-like
twitter.

Habitat: Tundra; flats, grassy pools, wet
meadows, and shores in winter.

Nesting: 4 brown-spotted olive eggs in a grass-
lined nest in a slight depression on the
ground. Because of the remoteness of
its breeding grounds relatively few nests
have been found.

Range: Northern Alaska, Yukon and the Arctic
islands south to northern Hudson Bay.
Winters in southern South America,
east of the Andes from southern Brazil
southward.

A long-distance flyer, it performs
annual migrations between the Arctic
and the subantarctic. On the wintering
grounds in Argentina this is the
commonest of the smaller sandpipers.
With its conspicuous white rump this
species is the easiest to identify of the
"peeps," as these smaller sandpipers
are called.

233 Snowy Plover
(*Charadrius alexandrinus*)
Plovers (Charadriidae)

Description: 5–7" (13–17 cm). Whitish with pale
brown upperparts, black legs, *slender
black bill,* and a small black mark on
each side of the breast. The similar
Piping Plover has a stubbier, yellow
bill and yellow legs.

Voice: Plaintive *chu-we* or *o-wee-ah*.
Habitat: Flat, sandy beaches; alkali beds; and sandy areas with little vegetation.
Nesting: 2 or 3 black-spotted buff eggs in a sand scrape lined with a few shell fragments or bits of grass.
Range: Locally from Washington, Colorado, and Oklahoma to South America, and along the Gulf Coast as far east as northwestern Florida. Winters from California and the Gulf Coast south. Also breeds in the Old World.

The Snowy Plover's patchy distribution, not only in North America but elsewhere in the world, is due to its specialized habitat requirements. Keeping to large, flat expanses of sand, it avoids competition for food in a habitat in which few other species can exist. Here these tiny birds, with their pale coloration, are difficult to see even when they run nimbly over the hard, pavement-like ground. In England the species is usually found only on the southern coast in the counties of Kent and Sussex, and is called the Kentish Plover.

234 **Piping Plover**
(*Charadrius melodus*)
Plovers (Charadriidae)

Description: 6–7″ (15–17 cm). Sparrow-sized. Pale whitish with complete or incomplete black breast band; yellow legs; bill yellowish in spring, dark in fall.
Voice: Clear, whistled *peep-lo*.
Habitat: Bare, dry, sandy areas, both inland and on the coast.
Nesting: 4 buff-white eggs evenly marked with small dark spots, laid in a depression in the sand that is often lined with pebbles and bits of shells. Usually in loose colonies.
Range: Lakes in interior Canada and Newfoundland south along the Atlantic

375

Coast to Virginia, rarely to the
Carolinas. Winters on the Atlantic and
Gulf coasts, north regularly as far as the
Carolinas. Also south to the West
Indies and Mexico.

The color of dry sand, the Piping
Plover is difficult to see on the beach.
The eggs and downy chicks also blend
with the sand. With the rapid
expansion of summer resorts along the
Atlantic Coast, many of the former
nesting sites have been destroyed. This
species arrives much earlier in spring
and departs for the South much earlier
in fall than does the Semipalmated
Plover.

236 Semipalmated Plover
(*Charadrius semipalmatus*)
Plovers (Charadriidae)

Description: 6–8" (15–20 cm). A dark-backed
shorebird with white underparts and a
conspicuous black breast band from which
it gets its common name of "Ring-
necked Plover." Bill stubby, yellow-
orange, with dark tip. The Piping Plover
is similar but is much paler above. The
larger Killdeer has two black breast
bands.

Voice: Plaintive two-noted whistle: *tsuwee.*
Also a soft, rather musical chuckle.

Habitat: Beaches and tidal flats, shallow pools in
salt marshes; lakeshores in the interior
during migration.

Nesting: 4 brown-spotted buff eggs in a shallow
scrape lined with shell fragments,
pebbles, or bits of vegetation on the
tundra or on a beach.

Range: Breeds from the Aleutians, Alaska and
the islands of the Canadian Arctic south
to Nova Scotia, Quebec, northern
Manitoba, and northern British
Columbia. Winters regularly from
California and the Gulf Coast south;
in smaller numbers farther north.

This is one of the most familiar
American shorebirds. The birds usually
migrate in flocks, but otherwise tend to
scatter when feeding. They have the
typical plover habit of running along
the beach for several paces, then
stopping abruptly and raising their
heads.

---

237 Wilson's Plover
(*Charadrius wilsonia*)
Plovers (Charadriidae)

Description: 7–8″ (17–20 cm). Starling-sized. Male
brown above and white below with a
broad black eye patch and neck band;
heavy black bill and *pinkish-gray legs*.
Female similar but bands are gray.

Voice: Clear, whistled *queet*. Also *quit-quit*.

Habitat: Sand beaches and mud flats.

Nesting: 3 or 4 buff eggs with small spots and
blotches placed in a slight depression
on the open sand or occasionally in the
dunes.

Range: Atlantic and Gulf coasts from southern
New Jersey (rare) to Florida and Texas.
Winters chiefly along the Gulf Coast
south to northern South America.

Its stouter, longer bill enables this bird
to partake of a more varied diet than
other plovers, including small crabs,
shrimps, beach fleas, beetles, spiders,
and the smaller shellfish. This is the
largest of the "ring-necked" plovers and
can be most easily identified by its
thick black bill.

---

242 American Oystercatcher
(*Haematopus palliatus*)
Oystercatchers (Haematopodidae)

Description: 17–21″ (43–53 cm). Chicken-sized.
Boldly patterned in blackish-brown and
white. Long red bill, pink feet. Shows a

bold white wing patch in flight.

Voice: Piercing *kleep!* Also a plover-like *cle-ár*.

Habitat: Sandy and pebbly beaches, mud flats, borders of salt marshes.

Nesting: 2–4 spotted blackish-buff eggs in a shallow scrape lined with a few shell fragments on beaches.

Range: Along the coast from Baja California and Massachusetts south to Argentina and Chile. Winters from North Carolina southward.

Oystercatchers are large, conspicuous birds that were quickly shot out along the Atlantic Coast. Given total protection, they have once again become numerous and now nest in numbers as far north as Massachusetts, where just a few years ago they were very rare. Oystercatchers insert their long, bladelike bills into mussels and other bivalves, severing the powerful adductor muscles before the shells can close. They also feed on barnacles and snails. Although they do not breed in colonies, these birds gather in large flocks on migration and in winter.

580 Fish Crow
(*Corvus ossifragus*)
Jays, Magpies, Crows (Corvidae)

Description: 17" (43 cm). All black, somewhat smaller than the American Crow, but size is deceptive in the field. May be best told by its voice.

Voice: Two calls, both distinct from the American Crow's familiar *caw*—a nasal *kwok* and a two-noted nasal *ah-ah*—but in the breeding season young American Crows have a similar *kwok* call.

Habitat: Low coastal country, near tidewater in the North; in the South also lakes, rivers, and swamps far inland.

Nesting: 4 or 5 greenish eggs with brown blotches in a stick nest lined with pine needles, grass, hair, or bark flakes

placed in an evergreen or deciduous
tree.

Range: Atlantic and Gulf coasts from
Massachusetts and extreme southern
New England south to Florida and west
to Texas. Also inland along the larger
rivers north to Arkansas, southwestern
Tennessee, central Virginia, and south-
central Pennsylvania.

Nearly all the heronries on the coast
have attendant Fish Crows ever ready to
plunder the heron nests for eggs. An
omnivorous feeder like all crows, it
consumes corn, insects, lizards, wild
and cultivated fruits, and often carrion
and dead fish—hence its name.

Salt Marshes

Tidal marshes of brackish or salt water,
along creeks and estuaries and behind
barrier beaches. At low tide there are
often extensive mudflats.
Besides the birds treated in this section,
one may find some of the birds of
freshwater marshes, and during
migration, hawks and swallows are
sometimes numerous here.

1, 5 Snowy Egret
(*Egretta thula*)
Herons, Bitterns (Ardeidae)

Description: 20–27" (51–68 cm). W. 38" (1 m). A small white heron with a *slender black bill,* black legs, and *yellow feet.* In the breeding season it has long lacy plumes on its back. Similar to young of the Little Blue Heron, but that species has a stouter, bluish-gray bill and greenish-yellow legs and feet.

Voice: Harsh squawk.

Habitat: Salt marshes, ponds, rice fields, and shallow coastal bays.

Nesting: 3 or 4 pale blue eggs on a platform of sticks in a bush or reedbed. In colonies, often with other species of herons.

Range: Northern California, Oklahoma, and Maine to southern South America. Winters regularly north to California and South Carolina.

During the 19th and early 20th centuries, Snowy Egrets were slaughtered almost to extinction for their fine plumes, used to decorate hats. Fortunately, complete protection has enabled them to increase their numbers again. Snowies are agile, often seen sprinting about in shallow water, or even hovering as they seek small shrimps and minnows. Although they breed on freshwater marshes in the West, in the eastern states, where large freshwater marshes are scarce, they are best known as salt marsh birds.

11 Roseate Spoonbill
(*Ajaia ajaja*)
Ibises, Spoonbills (Threskiornithidae)

Description: 30–32" (76–81 cm). W. 53" (1.3 m) Brilliant pink with white neck and back, orange tails. Straight bill with broad spatulate tip, hence its name. Immatures are white.

Voice: Low croak or cluck.
Habitat: Mangroves.
Nesting: 3–5 dull white eggs with dark spots
and blotches in stick nest, in low dense
bushes or trees.
Range: Locally on the coasts of southern
Florida, Louisiana (rare), and Texas.
Also West Indies, Mexico, and Central
and South America.

These birds spend much time feeding
on shrimps and fish in the shallow
waters of Florida Bay and the Gulf of
Mexico. They obtain food by sweeping
their bills from side to side and
scooping up whatever they encounter.
Early in the century their numbers were
severely depleted by plume hunters
but, with protective laws, they have
increased once again.

13 Louisiana Heron
(*Egretta tricolor*)
Herons, Bitterns (Ardeidae)

Description: 25–30″ (63–76 cm). W. 38″ (1 m).
A gray-blue heron with rufous neck and
white belly.
Voice: Guttural croaks and squawks.
Habitat: Swamps, bayous, coastal ponds, salt
marshes, mangrove islands, mud flats,
and lagoons.
Nesting: 3 or 4 blue-green eggs in a stick nest in
a tree, on the ground, or among reeds.
Range: Atlantic and Gulf coasts from
Massachusetts southward. Winters
north to Virginia. Also in South
America.

Also called the "Tricolored Heron," this
is one of the most numerous herons in
the Deep South. It is extremely slender
and with graceful movements searches
about for frogs or fish. Like bitterns, it
has a habit of standing motionless
among the grasses with bill pointing
straight up in an attempt to avoid
detection.

25, 26 White Ibis
(*Eudocimus albus*)
Ibises, Spoonbills (Threskiornithidae)

Description: 23–27" (58–68 cm). W. 38" (1 m).
Adult white with black wing tips
(usually hidden at rest); bare face and
downcurved, red bill; red legs in
breeding seasons, otherwise slate-
colored. Immature birds are brown
above and white below with brown bill
and legs.

Voice: Grunts and growls.

Habitat: Marshy sloughs, mud flats, lagoons,
and swamp forests.

Nesting: 3–5 pale blue, green, or buff eggs with
dark spots or blotches in a stick nest in
trees over water.

Range: Coastal from South Carolina to Florida
and Texas. South to northern South
America.

Around their colonies, ibises eat crayfish
which in turn devour quantities of fish
eggs. By keeping down the numbers of
crayfish, the birds help increase fish
populations. In addition, their
droppings fertilize the water, greatly
increasing the growth of plankton, the
basic food of all marsh life.

27 Glossy Ibis
(*Plegadis falcinellus*)
Ibises, Spoonbills (Threskiornithidae)

Description: 22–25" (56–63 cm). W. 37" (0.9 m).
A large, all-dark marsh bird with a
downcurved bill. Plumage rich chestnut
wings glossy greenish. The White-
faced Ibis of the Southwest is similar
but has a narrow band of feathers
around the base of the bill and around
the eye.

Voice: Low grunt and higher-pitched bleats.

Habitat: Marshes, swamps, flooded fields, coastal
bays, and estuaries.

Nesting: 2–4 pale blue eggs in stick nests in

bushes and trees, rarely on the ground. In colonies, often along with herons.

Range: On or near the coast, chiefly from Maine to Florida and Texas. In recent years, inland to the Great Lakes. Also in the Old World.

The Glossy Ibis probably crossed the Atlantic from Africa to northern South America in the 19th century, dispersing northward into the United States by way of the Caribbean region. In recent years it has expanded its range considerably and is now a common breeder in areas where it was rare or absent. Inland it frequently eats crayfish, but along the coast it feeds mostly on fiddler crabs. It also eats insects and snakes, including the poisonous water moccasin.

28 White-faced Ibis
(*Plegadis chihi*)
Ibises, Spoonbills (Threskiornithidae)

Description: 22–25" (56–63 cm). W. 37" (0.9 m). A large, chestnut-bronze marsh bird with a long, curved bill. Very similar to the Glossy Ibis but has a *band of white feathers around the base of the bill, under the chin, and behind the eye*. The Glossy Ibis may show white skin at base of bill. In winter the White-faced loses this band and becomes virtually impossible to distinguish from the Glossy.

Voice: Low croak or grunt.

Habitat: Salt marshes and brushy coastal islands in Louisiana and Texas, freshwater marshes in the West.

Nesting: 3–5 pale blue eggs in a shallow cup of reeds lined with grass and placed in low bushes in a marsh.

Range: Oregon and Nebraska south into Mexico and east to coastal Louisiana. Winters north to the Gulf Coast. Also breeds in South America.

This western bird enters our area only in western Louisiana and Texas where the White-faced Ibis is common and the Glossy Ibis is rare; therefore most dark ibises can be assumed to be the White-faced. This bird probably represents an earlier invasion of the New World by the Glossy Ibis, which in isolation evolved into a separate species.

29 Whooping Crane
(*Grus americana*)
Cranes (Gruidae)

Description: 45–50" (114–127 cm). W. 90" (2.3 m) A very large bird, *pure white with jet-black wing tips* and red on forehead and cheeks. Immature birds are similar but head and neck are brown.

Voice: Trumpet-like call that can be heard for several miles.

Habitat: Breeds in northern freshwater bogs; winters on coastal prairies.

Nesting: 2 dark-blotched buff eggs in a mound of marsh vegetation.

Range: South-central Mackenzie, Canada (Wood Buffalo Park). Winters on the Gulf Coast of Texas at Aransas National Wildlife Refuge.

This extremely rare crane is one of our most spectacular birds. In the last few years a few eggs have been taken and placed in the nests of Sandhill Cranes. The young Whooping Cranes are reared by their foster parents. In this way it is hoped that the population of Whooping Cranes can be increased beyond its present limit of about 50.

43, 56 Laughing Gull
(*Larus atricilla*)
Gulls, Terns (Laridae)

Description: 15–17" (38–43 cm). In summer the adult has a *black hood* and dark gray back and wings; hind edge of wing is white; *wing tip is black, without white spots.* Lacks a hood in winter. Young bird is dark brown with *contrasting white rump.* The similar Franklin's Gull has a black wing tip separated from the gray wing by a white band.

Voice: Loud, high-pitched *ha-ha-ha-ha-haah-haah-haah-haah.*

Habitat: Salt marshes, bays, and estuaries. Very rare inland.

Nesting: 3 olive-brown eggs with dark blotches in a ground nest lined with grass and weed stems on sand or salt marsh.

Range: Maine to the Caribbean. Winters regularly north to Virginia, in smaller numbers farther north.

The common summer gull along the Atlantic and Gulf coasts, it has declined in numbers in recent years perhaps due to the destruction of coastal marshes and the increase in Herring Gulls, which prey on its eggs and young. Very agile on the wing, Laughing Gulls easily catch bits of food tossed into the air. In winter they feed on beaches and in harbors.

60, 66 Forster's Tern
(*Sterna forsteri*)
Gulls, Terns (Laridae)

Description: 14–15" (35–38 cm). White with pale gray back and wings, black cap, and deeply forked tail. Orange bill with black tip. Similar to the Common Tern, but *wing tips* are *frosty white* and, at very close range, outer web of outermost tail feathers white instead of dusky. Lacks black cap in winter but has distinctive black mark behind eye.

Voice: Harsh nasal *beep*.

Habitat: Salt marshes in the East; freshwater marshes in the West.

Nesting: 3 or 4 buff, spotted eggs on a large platform of dead grass lined with finer grasses. Usually placed on masses of dead marsh vegetation. In colonies.

Range: Breeds along the Atlantic Coast from Maryland to Texas and in the interior from Alberta and California east to Illinois. Winters from Virginia to Guatemala.

One of the few exclusively North American terns, it is so similar to the Common Tern that, until 1831, it was not recognized as a distinct species. Its preference for marshes enables it to avoid competition with the Common Tern, which favors sandy or pebbly beaches and rocky islands. It was named after Johann Reinhold Forster (1729–1798), a German pastor-naturalist who accompanied Captain Cook around the world, in 1772.

68 Gull-billed Tern
(*Gelochelidon nilotica*)
Gulls, Terns (Laridae)

Description: 13–15″ (33–38 cm). Pigeon-sized. Very pale with almost white back and wings, black cap, and *stout black bill*; tail not as deeply forked as in other terns. Winter birds lack the black cap.

Voice: Rasping *katy-did* similar to the sound made by that insect.

Habitat: Coastal marshes and sandy beaches.

Nesting: 2 or 3 spotted buff eggs in a shell-lined shallow depression (occasionally a well-made cup of dead marsh grasses) on a sandy island in a salt marsh. In colonies. Often breeds with other species of terns.

Range: Long Island south to the Gulf of Mexico and the West Indies. Winters from the Gulf Coast to northern South America. Also in Eurasia, Africa, and Australia.

In addition to the usual tern diet of fish and crustaceans, this bird catches insects in flight, and pursues them on the ground in plowed fields or croplands. Although not numerous, it is widespread, breeding in scattered colonies. In America it was one of the species hardest hit by the millinery trade and has never recovered its former numbers, although recently it has slowly extended its range to the north.

133 Black Duck
(Anas rubripes)
Swans, Geese, Ducks (Anatidae)

Description: 19–22″ (48–56 cm). Sooty brown with conspicuous white wing linings, olive or greenish bill. Sexes alike. The female Mallard is paler and sandier and has the bill mottled with orange.
Voice: Typical duck quack.
Habitat: Marshes, lakes, streams, coastal mud flats, and estuaries.
Nesting: 9–12 greenish-buff eggs in a ground nest of feathers and down.
Range: Eastern and central North America, from Manitoba and Labrador to Texas and Florida.

It is believed that widespread inter-breeding between Black Ducks and Mallards has resulted in recent years in a decrease of "pure" Blacks. Actually the name is a misnomer, for the bird appears black only at a distance; it was formerly more aptly known as the "Dusky Duck." In areas of heavy shooting, these and other dabbling ducks ingest enough lead shot to cause extensive mortality from lead poisoning. If hunters used steel shot such damage would be much reduced.

Mottled Duck
(*Anas fulvigula*)
Swans, Geese, Ducks (Anatidae)

Description: 21″ (53 cm). Mottled dark brown and sandy. Similar to a female Mallard, but bill clear yellow or orange yellow, and tail dark, rather than sandy brown.

Voice: A loud *quack,* like that of a Mallard.

Habitat: Coastal marshes and lagoons.

Nesting: 9–13 pale greenish eggs, in a down-lined nest of grass, concealed in vegetation near a shore.

Range: Resident in southern Florida and along the Gulf Coast of Louisiana and Texas.

This southern duck is a very close relative of the more widespread Mallard. Until recently, no other duck of the genus *Anas* nested in these coastal marshes, and so the distinctive male plumage, which among these birds serves in species recognition, was gradually lost. After thousands of years of evolutionary change, the two sexes are colored alike.

171 **Snow Goose**
including "Blue Goose"
(*Chen caerulescens*)
Swans, Geese, Ducks (Anatidae)

Description: 22–30″ (56–76 cm). The white color phase with black wing tips is most common in the East, while in the West and along the Gulf Coast the "Blue Goose"—dark gray with white head and neck—is numerous. Pinkish bill and feet.

Voice: High-pitched nasal barking.

Habitat: Breeds on the tundra and winters in salt marshes and marshy coastal bays; less commonly in freshwater marshes and adjacent grain fields.

Nesting: 5–7 whitish eggs in a large cup of grass and moss lined with down. Often in loose colonies.

Range: Arctic regions of North America and extreme eastern Siberia. Winters on the Pacific Coast south to Baja California and along the Atlantic Coast from New Jersey to Texas. In smaller numbers in the interior.

Until recently the two color phases were considered separate species, but it is now known that they interbreed where their ranges overlap. The nesting grounds of the "Blue Goose" were unknown until 1929, when large numbers were discovered breeding on the shores of Foxe Basin, west of Baffin Island. They are now known to breed on Baffin Island and nearby Southampton Island. Each fall virtually the entire population gathers at the southern end of Hudson Bay and makes a single nonstop flight to the Gulf Coast.

Ross' Goose
(Chen rossii)
Swans, Geese, Ducks (Anatidae)

Description: 24″ (60 cm). A Mallard-sized edition of the Snow Goose. White wings, black wing tips, pink bill and pink legs. Differs from the Snow Goose in its smaller size, *very stubby bill,* and rounder head.

Voice: Soft cackling and grunting notes.

Habitat: Arctic tundra in the breeding season, salt or fresh marshes in the winter.

Nesting: 4 creamy white eggs in a nest of grass lined with down, placed on a small island in a lake or river.

Range: Breeds in northeastern Mackenzie and on Southampton Island; winters mainly in central California; but occurs occasionally in the lower Mississippi Valley and on the east coast.

This species is very similar to the white phase of the Snow Goose, and occasionally hybridizes with that species. There is some evidence that many of the Ross' Geese that appear in the eastern United States in the winter are actually hybrids. The great majority of Ross' Geese spends the winter in the Sacramento Valley in California.

172 **Brant**
     including "Black Brant"
     (*Branta bernicla*)
     Swans, Geese, Ducks, (Anatidae)

Description: 22–30" (56–76 cm). Similar to the Canada Goose but smaller, shorter-necked, and lacking the conspicuous white cheek patch. Dark brown above with black head and neck, and an inconspicuous white mark on the side of the neck.

Voice: Low, guttural croaking, unlike the clear, rich honking of Canada geese.

Habitat: Tundra and coastal islands in the Arctic; salt marshes and estuaries in winter.

Nesting: 4 or 5 cream-colored eggs in a large mass of moss and down on the tundra. Often nests in loose colonies.

Range: Breeds in the Arctic; winters along the coasts south to California and the Carolinas.

Its favorite winter food is eelgrass. In the 1930s a disease virtually wiped out this abundant underwater plant in the North Atlantic and the Brant declined drastically, but it is once again a fairly common visitor to our shores.
Migrating flocks can be identified at a great distance as they travel in erratic, constantly shifting bunches unlike the V-shaped flocks of Canada Geese or the long, irregular lines of Snow Geese. Birds from far western North America have black underparts and until recently were considered a separate species, the "Black Brant."

200, 230 Stilt Sandpiper
(*Micropalama himantopus*)
Sandpipers (Scolopacidae)

Description: 8½" (21 cm). Robin-sized. *Chestnut head stripes and barring below* are diagnostic in breeding plumage. Nonbreeding birds have much paler plumage with a white line over the eye. Long bill, slightly downcurved at the tip. Has long, greenish legs. Wings unpatterned.

Voice: Simple *tu-tu* similar to that of Lesser Yellowlegs.

Habitat: Grassy pools and shores of ponds and lakes.

Nesting: 4 pale buff eggs with brown markings on open ground in grass tussocks near water.

Range: Breeds in northern Alaska and Canada. Winters in Florida and South America. Uncommon along the Atlantic Coast.

Often associated with dowitchers and yellowlegs, Stilt Sandpipers resemble both species and appear to be intermediate between the two. While yellowlegs move about continually in nervous, jerky motions and dowitchers feed slowly, probing deep into the mud, Stilt Sandpipers move like yellowlegs but cover more ground, at the same time feeding deliberately like dowitchers.

201, 212 Short-billed Dowitcher
(*Limnodromus griseus*)
Sandpipers (Scolopacidae)

Description: 12" (30 cm). Rich rust-brown in spring, gray in fall; very long bill, greenish legs, barred tail, white rump and back.

Voice: Loud, rapid, whistled *tu-tu-tu*.

Habitat: Mud flats, creeks, salt marshes, and tidal estuaries.

Nesting: 4 greenish eggs, spotted with brown,

in a nest lined with grass and moss in a ground depression on open wet tundra.

Range: Southern Alaska to eastern Canada. Winters from southern United States to central South America.

Dowitchers often occur in large flocks—sometimes in the thousands— on coastal flats during migrations, remaining well bunched whether in flight or feeding in the mud. They probe deeply with their long bills with rapid up-and-down movements like sewing machines, seeking marine worms, snails, tiny crustaceans, and aquatic larvae.

202, 229 Willet
(*Catoptrophorus semipalmatus*)
Sandpipers (Scolopacidae)

Description: 15″ (38 cm). Pigeon-sized. Grayish-brown with *gray legs*. Best told in flight by its flashy *black-and-white wing pattern*. The gray legs and thicker bill distinguish it from the Greater Yellowlegs.

Voice: Extremely vocal; their *will-will-willet* calls identify them immediately. They also utter a rapid *kuk-kuk-kuk-kuk-kuk*.

Habitat: Coastal beaches, freshwater and salt marshes, lakeshores, and wet prairies.

Nesting: 4 brown-spotted olive-buff eggs in a nest lined with weeds or bits of shell in a depression on open ground or in a grass clump.

Range: Breeds locally in southern Canada, United States, and the West Indies. Winters from southern United States to central South America.

Willets look quite nondescript on the ground and superficially resemble yellowlegs; but once in flight or even with wings spread out, they are distinguished by their striking black-and-white color pattern. They frequently accompany godwits on migration.

213 Long-billed Dowitcher
(*Limnodromus scolopaceus*)
Sandpipers (Scolopacidae)

Description: 12¼" (31 cm). A stocky shorebird with a very long, straight bill. Breeding birds have rusty underparts and dark, streaked upperparts; winter birds are gray. In all plumages shows a conspicuous white rump and lower back, most easily seen in flight. Very similar to Short-billed Dowitcher, but darker and more coarsely streaked above, and with a longer bill. Voices also different.

Voice: A sharp, thin *keek*, very different from soft *tu-tu-tu* of Short-billed Dowitcher.

Habitat: Breeds in muskeg; in migration and winter occurs on mud flats, marshy pools, and margins of freshwater ponds.

Nesting: 4 olive eggs spotted with brown, in a grass and moss-lined nest on the ground.

Range: Northeastern Siberia, northern Alaska, and northwestern Canada. Winters from southern United States south to Guatemala.

Dowitchers are most often seen during migration, when this species favors freshwater habitats, and the Short-billed Dowitcher is more partial to salt water. The main fall migration of Long-bills takes place in September and October, when a majority of Short-bills have already departed.

214 Ruff
(*Philomachus pugnax*)
Sandpipers (Scolopacidae)

Description: 11″ (28 cm). The breeding males have
extraordinarily variable plumage,
showing any combination of black,
white, chestnut, gray, buff, etc. ear
tufts, ruffs, and gorgets; females (called
Reeves) and winter males are much
duller—gray or brown above, white
below; leg color varies from yellow to
green, brown, and red. In flight, two
oval white tail patches are visible. In all
seasons the male is noticeably larger
than the female.

Voice: Usually silent, but occasionally a soft
tu-whit when flushed.

Habitat: Short grassy meadows and marshy
ponds.

Nesting: 4 gray, green, or buff eggs, heavily
marked with deep brown blotches.

Range: Subarctic Europe and Asia south to the
central portions of those continents;
winters south to South Africa, Ceylon,
and Indonesia. In America, a rare but
regular migrant on or near the Atlantic
Coast.

The Ruff is one of the most remarkable
of all shorebirds. It is the only wader in
which the two sexes are different in
color, pattern, and size during the
breeding season. The males also form
leks or "dancing" grounds and engage
in courting. After mating, the females
build their nests away from the
courtship area.

227 Lesser Yellowlegs
(*Tringa flavipes*)
Sandpipers (Scolopacidae)

Description: 10½″ (26 cm). A smaller edition of the
Greater Yellowlegs, with a shorter bill.

Voice: Call is quite different from that of the

Greater Yellowlegs: a flatter, less melodious *tu-tu*, given in doublets rather than triplets.

Habitat: Marshy ponds, lake and river shores, mud flats; in the breeding season, boreal bogs.

Nesting: 4 buff eggs blotched with brown in a slight depression on the open ground near damp places.

Range: Alaska and Canada. Winters from southern United States to southern South America.

This species usually occurs in larger flocks and is a tamer bird than the Greater Yellowlegs, allowing an observer a much closer approach before flying off a short distance. Both species of yellowlegs nod up and down when watching an intruder or just before.

228 Greater Yellowlegs
(*Tringa melanoleuca*)
Sandpipers (Scolopacidae)

Description: 14″ (35 cm). A slender, gray-streaked wader with conspicuous white upper tail coverts and long *yellow legs*. The Lesser Yellowlegs is similar, but smaller, with a more slender bill.

Voice: Far-reaching, penetrating—though musical—series of whistled *whew-whew-whews*, usually given in threes or fours. This call easily differentiates the Greater Yellowlegs from its relative, the Lesser Yellowlegs.

Habitat: Prefers pools, lakeshores, and tidal mud flats on migration, but open wet tundra and marshy ground in the breeding season.

Nesting: 4 eggs—rich, tawny-colored, heavily marked with brown—in a slight depression on the ground in open, damp areas.

Range: Breeds in southern Alaska and central and southern Canada. Winters along coast from Carolinas to southern South America.

The larger of the two yellowlegs is a noisy and conspicuous bird. It is also more wary than its smaller relative and flushes at a greater distance. It often wades up to its belly and occasionally even swims. With its long legs it easily obtains food in pools.

---

231 Marbled Godwit
(*Limosa fedoa*)
Sandpipers (Scolopacidae)

Description: 18″ (46 cm). Crow-sized. A large, pale, buff-brown wader with *cinnamon wing linings* and buffy underparts, and a *long, pinkish upturned bill.*

Voice: Prolonged, far-reaching, whistled *god-wit, god-wit,* or *go-wit, go-wit*—hence its name.

Habitat: Extensive grasslands; on migration, salt marshes, tidal creeks, mud flats, and sea beaches.

Nesting: 4 olive-buff eggs, blotched with brown, in a slight depression on the ground in a grass-lined nest.

Range: South-central Canada and north-central United States. Winters from southernmost United States to Central America and on the Pacific Coast of South America to Chile.

One of our largest shorebirds, it breeds on the vast grassy plains of the West but less abundantly than in former days. Like the Long-billed Curlew, it is a rich buff color, blending perfectly with the brown grass of the plains.

232 Hudsonian Godwit
(*Limosa haemastica*)
Sandpipers (Scolopacidae)

Description: 15″ (38 cm). *Underparts rufous* in the
breeding season, otherwise gray above,
whitish below. Conspicuous *black-and-white tail,* broad white wing stripe, and
black wing lining. Long, slightly
upturned bill.

Voice: Similar to the Marbled Godwit but
higher pitched. Reported as *chip-ta-it*
and *quit-quit.* Usually silent.

Habitat: Tundra; chiefly mud flats on migration.

Nesting: 4 olive-buff eggs in a shallow grass-lined hollow on the ground.

Range: Breeds on the Canadian tundra and
migrates through the United States;
winters in the southern parts of South
America.

Never common, the Hudsonian Godwit
was for many years hunted for food and
became scarce. Now completely
protected, its numbers have increased
considerably. This large shorebird can
be seen in flocks of up to several dozen
or more during fall passage on the
coastal mud flats of the northeastern
states.

243 Black-necked Stilt
(*Himantopus mexicanus*)
Avocets, Stilts (Recurvirostridae)

Description: 13–16″ (33–40 cm). Black above, white
below; head patterned in black and
white; long neck; *very long red legs;*
straight, very thin bill.

Voice: Sharp *kip-kip-kip-kip.*

Habitat: Salt marshes and shallow coastal bays in
the East; also freshwater marshes in the
West.

Nesting: 3 or 4 brown-spotted buff eggs in a
shallow depression lined with grass or
shell fragments in a marsh. In small,
loose colonies.

Range: Oregon and Saskatchewan to the Gulf
Coast, and along the Atlantic Coast
from Delaware and the Carolinas to
northern South America. Winters
mainly south of the United States.

These stilts once bred as far north as
New Jersey. Noisy and conspicuous,
their decline was due to excessive
hunting. In the nesting season they are
particularly aggressive and will often fly
low over an approaching human being,
uttering a loud alarm call with their
long red legs trailing behind them.

245 **Whimbrel**
(*Numenius phaeopus*)
Sandpipers (Scolopacidae)

Description: 17″ (43 cm). Crow-sized, with long
legs. Gray-brown with *striped crown* and
medium-length *curved bill*.
Voice: 5–7 loud, clear, whistled notes.
Habitat: Arctic tundra, preferring freshwater
pools near the coast. On migration,
chiefly coastal salt meadows, mud flats,
and grassy slopes along the coast.
Nesting: 4 olive eggs heavily marked with brown
in a depression in a moss or sedge
clump on the ground.
Range: Northern America and Eurasia. In
America winters from Florida and
California to southern South America.

The Whimbrel, or Hudsonian Curlew,
is found not only along both coasts but
in the center of the continent. It is
numerous because of its wary behavior,
its remote nesting grounds on the
Arctic tundra, and its successful
competition with other big shorebirds
for food and breeding territory. Like
many other tundra breeders, those in
the east fly offshore during their
autumn migration to South America,
returning in spring mainly through the
interior.

246 Long-billed Curlew
(*Numenius americanus*)
Sandpipers (Scolopacidae)

Description: 23" (58 cm). Very large, buff-brown shorebird with *very long sickle-shaped bill* and cinnamon wing linings.

Voice: *Cur-lew*, with the second note higher.

Habitat: Chiefly grass plains and prairies; in migration, lake and river shores, mud flats, salt marshes, and sand beaches.

Nesting: 4 brown-spotted olive-buff eggs in a grass-lined nest in a hollow on the ground.

Range: Breeds chiefly in western North America from southern Canada to New Mexico and Texas. Winters from California and Louisiana to Guatemala, and from South Carolina to Florida.

Our largest shorebird, the "Sicklebill," as it was called by hunters, was once a plentiful gamebird of the Great Plains and the formerly extensive prairies to the east. They are now so scarce that they must be protected by law. Their prolonged, musical whistles carry far, signaling their arrival in spring. While they incubate, their golden colors blend with the brown grass, making them difficult to detect. On grasslands they consume grasshoppers, crickets, and beetles; on shores and beaches, during their migration, they feast on small crustaceans and mollusks or on berries and seeds.

253 Clapper Rail
(*Rallus longirostris*)
Rails, Gallinules, Coots (Rallidae)

Description: 14–16" (35–40 cm). Chicken-sized. Long-billed, grayish-brown bird without the rusty underparts of the similar King Rail.

Voice: Harsh clattering *kek-kek-kek-kek-kek*.

Habitat: Salt marshes.

Nesting: 5–15 spotted buff eggs in a shallow saucer or deep bowl of dead marsh grasses, often domed.

Range: Breeds along the coasts from California and Massachusetts to South America. Winters north to New Jersey, rarely farther north.

Its call is one of the most familiar sounds in the salt marshes in summer. Although generally secretive, the birds are sometimes forced into view by high tides, when they may be seen along roads in the marsh or standing on floating boards. Otherwise they are most often glimpsed as they dart across a tidal creek between sheltering grasses. This bird may be confused with the rusty King Rail when the latter enters the salt meadows for the winter.

Black Rail
(*Laterallus jamaicensis*)
Rails, Gallinules, Coots (Rallidae)

Description: 5–6″ (13–15 cm). Sparrow-sized. Black with rusty nape and white flecks on the back; black bill; legs and feet greenish. Can be confused with the glossy black young of larger rails.

Voice: *Kee-kee-kerr,* the last note lower in pitch.

Habitat: Coastal salt marshes, more rarely in inland freshwater marshes.

Nesting: 4–8 lightly spotted pale buff eggs in a loose cup of grass concealed under a mat of dead marsh vegetation.

Range: Breeds along the Atlantic and Pacific coasts from Long Island and California to southern South America, locally in the interior. Winters north to the Gulf Coast.

This tiny rail may be common in some areas, but is so secretive that many consider it rare. The birds spend much of their time creeping about under mats

Habitat: Exclusively grassy salt marsh, favoring the wetter portions.

Nesting: 4 or 5 white eggs with brown blotches in a woven grass nest placed in a grass tussock above the high-tide line.

Range: Salt marshes of the Atlantic and Gulf coasts from southern New England to Florida and Texas, wintering in the southern portions of this range.

Literally a seaside bird, few other sparrows have so restricted a habitat. Favoring the wetter sections of salt marsh, it feeds much less on seeds than do other sparrows, but eats tiny young crabs, snails, and other small marine animals along the tidal creeks of salt meadows. Like all birds living near the ground in grass, it is difficult to detect until almost underfoot, whereupon it flushes, flies for a short distance, drops down into the thick grass, and runs along like a mouse. The best opportunity to view one is when it is in song atop a grass stem or small shrub. Two distinctively plumaged populations of this bird in Florida were formerly considered separate species, called the "Dusky Seaside Sparrow" and the "Cape Sable Seaside Sparrow."

Freshwater Marshes

Shallow fresh water with a growth of
cattails, sedges, reeds, or bulrushes.
Such marshes often include some open
water; in these may be found the birds
we cover in our Lakes, Ponds, Rivers
section. Around the edge of the marsh,
on damp ground, there may be stands
of willows, alders, or red maples, in
which may be found birds treated in
our Thickets and Second Growth
section. Finally, during migration,
flocks of swallows may often inhabit
such marshes.

2, 6 Great Egret
(*Casmerodius albus*)
Herons, Bitterns (Ardeidae)

Description: 35–41" (89–104 cm). W. 55" (1.4 m
A large, all-white heron with a *yellow
bill and black legs.* In Florida the white
form of the Great Blue Heron, known
as the "Great White Heron," is simila
but larger, with greenish-yellow legs.

Voice: Deep guttural croak. Also loud
squawks when in the nesting colony.

Habitat: Freshwater and salt marshes, marshy
ponds, and tidal flats.

Nesting: 3 or 4 pale blue eggs on a platform
sticks in a tree or bush. In colonies,
often with other species of herons.

Range: Oregon, Wisconsin, and Massachuset
to southern South America. Winters
regularly north to South Carolina and
the Gulf Coast. Also breeds in warmer
parts of the Old World.

Formerly known as the "American
Egret," "Common Egret," "Large
Egret," "White Egret," "Great White
Egret," and "Great White Heron," its
official name in North America is now
Great Egret. One of the most
magnificent of our herons, it has
fortunately recovered from long
persecution by plume hunters. Like the
Great Blue Heron, it feeds alone,
stalking fish, frogs, snakes, and crayfis
in shallow water. Each year individual
birds wander far to the north of the
breeding grounds.

7, 16 Little Blue Heron
(*Egretta caerulea*)
Herons, Bitterns (Ardeidae)

Description: 25–30" (63–76 cm). W. 41" (1 m).
Adult slate blue with maroon neck;
immature is white, usually with dark
tips to primaries. Grayish bill with
black tip; greenish legs. Young birds

acquiring adult plumage have a piebald
appearance.

Voice: Usually silent. Squawks when alarmed.
Croaks, grunts, and screams at the nest
site.

Habitat: Freshwater swamps and lagoons in the
South; coastal thickets on islands in the
North.

Nesting: 4 or 5 pale bluish-green eggs in a stick
nest in small trees or bushes near the
ground.

Range: East coast from New York to Texas and
inland to Oklahoma. Winters north to
South Carolina. Also in South America.

This is one of the most numerous
herons in the South and may be
observed in large mixed concentrations
of herons and egrets. It eats more
insects than the larger herons and is
sometimes seen following a plow to
pick up exposed insect larvae. Unlike
the egrets, it has no fancy plumes and
was thus spared by plume hunters.

17 **Least Bittern**
(*Ixobrychus exilis*)
Herons, Bitterns (Ardeidae)

Description: 11–14″ (28–35 cm). A tiny heron with
blackish back and *conspicuous buff wing
patches* and underparts. Female and
young are similar but duller.

Voice: Soft *coo-coo-coo,* easily unnoticed.

Habitat: Freshwater marshes where cattails and
reeds predominate.

Nesting: 4 or 5 small bluish eggs on a flimsy
platform of dead cattails or reeds,
usually over water.

Range: Southern Canada and northern United
States to southern Texas and the West
Indies. Winters from the Gulf Coast
south. Also breeds in South America.

Although locally common, this heron is
very secretive. It is reluctant to fly,

depending on its cryptic color pattern to escape detection. It often runs and climbs rapidly through reeds and cattails. The best way to see it is to wait at the edge of a cattail marsh—eventually one may rise, fly over the cattails, and drop out of sight again. The very rare rufous form, once thought to be a separate species, is called "Cory's Least Bittern."

19, 21 Yellow-crowned Night Heron
(*Nycticorax violacea*)
Herons, Bitterns (Ardeidae)

Description: 22–27" (56–68 cm). W 44" (1.1 m). Medium-sized heron. Adult is slate-gray with black head, *white cheeks, yellowish crown and plumes,* black bill, and orange legs. In flight the feet extend beyond the tail. Immature birds are grayish, finely speckled with white above, like young Black-crowned Night Herons but with a thicker bill and longer legs.

Voice: *Quawk* like that of Black-crowned Night Heron but higher in pitch.

Habitat: Wooded swamps and coastal thickets.

Nesting: 4 or 5 pale blue-green eggs in stick nest in trees or on the ground. Singly or in small colonies; occasionally with other herons.

Range: Massachusetts to Florida and west to Texas; mainly near the coast, but north along the Mississippi River and its larger tributaries, rarely to the central states. Also warmer portions of Middle and South America and West Indies.

As with several herons having a southerly distribution, this species has increased and expanded its range northward. Contrary to popular opinion, herons do not stab a fish (it would then be difficult to release) but grasp it in their bill, toss it in the air, and swallow it head-first.

20, 22 Black-crowned Night Heron
(*Nycticorax nycticorax*)
Herons, Bitterns (Ardeidae)

Description: 23–28″ (58–71 cm). W. 44″ (1.1 m).
A medium-sized, stocky, rather short-necked heron with *black crown and back,* gray wings, and *white underparts;* short, black bill; pinkish or yellowish legs. In breeding season it has two or more long white plumes on back of head. Young birds are dull gray-brown lightly spotted with white. May be confused with young Yellow-crowned Night Herons and American Bitterns.

Voice: Harsh, barking *quawk!,* most often heard at night or at dusk. A bewildering variety of croaking, barking, and screaming calls are uttered in the nesting colony.

Habitat: Marshes, swamps, and wooded streams.

Nesting: 3–6 pale blue-green eggs in a shallow saucer of sticks or reeds in a thicket or reedbed; occasionally in tall trees. In colonies, sometimes with other species of herons.

Range: Washington, Saskatchewan, Minnesota, and New Brunswick, to southern South America. Winters in southern half of the United States. Also occurs in southern Eurasia, Africa, and East Indies.

As its name implies it is largely nocturnal, spending daylight hours roosting in trees or reedbeds. It is therefore best known for its call. These birds are less likely to nest in mixed colonies than other herons. When they do, they usually keep a separate corner for themselves.

24 American Bittern
(*Botaurus lentiginosus*)
Herons Bitterns (Ardeidae)

Description: 23–34" (58–86 cm). A medium-sized brown heron. *Outer wing appears blackish in flight,* contrasting with mustard brown of inner wing and body. At close range the bird shows a black streak on each side of the throat.

Voice: Peculiar pumping sound, *oong-KA-chunk!,* repeated a few times and often audible for half a mile.

Habitat: Freshwater and brackish marshes and marshy lake shores.

Nesting: 3–7 olive eggs on a platform of reeds concealed in the marsh. Not in colonies.

Range: British Columbia, Manitoba, and Newfoundland to Maryland, Kansas, and southern California; also in Texas, Louisiana, and Florida. Winters north to British Columbia, Ohio, and Delaware, occasionally farther north.

Its call has given such names to the bird as "Thunder-pumper" and "Stake-driver." It is secretive, preferring to freeze and trust its concealing coloration when approached rather than flush like other herons. When an observer is nearby it will often raise its head, point its bill skyward, and sway slowly from side to side, as if imitating waving reeds. If the observer gets too close the bittern will fly off, uttering a low barking call.

30 Sandhill Crane
(*Grus canadensis*)
Cranes (Gruidae)

Description: 34–48" (86–122 cm). W. 80" (2 m). Very tall, with long neck and long legs. Largely gray with red forehead. Plumage often appears rusty because of iron stains from the water of tundra ponds. Unlike herons, cranes fly with the neck outstretched and with the upstroke faster than the downstroke.

Voice: Loud, rattling *kar-r-r-o-o-o*.

Habitat: Large freshwater marshes, prairie ponds, and marshy tundra; also on prairies and grainfields during migration and in winter.

Nesting: 2 brown-spotted buff eggs in a large mound of grass and uprooted plants in an undisturbed marsh.

Range: Northeastern Siberia, Alaska, and Arctic Islands south to Michigan, Minnesota, and California; also in Gulf states from Florida to Texas. Winters in Arizona, Texas, Mexico, and California. Also breeds in Cuba.

Apparently this species was always more numerous than the larger Whooping Crane, and the fact that it breeds mostly in the remote Arctic has saved it from the fate of its relative. It is sensitive to human disturbance, and the draining of marshes has reduced nesting populations in the United States. These cranes migrate in great flocks and assemble in vast numbers at places like the Platte River in Nebraska. Here it is possible to see what must have been a common sight when the species bred over most of the interior United States.

The mating dance of the cranes is spectacular. Facing each other, they leap into the air with wings extended and feet thrown forward. Then they bow to each other and repeat the performance, uttering loud croaking calls.

45 Franklin's Gull
(Larus pipixcan)
Gulls, Terns (Laridae)

Description: 13–15" (33–38 cm). Adult has black
hood and gray back and wings. Similar
to Laughing Gull of seacoasts but
smaller, paler, with *black wing tip
separated from gray by a white band.*
Young bird much like young Laughing
Gull but breast and forehead whiter.

Voice: A strident *ha-ha-ha-ha-ha-ha,* similar
Laughing Gull's but higher in pitch.
Also utters clucks, screams, and mews.

Habitat: Prairie marshes and sloughs. Often
feeds in plowed fields.

Nesting: 3 buff-brown, spotted eggs on a loose
platform in a marsh. Breeds in large,
noisy colonies.

Range: Prairie marshes from southern Canac
to South Dakota and southwestern
Minnesota. Migrates to Gulf Coast and
winters south to Chile.

A freshwater version of the Laughing
Gull, it is sensitive to habitat
destruction and will breed only in larg
colonies. When agriculture encroaches
on prairie marshes and these become
too small for a large colony, the birds
move elsewhere. They are much less
numerous than formerly, but migratin
flocks of these "Prairie Doves" are still
familiar sight in spring on the souther
plains.

75 Black Tern
(Chlidonias nigra)
Gulls, Terns (Laridae)

Description: 9–10" (23–25 cm). A medium-sized
tern with *solid black head and underparts,*
gray wing and moderately forked gray
tail; in fall and winter the head and
underparts are white, with dusky
smudging around the eyes and back of
the neck.

Voice: Sharp *kick;* when disturbed, a shrill *kreek.*

Habitat: Freshwater marshes and marshy lakes in summer; sandy coasts in migration and in winter.

Nesting: 2 spotted olive-buff eggs in a hollow on a mass of floating marsh vegetation or a well-made cup of dead grass. Colonial.

Range: Breeds from Quebec, Alaska, Mackenzie, and south to Pennsylvania, Missouri, and California. Winters in South America.

This tern usually nests in small groups and in shallow water. The nests are sometimes conspicuous; perhaps this is why the young often leave the nest at the first sign of an intruder, swimming quietly away to hide in the surrounding marsh vegetation. It is not unusual to visit an active colony and find all the nests empty. Unlike other terns, Blacks frequently fly over land areas as they hawk for insects. Small fish and crustaceans are also taken.

105, 144 **Green-winged Teal including "Common Teal"** (*Anas crecca*) Swans, Geese, Ducks (Anatidae)

Description: 12–16" (30–40 cm). A small, dark duck. Male has chestnut head, green ear patch, flashing *green speculum,* pale gray sides, and pinkish breast with a vertical white stripe down the side. Female is dark brown without distinctive markings.

Voice: Clear repeated whistle. Females quack.

Habitat: Marshes, ponds, and marshy lakes.

Nesting: 10–12 whitish or pale buff eggs in a down-lined cup in tall grass, often several hundred yards from water.

Range: Aleutians, northern Alaska, Manitoba, and Quebec south to New York, Nebraska, and California. Winters south to Central America and the West Indies. Also breeds in temperate Eurasia.

Until recently the North American and Eurasian forms were considered distinct species. Eurasian males have a horizontal white stripe along the side of their bodies instead of a vertical stripe down the breast. Each year a few males—and probably females—of the Eurasian form turn up in North America, giving rise to speculation that somewhere in North America a few of these so-called "Common Teal" may be breeding. Green-winged Teal are among the fastest flying ducks and are therefore popular gamebirds. They wheel in compact flocks like shorebirds. They are hardy, being among the last ducks to reach their winter habitat in fall and the first to depart in spring.

106, 140 **American Wigeon**
(*Anas americana*)
Swans, Geese, Ducks (Anatidae)

Description: 18–23" (46–58 cm). Male is brownish with *white crown,* green ear patch, and bold white shoulder patches easily visible in flight. Female is mottled brown with grayish head and whitish shoulder patch. Pale blue bill and feet in both sexes.

Voice: Distinctive whistled *whew-whew-whew.* Also quacks.

Habitat: Marshes, ponds, and shallow lakes.

Nesting: 8–10 whitish or cream-colored eggs in a down-lined hollow in grass, often several hundred yards from water.

Range: Alaska, Mackenzie, and Minnesota south to Nebraska and northern California. Rarely farther east. Winters south to Central America and the West Indies.

The American Wigeon, or "Baldpate,"
is a wary species, often seen on marshy
ponds in the company of diving birds
such as coots, Redheads, and
Canvasbacks. They wait at the surface
while the other birds dive, then snatch
the food away when the birds reappear.
They also visit grain fields and
meadows to graze, like geese, on tender
shoots. The birds found in winter along
the Atlantic coast seem to come mainly
from the Far North, while birds in the
interior of the continent move south to
the Gulf Coast and West Indies.

132 European Wigeon
(*Anas penelope*)
Swans, Geese, Ducks (Anatidae)

Description: 18–20" (46–50 cm). Male has *rusty
head, buff crown,* pinkish-buff breast,
and gray body. Female is streaked
brown. Bill dull blue. The female
American Wigeon is very similar but
has a gray-tinged head.

Voice: Piping *whee-ouu;* seldom heard in
America.

Habitat: Marshes, ponds, and lakes; resorts to
tidal flats in nonbreeding season.

Nesting: 7 or 8 buff-cream eggs in a nest lined
with grass and down, concealed in
vegetation often some distance from
water.

Range: Eurasia; an uncommon visitor to North
America, mainly along the coast.

An Old World relative of the American
Wigeon, this bird in recent years has
become an uncommon but regular
visitor to our area, usually found in a
flock with its American cousin. Known
in Europe as one of the shyest of ducks,
it is a popular gamebird. Wigeons
often feed at night, and unlike most
other ducks they obtain a good deal of
food by grazing.

108, 143   Northern Shoveler
"Shoveler"
(*Anas clypeata*)
Swans, Geese, Ducks (Anatidae)

Description: 17–20" (43–51 cm). Large "shovel"
bill. Male has green head, white body,
and *chestnut flanks*. Female streaked
brown with pale blue wing patches;
similar to female Blue-winged Teal but
larger, with the distinctive bill. Both
sexes have *pale blue shoulder patches*.
Voice: Low croak, cluck, or quack.
Habitat: Marshes and prairie potholes.
Sometimes on salt or brackish marshes.
Nesting: 8–12 pale olive or greenish eggs in a
down-lined cup of grass concealed in
vegetation, often some distance from
water.
Range: Alaska, northern Mackenzie and
Manitoba, south to Nebraska, Colorado
and Southern California; occasionally
farther east and south. Winters north to
British Columbia and Georgia, and in
smaller numbers to New England. Also
breeds in Eurasia.

Like the closely related Blue-winged
Teal, the Northern Shoveler, formerly
called "Shoveler," is among the first
ducks to arrive in the fall and the last
to leave in the spring. It feeds on
minute aquatic animals by straining
water through comblike teeth along the
sides of its long, expanded bill. It also
eats seeds and aquatic plants. Because it
often feeds in stagnant ponds, it is
particularly susceptible to botulism, a
fatal bacterial food poisoning.

111, 159   Ruddy Duck
(*Oxyura jamaicensis*)
Swans, Geese, Ducks (Anatidae)

Description: 14–16" (35–40 cm). A small, chunky
duck with a long tail that is often held
straight up. Male in breeding plumage

has a chestnut body, black crown, and *white cheeks.* Female and winter male are dusky brown with whitish cheeks—crossed by a brown stripe in the female. Bill of male is blue in breeding season, black at other times.

Voice: Mostly silent. Courting male makes a series of clucking notes.

Habitat: Freshwater marshes, marshy lakes and ponds; sometimes shallow salt bays and rivers in winter.

Nesting: 5–15 buffy-white eggs in a floating nest of dry stems of water plants lined with down, concealed among reeds or bulrushes in a marsh.

Range: Breeds from British Columbia, Mackenzie, and Quebec south to the Gulf Coast and through Central America to northern South America. Winters north to British Columbia and Massachusetts.

This duck is one of the most aquatic members of the family, and like a grebe can sink slowly out of sight. They seldom fly, escaping from danger by diving or concealing themselves in marsh vegetation. Once airborne, however, they are fast fliers, annually covering long distances in migration. Largely vegetarian, they favor marsh plants and seeds in summer, wigeon grass in winter. The male has a bizarre courtship display, raising and spreading his tail as he produces bubbles by expelling air trapped under his breast feathers.

112, 141 **Cinnamon Teal**
(*Anas cyanoptera*)
Swans, Geese, Ducks (Anatidae)

Description: 14–17″ (35–43 cm). Male bright rufous, with a pale blue patch along the leading edge of each wing. Female mottled sandy brown and dusky, with pale blue wing patches; not distinguishable in the field from female Blue-winged Teal.

Voice: A soft *quack;* various chattering and clucking notes.

Habitat: Prairie marshes, ponds, and slow-moving streams bordered with reeds.

Nesting: 4–16 pale buff eggs in a cup nest of grass and feathers concealed in grass or weeds, usually near water.

Range: Western North America from Aleutian Islands, regularly east to Saskatchewan, Nebraska, and western Texas, and casually east to New York and the Carolinas. Also in South America.

This western relative of the Blue-winged Teal often associates with that species in areas where both occur. Like the Blue-wing, these birds migrate south in late summer and early fall, a month or two ahead of the other dabbling ducks. Records of the Cinnamon Teal from east of their normal range are based on sightings of adult males, because the females are indistinguishable from female Blue-wings.

115, 138 Pintail
(*Anas acuta*)
Swans, Geese, Ducks (Anatidae)

Description: Males 25–30″ (63–76 cm), females 21–23″ (53–58 cm). Slim, graceful duck with a slender neck. Male has *brown head and white neck with white line extending up the side of the head.* Central tail feathers long, black, and pointed. Female streaked brown, similar to female Mallard but paler, grayer, and slenderer, with brown speculum that is bordered with white at the rear edge only; tail is more pointed than in female Mallard.

Voice: Distinctive two-toned whistle. Females quack.

Habitat: Marshes, prairie ponds, and tundra;

sometimes salt marshes in winter.

Nesting: 7–10 pale greenish-buff eggs in a
shallow grass bowl lined with down and
hidden in grass, often some distance
from water.

Range: Breeds from Alaska and Greenland
south to western Pennsylvania,
Nebraska, and California. Locally and
occasionally farther east. Winters south
to Central America and the West
Indies. Also breeds in Eurasia.

The Pintail, a widely distributed and
common duck, is a strong flier and
long-distance migrant like the Mallard.
Seeds of aquatic plants are its main
food, but in winter small aquatic
animals are also taken; when freshwater
habitats freeze over, it resorts to tidal
flats, where it feeds on snails and small
crabs. A popular gamebird because of
its tasty flesh and fast flight, it is one of
our wariest ducks.

134 American Coot
(*Fulica americana*)
Rails, Gallinules, Coots (Rallidae)

Description: 15″ (38 cm). *Slate-gray* with a
conspicuous *white bill;* greenish legs and
lobed feet.

Voice: Variety of calls, some fowl-like
clucking, and cackles, grunts, and
other harsh notes.

Habitat: Open ponds and marshes; in winter,
also in saltwater bays and inlets.

Nesting: 8–10 brown-spotted pinkish eggs in a
shallow platform of dead leaves and
stems of marsh plants, usually on the
water but anchored to a clump of reeds.

Range: Southern Canada to northern South
America.

Coots are the most aquatic members of
their family, moving on open water like
ducks and often feeding with them.
They are excellent swimmers and

divers, and they eat various aquatic plants. They also come out on land to feed on seeds, grass, and waste grain. They often become tame when fed scraps and bits of bread. These birds must patter over the water before becoming airborne.

135, 139   Gadwall
(*Anas strepera*)
Swans, Geese, Ducks (Anatidae)

Description: 18–21″ (46–53 cm). A medium-sized duck with a *white patch on hind edge of wing.* Male mottled gray with a black rump and sandy brown head. Female similar but brown.

Voice: Duck-like quack. Also utters *kack-kacks* and whistles.

Habitat: Freshwater marshes, ponds, and rivers; locally in salt marshes.

Nesting: 7–12 whitish eggs in a nest made of dead grass, usually well concealed near water but sometimes in upland fields.

Range: Alaska and New England south to North Carolina and California. Winters north to southern New England. Also breeds in Eurasia and North Africa.

This relative of the Mallard has the widest range of any duck, breeding almost throughout the North Temperate Zone. Known to hunters as the "Gray Duck," it is a popular gamebird and is abundant in winter in southern marshes. It feeds mainly on seeds, leaves, and stems of aquatic plants. This species has recently appeared as a breeder on the Eastern seaboard, and now nests along the coast from Nova Scotia to the Carolinas.

136, 142 Blue-winged Teal
(*Anas discors*)
Swans, Geese, Ducks (Anatidae)

Description: 14–16" (35–40 cm). A small brownish
duck with *pale blue shoulder patches*.
Male has a gray head and *white crescent*
in front of eye. Female mottled brown,
similar to female Green-winged Teal
but grayer, with pale blue shoulder
patches like the male.

Voice: Soft lisping or peeping note. Female
utters a soft quack.

Habitat: Marshes, shallow ponds, and lakes.

Nesting: 7–10 whitish eggs in a down-lined
hollow concealed in grass near the edge
of water.

Range: British Columbia, Quebec, and
Newfoundland to North Carolina, the
Gulf Coast, and southern California.
Winters south to northern South
America.

On low marshy prairies in the central
part of the continent, where this duck
is most numerous, virtually every pond
and pothole has a breeding pair. The
male commonly "stands guard" on the
pond while the female is incubating.
Unlike other dabbling ducks that form
pairs in the fall, this teal begins
courting in the spring and often does
not acquire the familiar breeding
plumage until December or January.
Like most ducks they go through an
eclipse plumage and molt most of their
feathers, including the primaries, and
so are flightless until new feathers grow
in. This species migrates early, often
passing through the United States in
August and September; most Blue-
wings winter south of the United
States.

165, 166 Fulvous Whistling-Duck
"Fulvous Tree Duck"
(Dendrocygna bicolor)
Swans, Geese, Ducks (Anatidae)

Description: 18–21" (46–53 cm). A long-legged, long-necked, goose-like duck. Body mainly *tawny, with a white stripe on the side;* rump and undertail coverts are white.

Voice: Clear double whistle. Called "Squealer" by hunters.

Habitat: Rice fields, freshwater marshes, and wet meadows.

Nesting: 12–15 buff-white eggs in a shallow cup of grass or a well-woven basket of reeds in a marsh.

Range: Resident in southern California, Texas, and southern Florida, and locally southward to Brazil. Also breeds in East Africa and India.

Although Fulvous Whistling-Ducks in North America breed only in southern Texas and southern California, they occasionally wander; small flocks have turned up as far away as Utah and Nova Scotia. These long-legged ducks do most of their feeding on land, eating green grass, seeds, and acorns. This species was formerly known as "Fulvous Tree Duck." The name "fulvous" refers to its tawny color.

167, 168 Black-bellied Whistling-Duck
"Black-bellied Tree Duck"
(Dendrocygna autumnalis)
Swans, Geese, Ducks (Anatidae)

Description: 20–22" (51–56 cm). Long neck and legs; rich chestnut crown, back, and breast; gray face and throat; black lower belly; bright red bill; pink legs; large white wing patch in flight. Female duller.

Voice: Shrill, often repeated whistle.

Habitat: Wooded streams and ponds.

Nesting: 12–14 white eggs, placed without a nest lining, in tree cavity or nest box, occasionally on the ground.

Range: Extreme southern Texas and Arizona to tropical portions of South America.

These handsome, conspicuous birds often rest on large tree branches, stakes, or poles in the water or, less commonly, on the ground. Almost entirely herbivorous, they feed in shallow water on tubers and other aquatic vegetation, as well as in grain fields. Unlike many ducks, this species is largely nocturnal, migrating at night and resting and feeding during the day. They are easily domesticated and are quite tame even in the wild. This species was formerly known as "Black-bellied Tree Duck."

169 **White-fronted Goose**
(*Anser albifrons*)
Swans, Geese, Ducks (Anatidae)

Description: 27–30" (68–76 cm). A dusky-brown goose with conspicuous white belly and undertail covers; *white patch on front of face;* underparts barred and flecked with black. *Only goose in the East with orange legs.*

Voice: Distinctive two-note or three-note bark, *kla-ha!* or *ka-la-ha!,* very different from the calls of other geese.

Habitat: Marshy tundra; winters on marshes and bays.

Nesting: 4–6 creamy-buff eggs in a down-lined grassy depression on the tundra.

Range: Breeds in Alaska, the Northwest Territories, and Greenland. Winters from British Columbia and Illinois to southern Mexico and the Gulf Coast. Also breeds in northern Eurasia.

This is the least common goose in the eastern states, occurring in numbers only along the western Gulf Coast in

Louisiana and Texas; its winter
headquarters is the Sacramento Valley
of California. Along the eastern edge of
the Great Plains the birds often migrate
at night, when they are identified by
their distinctive call. Like other geese,
they often leave the marshes to feed in
nearby stubble fields; here they are
frequently concealed from view until
the observer is very close, when they
explode noisily into the air. Hunters
call them "Speckle Bellies." The Tule
Goose of the west coast is considered a
large race of the White-fronted Goose,
but its status is still uncertain and its
nesting ground is unknown.

173 Mute Swan
(*Cygnus olor*)
Swans, Geese, Ducks (Anatidae)

Description: 58–60" (147–152 cm). W. 95" (2.3m)
All white; bill of adults is orange with
black knob at the base. Young birds are
similar, but dingy.

Voice: Unlike other swans, it is usually silent
except for some hissing and grunting
notes. It does have a loud trumpeting
call, but this is rarely heard.

Habitat: Ponds, rivers, coastal lagoons, and
bays.

Nesting: 6–8 eggs in a huge mound-like nest
lined with feathers and down,
conspicuously placed at the edge of a
pond or marsh.

Range: Introduced from Europe into the
northeastern United States; most
frequent in southern New England,
southeastern New York, New Jersey,
and Maryland; also established
locally in Michigan.

With its wings arched over its back and
its neck in a graceful S-curve, the male
is extremely handsome on the water. A
breeding pair will defend the nest and
young against all comers, including

humans, using their powerful wings
and strong bills.

---

175 **White Pelican**
(*Pelecanus erythrorhynchos*)
Pelicans (Pelecanidae)

Description: 55–70" (140–179 cm). W. 96" (2.8 m).
Huge white bird with a massive yellow
bill and black wing tips. Usually rests
bill on breast.

Voice: Low grunts or croaks on the nesting
ground, but usually silent.

Habitat: Marshy lakes and along the Pacific and
Texas coasts. Winters chiefly in coastal
lagoons.

Nesting: 2 or 3 whitish eggs on a low mound of
earth and debris on a marshy island;
occasionally on barren islands in desert
lakes. In colonies.

Range: Breeds from British Columbia and
Mackenzie south to western Ontario
and California; also on the Texas coast.
Winters from Florida and southern
California south to Panama.

A flock of migrating White Pelicans is
a majestic sight—a long line of
ponderous birds, flapping and sailing in
unison. These birds ride rising air
currents to great heights, where they
soar gracefully in circles. They often
capture fish cooperatively, forming a
long line, beating their wings and
driving the prey into shallow water,
where they seize the fish in their large,
pouched bills. They take in water as
well as fish, and so first hold their bills
vertically to drain the water out before
swallowing the food.

178, 180   Pied-billed Grebe
(*Podilymbus podiceps*)
Grebes (Podicipedidae)

Description: 12–15″ (30–38 cm). Pigeon-sized. A
stocky, uniformly brownish water bird;
stubby bill, whitish with a prominent
black band, lacking in winter.

Voice: Series of hollow *cow-cow-cow* notes
somewhat like those of the Yellow-
billed Cuckoo.

Habitat: Marshes, ponds; salt water in winter if
freshwater habitats freeze.

Nesting: 5–7 whitish, stained eggs in a well-
concealed floating mass of dead marsh
vegetation anchored to adjacent plants.

Range: British Columbia to southern
Mackenzie and Nova Scotia to southern
Argentina. Winters as far north as New
England.

This is the most common grebe in
eastern North America. Although easily
overlooked, it announces itself in the
breeding season with its loud barking
call notes. It eats small fish,
crustaceans, and aquatic insects but is
especially fond of crayfish, which it
easily crushes with its stout bill. When
alarmed, it slowly sinks below the
water, surfacing again out of sight
among the reeds; this trick has earned
it the local name of "Hell-diver." It is
also called "Dabchick" and "Water
Witch."

199, 223   Least Sandpiper
(*Calidris minutilla*)
Sandpipers (Scolopacidae)

Description: 6″ (15 cm). Sparrow-sized; smallest of
American shorebirds. Brownish with
yellowish or greenish legs, a short thin
bill, and a streaked breast. Grayer in
winter plumage.

Voice: A loud clear *treep;* when feeding, a soft
chuckle.

Habitat: Grassy pools, bogs, and marshes with open areas; also flooded fields and mud flats.

Nesting: 4 brown-spotted pinkish-buff eggs in a nest lined with moss and grass on a dry hummock in a depression on boggy tundra.

Range: Breeds in Aleutians, Alaska and Canada. Winters from southern United States to central South America.

These are probably the tamest of shorebirds and at times fly off only when almost underfoot. They look like miniature Pectoral Sandpipers, and like Pectorals they prefer grassy areas to the more open flats frequented by most shorebirds. The name *minutilla* is Latin for "tiny."

204, 207 Wilson's Phalarope
(*Phalaropus tricolor*)
Sandpipers (Scolopacidae)

Description: 9″ (23 cm). A strikingly patterned shorebird with pearl gray head and back, white underparts, *a black stripe through eye and down the neck, and chestnut markings on breast and back.* In fall plumage pale gray above, white below; in this plumage its pale color, more terrestrial habits, and slender bill distinguish it from other phalaropes.

Voice: Soft *quoit-quoit-quoit.*

Habitat: Prairie pools and marshes, lake and river shores, marshy pools along the coast.

Nesting: 4 pale buff, brown-spotted eggs in a grass-lined nest in a slight depression on the ground near water.

Range: From southwestern and south-central Canada to central and western United States. Winters chiefly in southern South America.

Wilson's is larger than the Red and Northern phalaropes and has a much longer, thinner bill. Unlike the others, this species does not have fully lobed toes and so rarely swims, spending no time at sea. When it does feed in water, however, it spins more rapidly than the other two. It is limited to the Western Hemisphere and breeds much farther south than the others.

216 Solitary Sandpiper
(*Tringa solitaria*)
Sandpipers (Scolopacidae)

Description: 8½″ (21 cm). Dark legs, white tail barred with black, *prominent eye-ring;* wing linings dark. Has distinctive, swallow-like flight when flushed.

Voice: *Peet-weet-weet,* like that of the Spotted Sandpiper but higher pitched.

Habitat: Inland ponds and bogs, wet swampy places, and woodland streams.

Nesting: 4 pale green or buff eggs thickly spotted with gray and brown, laid in deserted tree nests of thrushes, jays, or blackbirds in northern spruce forests.

Range: Breeds in Alaska and Canada. Winters from Central America to southern South America.

As its name suggests, this bird is most often seen by itself—a single migrant foraging along the margin of a wooded pond or stream. It is rather shy, and when approached will spring quickly into the air, uttering its ringing call note, and dart away. In the spring, most Solitary Sandpipers seem to migrate north through Central America, and here an observer may be surprised to see flocks of several dozen feeding in flooded fields.

219 Pectoral Sandpiper
(*Calidris melanotos*)
Sandpipers (Scolopacidae)

Description: 9" (23 cm). A chunky, somewhat short-legged wader, with *heavily streaked breast* sharply delimited by the *unmarked white of the belly. Yellow legs.* In flight the wings are dark and have no stripe.

Voice: Sharp *brrrrp.* Courting males inflate the throat and breast and utter a series of booming, resonant calls.

Habitat: Wet, short-grass areas; grassy pools; golf courses and airports after heavy rains; and salt creeks and meadows.

Nesting: 4 buff-white, dark-spotted eggs on the ground in a slight depression in boggy tundra.

Range: Breeds on the Arctic coasts of eastern Siberia, Alaska, and Canada south to Hudson Bay. Winters chiefly in southern South America.

In the days when shorebirds were shot as game, hunters called this species the "Grass Snipe," referring to its liking for grassy meadows, or "Krieker" because of its grating snipe-like call when in flight. They are as numerous in the interior as on the coasts and are another of the many shorebirds that make the long migration from the Arctic to the Antarctic and back again.

244 American Avocet
(*Recurvirostra americana*)
Avocets, Stilts (Recurvirostridae)

Description: 16–20" (40–51 cm). Pigeon-sized. Slender and long-legged. Upperparts and wings patterned in black and white; underparts white. Head and neck rust-colored in summer, white in winter. *Bill very thin and strongly upturned.*

Voice: Loud repeated *wheep.*

Habitat: Freshwater marshes and shallow marshy

lakes; breeds locally in salt or brackish marshes. Many move to the coast in winter.

Nesting: 4 spotted buff eggs in a shallow scrap on a beach or mud flat, with sparse lining of grass. Often in loose colonies

Range: Washington and Manitoba south to Texas and California. Winters from southern Texas and California to Guatemala. Uncommon but regular on Atlantic coast in fall.

During their southward migration every fall, a few Avocets stray eastward to the Atlantic coast, where they may be seen singly or in small flocks on shallow lagoons and coastal ponds. In the 19th century there was a small breeding population in southern New Jersey, but they were shot out by hunters. Avocets feed much like Spoonbills, sweeping their bills from side to side along the surface of the water to pick up crustaceans, aquatic insects, and floating seeds. Recently given complete protection, they seem to be gaining in numbers and before long may be reported breeding on the Atlantic coast once again.

---

247 **Common Gallinule**
(*Gallinula chloropus*)
Rails, Gallinules, Coots (Rallidae)

Description: 13″ (33 cm). A duck-like swimming bird that constantly bobs its head while moving. Slaty gray with a prominent red bill with yellow tip and red frontal shield (adults); *white under its tail* which it cocks up.

Voice: Squawking notes similar to those of coots. Other calls sound like frogs and are rather harsh in tone.

Habitat: Freshwater marshes and ponds with cattails and other aquatic vegetation.

Nesting: 9–12 cinnamon-buff eggs, lightly spotted with brown; in a shallow platform of dead cattails, rushes, and other marsh plants; usually built up a few inches above water level.

Range: Nearly cosmopolitan in distribution. In the Americas, from southern Canada to southern South America.

Gallinules—or "Moorhens" as they are known in the Old World—are closely related to coots and rails but do not swim out in the open water as much as coots and hide in reeds much less than rails. Males build several nests on the pair's territory; these are used by the female and newly hatched young as "dormitories" at night.

---

248 Purple Gallinule
(Porphyrula martinica)
Rails, Gallinules, Coots (Rallidae)

Description: 11–13″ (28–33 cm). Chicken-sized. Rich purplish-blue with green upperparts, white undertail coverts, yellowish-green legs, red-and-yellow bill, and light blue frontal shield.

Voice: Squawking and cackling. Also guttural grunts.

Habitat: Freshwater marshes with lily pads, pickerelweed, and other aquatic vegetation.

Nesting: 6–10 pinkish-buff eggs with fine dark spots in a nest of dead stems and leaves of water plants placed on a floating tussock or in a clump of sawgrass or thicket over water.

Range: The Carolinas and Tennessee to Florida and Texas; wanders to the northern states. South to southern South America.

This beautiful bird is often observed walking on lily pads, using its very long toes, and may even sometimes be seen climbing up into low bushes. When walking or swimming it constantly jerks its head and tail. Its flight is slow and weak, and its yellow legs hang down. On rare occasions these birds have wandered north and have been found in gardens or city parks. They have landed on ships 300 miles from shore and on remote oceanic islands.

---

249 Sora
(*Porzana carolina*)
Rails, Gallinules, Coots (Rallidae)

Description: 8–10″ (20–25 cm). Quail-sized. *Gray breasted* with a black face and *stubby yellow bill*. Upperparts mottled brown; lower abdomen banded with black and white. Young birds in fall lack the black face and have buff breasts.

Voice: Most familiar call is a musical series o piping notes rapidly descending the scale. When an intruder approaches a nest the adults come boldly into view, uttering an explosive *keek!*

Habitat: Chiefly freshwater marshes and marshy ponds; rice fields and salt marshes in winter.

Nesting: 6–15 pale yellow-buff, spotted eggs ir a cup of cattails and dead leaves, usually placed in a clump of reeds in a more open part of the marsh.

Range: British Columbia, Mackenzie, and Newfoundland south to Pennsylvania, Oklahoma, and Baja California; winters north to California and to the Carolinas.

These birds are especially numerous in fall and winter in southern marshes and rice fields, where they are primarily seed-eaters. Although shot in large numbers every year, their high reproductive rate enables them to maintain a stable population. The greatest threat to them is the destruction of the freshwater marshes where they breed: they have consequently become scarce in heavily populated areas.

251 Yellow Rail
(*Coturnicops noveboracensis*)
Rails, Gallinules, Coots (Rallidae)

Description: 6–8″ (15–20 cm). Sparrow-sized.
Brownish-buff with a short yellow bill
and yellow feet. Shows a *white wing
patch* in flight.

Voice: Series of clicks in groups of two or
three: *click-click, click-click-click.*
Usually heard at night.

Habitat: Grassy marshes and wet meadows.

Nesting: 7–10 buff eggs, with a ring of dark
spots around larger end, in a firm cup
of grass well-concealed in a grassy
marsh.

Range: Central Canada south to North Dakota,
and in New Brunswick, Quebec, and
Maine. Winters from the Carolinas,
Florida, and the Gulf Coast.

All rails are secretive, but none more
than this tiny bird. It is also rare, and
many veteran bird-watchers have never
seen one. It can conceal itself in very
short grass and can seldom be induced
to fly. The best way to see one is to
follow a mowing machine in a damp
meadow in the Deep South during
September or October. When the uncut
grass is reduced to a small patch, one or
more birds may flush into view, fly
weakly away, and disappear into the
nearest patch of tall grass.

252 Virginia Rail
(*Rallus limicola*)
Rails, Gallinules, Coots (Rallidae)

Description: 9–11″ (23–28 cm). A small rail with a
long *reddish bill,* rusty underparts, and
gray cheeks. The much larger King Rail
has buff cheeks. Fall immatures are
similar to adults, but have blackish
breasts.

Voice: Series of descending grunts and a far-carrying *ticket-ticket-ticket-ticket*.

Habitat: Freshwater and brackish marshes. May visit salt marshes in winter.

Nesting: 5–12 spotted pale buff eggs in a shallow and loosely constructed saucer often woven into surrounding marsh vegetation.

Range: Breeds from British Columbia, Minnesota, and Newfoundland south to Guatemala. Winters regularly north to Virginia, occasionally farther north.

This common but elusive marsh bird is most often detected by its call. It seldom flies, preferring to escape intruders by running through protecting marsh vegetation. When it does take wing, it often flies only a few yards before dropping out of sight into the marsh. Despite its apparently weak flight, it annually migrates long distances, having even been recorded as far offshore as Bermuda. Like all rails, its body is compressed laterally so that it can more easily slip between the stems of rushes and cattails.

254 King Rail
(Rallus elegans)
Rails, Gallinules, Coots (Rallidae)

Description: 15–19″ (38–48 cm). A secretive, chicken-sized marsh bird with a long, slightly curved bill. *Head, neck, and underparts rusty;* back mottled brown. Similar to Virginia Rail but larger and without gray face patch. Clapper Rail is grayer.

Voice: Series of deep resonant notes, *beep-beep-beep-beep,* etc., usually more rapid at the end.

Habitat: Freshwater marshes and roadside ditches; wanders to salt marshes in fall and winter.

Nesting: 6–16 spotted buff eggs in a deep bowl of grass, often with surrounding marsh grass pulled down and woven into a dome.

Range: Minnesota and Massachusetts south to
Florida, Texas, and northern Mexico.
Winters regularly from the Gulf Coast
southward. Also breeds in Cuba.

This large rail is common in the larger
freshwater marshes of the interior.
Although difficult to see, its loud call,
consisting of deep grunting and
clucking notes, often reveals its
presence. It occasionally hybridizes
with the Clapper Rail where freshwater
and salt marshes occur together. They
may eventually be found to be two
forms of a single species.

255 Common Snipe
(*Capella gallinago*)
Sandpipers (Scolopacidae)

Description: 10½–11½" (26–29 cm). A long-billed,
brownish shorebird with striped back,
usually seen when flushed from the
edge of a marsh or a pond. Fast, erratic
flight.

Voice: Sharp, rasping *scaip!* when flushed.

Habitat: Freshwater marshes, ponds, flooded
meadows, and fields; more rarely in salt
marshes.

Nesting: 4 pale olive-brown eggs, spotted with
black, in a grass-lined depression
concealed in a grass tussock in a marsh.

Range: Alaska, Hudson Bay, and Labrador
south to Massachusetts, Indiana, and
California; more rarely farther south.
Winters regularly north to British
Columbia and Virginia. Also breeds in
Eurasia.

Although snipes commonly migrate in
flocks at night, during the day they
scatter and usually feed alone. They
seek food early in the morning and in
late afternoon, and seem to be more
active on cloudy days. In addition to
the alarm note described above, these

birds have a variety of calls heard only on the breeding ground, and they perform a spectacular territorial display in which the feathers of the tail produce an eerie whistling sound. They are not as numerous as formerly but are still a popular gamebird. This species was formerly called "Wilson's Snipe," after the Scottish-American ornithologist Alexander Wilson (1766–1813).

284 Short-eared Owl
(*Asio flammeus*)
True Owls (Strigidae)

Description: 16" (40 cm). Crow-sized. A long-winged, tawny-brown owl of open country, rather heavily streaked, and with a blackish patch around each eye. The very short ear tufts are rarely visible.

Voice: Usually silent; on the nesting ground gives a variety of barks, hisses, and squeals.

Habitat: Freshwater and salt marshes; open grassland, prairies, dunes; open country generally during migration.

Nesting: 5–7 white eggs in a grass-lined depression on the ground, often concealed in weeds or beneath a bush.

Range: Breeds locally from Alaska and northern Canada south to New Jersey and California; winters in the southern part of the breeding range and south to Guatemala. Also in South America and most of the Old World.

This owl is most commonly seen late in the afternoon, as it begins to move about in preparation for a night of hunting. It can often be identified at a great distance by its habit of hovering; its flight is erratic and bounding. Occasionally several birds may be seen at once, an indication that small rodents—their major prey—are especially numerous.

Coast, and northern Mexico. Winters north to New Jersey, along the Gulf Coast, and on the Pacific coast north to Washington.

The male has a number of mates, each of which builds a nest of her own. In addition, the male may also build up to half a dozen "dummy" nests, often incomplete, one of which may be used as a roost. Thus a marsh frequented by these birds often contains many nests in various stages of completion. Locating a nest with eggs or young in it can take much time—which may be the purpose of these dummy nests.

518, 583 Yellow-headed Blackbird
(*Xanthocephalus xanthocephalus*)
Orioles, Blackbirds (Icteridae)

Description: 8–11" (20–28 cm). Robin-sized. Male much larger than the female; *head, neck and upper breast bright yellow, blackish elsewhere;* and conspicuous white markings on the wings. Female duller and lighter; yellow on the chest, throat, and face; no white wing marks.

Voice: Harsh, incessant *oka-wee-wee* and *kruck* call, coming from many individuals in a colony, blends into a loud, wavering chorus.

Habitat: Freshwater marshes.

Nesting: 3–5 brown-speckled whitish eggs in a basket woven around several strong stalks. Breeds in colonies.

Range: Basically a western bird, extending into the prairie states and provinces.

Visiting a blackbird colony in a marsh or slough in spring is an exciting experience. The surrounding water provides safety but often limits the nesting habitat; crowding is thus inevitable. Some males are always in display flight, with head stooped, feet and tail drooped, wings beating in a slow, accentuated way. Some quarrel with neighbors over boundaries while others fly out to feed. Approaching predators are mobbed by clouds of blackbirds and neighboring Redwings, which nest in the drier stands of cattails.

533   Sharp-tailed Sparrow
(*Ammospiza caudacuta*)
Grosbeaks, Buntings, Finches, Sparrows (Fringillidae)

Description: 5½" (14 cm). The combination of a dark cap, gray ear patch, and a bright orange-buff triangular area on the face distinguishes this species from the only other salt-marsh sparrow, the Seaside Sparrow.

Voice: A dry, insect-like *kip-kip-zeeeee*.

Habitat: Along the coast, in the drier, grassy portions of salt marsh and inland to grassy, freshwater marshes.

Nesting: 4 or 5 brown-dotted pale blue eggs in a loosely woven cup of grass set in tussock above the high-tide line or locally in freshwater marsh grass.

Range: Locally from central Canada to the middle Atlantic states; winters chiefly on the south Atlantic and Gulf coasts.

These birds spend most of their lives in dense, coarse marsh grass, and by the end of the breeding season their plumage is so badly worn that little of the distinctive pattern remains visible. Indeed, there are few birds more unprepossessing than a threadbare Sharp-tail in August. A month later, however, when they have acquired a fresh coat of feathers, they are among our most attractive sparrows.

541 Swamp Sparrow
(*Melospiza georgiana*)
Grosbeaks, Buntings, Finches,
Sparrows (Fringillidae)

Description: 5″ (13 cm). A chunky, *dark* sparrow
with unstreaked underparts, *bright
rufous cap, and rusty wings;* back and tail
dark brown; face and breast gray; throat
white. The White-throated Sparrow has
a striped crown and lacks rusty
coloration in the wings.

Voice: Sweet, musical trill, all on one note.

Habitat: Freshwater marshes and open wooded
swamps; in migration with other
sparrows in weedy fields, parks, and
brush piles.

Nesting: 4 or 5 blue-green eggs with brown
blotches in a grassy cup on the ground,
well hidden in dense tussocks or marsh
vegetation.

Range: From east-central Canada south to east-
central United States; winters south to
the Gulf of Mexico.

A bird of the wetlands during the
breeding season, the Swamp Sparrow
appears in a variety of other habitats
during migration and winter. It is
rather shy, but responds readily to any
squeaking noise, and can usually be
lured into view by a patient observer. It
is never seen in large flocks like the
White-throated and White-crowned
Sparrows, but is usually found singly,
foraging on the ground in rather dense
cover.

560, 568 Red-winged Blackbird
(*Agelaius phoeniceus*)
Orioles, Blackbirds (Icteridae)

Description: 7–9½″ (17–24 cm). Smaller than a
Robin. Male is black with *bright red
shoulder patches.* Female and young are
heavily streaked with dusky brown.

Voice: Rich, musical *O-ka-LEEEE!*

Habitat: Marshes, swamps, and wet and dry
meadows; pastures.

Nesting: 3–5 pale blue eggs spotted and
scrawled with dark brown and purple.
Nest a well-made cup of marsh grass or
reeds attached to growing marsh
vegetation or built in a bush in a
marsh.

Range: Breeds from Alaska and Newfoundland
south to Florida, the Gulf Coast, and
central Mexico. Winters regularly north
to Pennsylvania and British Columbia.

Although primarily a marsh bird, the
Red-wing will nest near virtually any
body of water and occasionally breeds in
upland pastures. Each pair raises two or
three broods a season, building a new
nest for each clutch. After the breeding
season, the birds gather with other
blackbirds in flocks sometimes
numbering in the hundreds of
thousands or millions and have come to
be viewed as a health hazard. Attempts
have been made to reduce such flocks
by spraying and other methods.

Lakes, Ponds, Rivers

Open water that supports swimming
and diving birds, as well as birds that
characteristically feed around its edges.

14 Great Blue Heron
(*Ardea herodias*)
Herons, Bitterns (Ardeidae)

Description: 39–52″ (99–132 cm). W. 70″ (1.8 m
A common, *large, grayish* heron with a
yellowish bill. Flies with neck folded,
whereas the Sandhill Crane flies with
the neck extended. In Florida an all-
white form, the "Great White Heron,'
differs from the Great Egret in having
greenish-yellow rather than black legs.

Voice: Hoarse, guttural squawk.

Habitat: Lakes, ponds, rivers, and marshes.

Nesting: 3–5 pale greenish-blue eggs on a
platform of sticks, lined with finer
material, usually in a tree but
sometimes on the ground or concealed
in a reedbed. In colonies.

Range: Alaska, Quebec, and Nova Scotia sout
to Mexico and the West Indies.
Winters as far north as New England
and southern Alaska. Also breeds in the
Galapagos Islands.

This large heron is frequently found
standing at the edge of a pond or
marshy pool, watching for fish or frogs
which are its principal food. It also
feeds on small mammals, reptiles, and
occasionally birds. Most Great Blue
Herons migrate south in the fall, but a
few remain in the North during the
winter; such lingering birds often fall
victim to severe weather.

18 Green Heron
(*Butorides striatus*)
Herons, Bitterns (Ardeidae)

Description: 15–22″ (38–56 cm). Crow-sized. A
small dark heron with *bright orange or
yellowish legs.* Head and neck chestnut,
crown black with a small crest, back
and wings dark green-gray.

Voice: Explosive, rasping *skyow!* Also croaks

cackles, and clucks.

Habitat: Lake margins, streams, ponds, and marshes.

Nesting: 3–6 pale blue-green eggs in a flimsy saucer of sticks and twigs in a bush or thicket near water. Occasionally breeds in colonies.

Range: British Columbia, Minnesota, and New Brunswick south to southern South America. Winters north to South Carolina, the Gulf Coast, and California. Also in tropical portions of Africa and Southeast Asia.

The most common heron in much of its range, all it requires is a pond or stream with thick bushes or trees nearby for nesting and soft, muddy borders in which to search for its prey. It stretches its neck and bill forward as if taking aim, nervously flicking its short tail, and, after a few elaborately cautious steps, seizes the fish with a jab of its bill. A retiring bird, it is often first noticed when it flushes unexpectedly from the edge of water and flies off uttering its sharp call note.

37, 50 Herring Gull
(*Larus argentatus*)
Gulls, Terns (Laridae)

Description: 23–26" (58–66 cm). Adult white with light gray back and wings; black wing tip with white spots. *Feet pink or flesh-colored.* First-year birds brownish.

Voice: Loud rollicking call, *kuk-kuk-kuk, yucca-yucca-yucca,* and other raucous cries.

Habitat: Lakes, rivers, estuaries, and beaches; common in all aquatic habitats.

Nesting: 2–4 heavily spotted olive-brown eggs in a mass of seaweed or dead grass on the ground or a cliff; most often on islands. In colonies.

Range: Breeds from Alaska and Greenland

south to the Carolinas, and is spreading. Also in Eurasia.

This is the common "sea gull" inland and along the coast. In recent years it has become abundant, probably due to the amount of food available at garbage dumps, and has extended its range southward along the Atlantic Coast, often to the detriment of colonial birds such as terns and Laughing Gulls. Although a scavenger, it also eats large numbers of aquatic and marine animals and feeds on berries. It often drops clams and other shellfish on exposed rocks or parking lots in order to break the shells and get at the soft interior.

38, 52 Ring-billed Gull
(*Larus delawarensis*)
Gulls, Terns (Laridae)

Description: 18–20″ (45–50 cm). Adult silvery gray on back, white on head, tail, and underparts. Similar to Herring Gull but smaller, with *yellow feet* and with narrow black ring around bill. Young birds are mottled brown, paler than a young Herring Gull, and have a blackish tail band and flesh-colored legs.

Voice: Loud, raucous mewing cry, like the Herring Gull but higher-pitched.

Habitat: Lakes and rivers; many move to salt water in the winter.

Nesting: 2–4 spotted buff or olive eggs in a hollow in the ground, sometimes lined with grass or debris. Usually on islands in lakes. In the North they sometimes nest in low trees. In colonies, often with other gulls or terns.

Range: Alaska and Labrador south to the Great Lakes and California. Winters from southern New England south to Cuba.

In most of the northern part of the United States the Ring-billed Gull is known as a winter visitor, less common than the Herring Gull. But in some inland areas and in the Deep South it is the more numerous of the two species. It often nests in very large colonies; as many as 85,000 pairs nest on a single island in Lake Ontario. By contrast, colonies of Herring Gulls seldom number more than a few score pairs.

46 Black-headed Gull
(*Larus ridibundus*)
Gulls, Terns (Laridae)

Description: 15″ (38 cm). A small gull with gray back and inner wings and *flashing white primaries.* In breeding plumage has a dark brown hood. Red bill and legs. Immature is darker above, but shows some white in primaries, and has narrow black tip to tail. *In all plumages, under surface of primaries is blackish.* Bonaparte's Gull is smaller, has black bill, and lacks dark undersurface of primaries.

Voice: A harsh *kwup;* various squealing notes.

Habitat: Bays and estuaries.

Nesting: 3 buff-brown eggs with black blotches, in a nest lined with grass, sticks, and seaweed in trees, bushes, on rocks, or on the ground. Colonies located on sand dunes, beaches, marshes, and open fields.

Range: Northern portions of Europe and Asia south to their southern parts; winters from the southern portions of the breeding range south to Africa and southern Asia. Uncommon but regular winter visitor to eastern North America.

Like the Bonaparte's Gull, with which it is almost always found in America, its flight is light and buoyant, resembling that of a tern more than a gull. Although this Old World gull is uncommon in North America, it may be seen regularly

in small numbers in northeastern coastal
waters. In Europe it is one of the most
familiar gulls.

---

47 **Little Gull**
(*Larus minutus*)
Gulls, Terns (Laridae)

Description: 11″ (28 cm). The *smallest* gull. Summer
adult has pale gray back and wings,
white underparts, a *black hood,* and
blackish underwings. Winter plumage
similar but head white with partial gray
cap and dark spot behind eye. Dark red
bill and legs. Immature has narrow
black tail tip, a diagonal dark bar on
forewing, and dark primaries.

Voice: A soft *kek-kek-kek-kek.*

Habitat: Inland marshes, meadows, lakes, and
rivers; also coastal bays, flats, harbors,
and estuaries.

Nesting: 3 olive-brown eggs with dark spots, in
a nest lined with grass and leaves,
placed among marsh vegetation.

Range: Central Europe east to southern Siberia;
in recent years, locally in Ontario and
Wisconsin; winters regularly in small
numbers in eastern North America,
especially along the coast from New
Brunswick to New Jersey and on the
Great Lakes.

This tiny gull was known for decades as
a rare winter visitor to the Northeast
before it was found nesting in Ontario.
Its flight is rather buoyant and tern-like,
and it often plucks food from the
surface while on the wing, or dives
from the air after minnows and aquatic
insects.

48, 53, 55 Bonaparte's Gull
(*Larus philadelphia*)
Gulls, Terns (Laridae)

Description:

12–14″ (30–35 cm). A small, delicate gull, silvery-gray above with conspicuous white patches on the leading edge of the outer wing. Black on head of breeding adults is lacking in winter. Young birds have dark markings on the upper surface of the wing and a black tail band. The Black-headed Gull is similar, but is larger, has a red bill (Bonaparte's is black), and has dark wing linings.

Voice: Rasping *tea-ar;* a soft, nasal snarling note.

Habitat: Forested lakes and rivers; winters along the coast, in estuaries, and at the mouth of large rivers.

Nesting: 2–4 olive or buff, spotted eggs in a well-made cup of grass, moss, and twigs in a spruce or fir tree near a lake or river.

Range: Breeds in interior of northwestern Canada and in Alaska. Winters along both coasts, on the Atlantic from southern New England southward.

Breeding in the Far North, these beautiful gulls are most often seen on lakes and rivers during migration or along the coast in winter. They keep to themselves, seldom joining the larger gulls at dumps. They feed in tidal inlets and at sewage outlets, picking scraps of food from the water. During spring migration they may often be seen flying northward up large rivers such as the Hudson and the Mississippi. The gull is named after a nephew of Napoleon, Charles Lucien Bonaparte, who was a leading ornithologist in the 1800s in America and Europe.

58, 61 Common Tern
(*Sterna hirundo*)
Gulls, Terns (Laridae)

Description: 13–16″ (33–40 cm). Pigeon-sized.
White with black cap and pale gray
back and wings. Red bill with black
tip. Deeply forked tail. Similar to
Forster's Tern but lacks frosty wing tip
Also similar to Arctic and Roseate
terns.

Voice: *Kip-kip-kip*. Also *TEEaar*.

Habitat: Lakes, ponds, rivers, coastal beaches,
and islands.

Nesting: 2 or 3 spotted olive-buff eggs in a
depression in sand or a shallow cup of
dead grass on sandy or pebbly beaches
or open rocky places; most often nests
on islands or isolated peninsulas. In
colonies.

Range: Labrador south to the Caribbean and
west to Wisconsin and Alberta.
Winters from Florida to southern South
America. Also in Eurasia.

A grasp of the field marks of other terns
is best gained by comparison with these
most common of "sea swallows." They
are a familiar sight on almost all large
bodies of water where protected nesting
sites exist. They are seen flying
gracefully over the water, searching for
small fish and shrimp, which they
capture by diving from the air.
Sensitive to disturbance during the
breeding season, whole colonies often
fail to breed successfully because of
disruption by humans and, as a result,
their numbers are slowly declining.
They will attack human intruders in the
nesting colonies, often striking them on
the head with their bills.

65 Caspian Tern
(*Sterna caspia*)
Gulls, Terns (Laridae)

Description: 19–23" (48–58 cm). Gull-sized.
Largely white, with black cap and pale
gray back and wings; heavy *bright red
bill* and *dusky underwing*. The similar
Royal Tern has an orange-red bill, paler
underwing, and is almost never seen
away from the coast.

Voice: Low, hoarse *kraa*. Also a shorter *kow*.

Habitat: Sandy or pebbly shores of lakes and
large rivers, and along seacoasts.

Nesting: 2 or 3 spotted buff eggs in a shallow
depression or a well-made cup of dead
grass, most often on a sandy or rocky
island. Solitary or in small colonies.

Range: Mackenzie, the Great Lakes and
Newfoundland south to the Gulf Coast
and Baja California. Winters north
to California and North Carolina.
Also breeds in Eurasia, Africa, and
Australia.

Much less gregarious than other terns,
Caspians usually feed singly. Pairs
breed by themselves, in small colonies,
or may attach themselves to colonies of
other birds such as the Ring-billed
Gull. Caspians are more predatory than
most other terns, readily taking small
birds or the eggs and young of other
terns.

99, 103 Double-crested Cormorant
(*Phalacrocorax auritus*)
Cormorants (Phalacrocoracidae)

Description: 30–35" (76–89 cm). Goose-sized.
Slender-bodied, dark bird with a long
neck and a slender, hooked bill that is
usually tilted upward when swimming.
Orange throat pouch. Stands upright
when perched. Larger than the
Olivaceous Cormorant of the Gulf
Coast, and lacks its white-bordered

throat pouch. Tufts on the crown, from
which it gets its name, are rarely visible.

Voice: Deep guttural grunt.

Habitat: Lakes, rivers, swamps, and coasts.

Nesting: 3 or 4 pale, chalky blue eggs in a well-
made platform nest of sticks (or
seaweed on the coast) in a tree or on a
cliff or rocky island. In colonies.

Range: Breeds from Alaska and Newfoundland
south to Mexico and the Bahamas.
Winters north to Long Island and
southern Alaska.

The Double-crested is the most familiar
cormorant in the East. Except in the
Northeast during the winter, and along
the Gulf Coast, it is the only cormorant
to be seen. Occupying a wide variety of
habitats, it replaces the Great Cormorant
(*Phalacrocorax carbo*) which is widespread
in the Old World but is here found as
a breeder only along the Canadian coast
south to the Gulf of Nova Scotia.
Cormorants migrate in large, V-shaped
flocks like migrating geese but are
silent when flying. The word
"cormorant" is derived, through
French, from the Latin name *corvus
marinus,* meaning "sea crow."

100, 104 **Anhinga**
(*Anhinga anhinga*)
Anhingas (Anhingidae)

Description: 34–36″ (86–91 cm). A blackish bird
of southern swamps with a very long,
slender neck and long tail. Male's
plumage has greenish iridescence; upper
surface of wings silvery gray. Female has
tawny brown neck and breast, sharply
set off from black belly.

Voice: Low grunt similar to that of the
cormorant.

Habitat: Freshwater ponds and swamps with
thick vegetation, especially cypress.

Nesting: 4 chalky blue eggs in a stick nest lined
with fresh green leaves, in trees; often

109, 153 Redhead
(*Aythya americana*)
Swans, Geese, Ducks (Anatidae)

Description: 18–22" (46–56 cm). Male *gray, with brick red head and black breast.* Female duller and browner, with a light area around base of bill; rounder-headed than female Ring-necked Duck. Both sexes have a pale gray wing stripe and a pale blue-gray bill. Similar Canvasback has a whitish body and sloping forehead and bill.

Voice: Like the meow of a cat; also quacks.

Habitat: Nests in marshes, but at other times is found on lakes and bays; often on salt water in winter.

Nesting: 10–15 buff eggs in a woven cup of reeds lined with white down and attached to marsh vegetation.

Range: Breeds from British Columbia, Mackenzie, and Manitoba south to New Mexico, and rarely in eastern states. Winters from California, the Great Lakes, and southern New England south to Guatemala and the West Indies.

Redheads do most of their feeding at night, spending the daylight hours resting on water. This beautiful duck has suffered greatly from hunting and the destruction of its habitat; it has declined in numbers until it is one of the least common North American ducks. In many areas the introduction of carp from Eurasia has caused the destruction of its aquatic food plants.

110, 154 Canvasback
(*Aythya valisineria*)
Swans, Geese, Ducks (Anatidae)

Description: 19–24" (48–61 cm). Male has a *whitish body,* black chest, and reddish head with low forehead. The *long bill gives the head a distinctive sloping profile.* Female gray-brown, with similar profile. At a distance males can be distinguished from Redheads by their white bodies, the male Redhead's body being largely gray.

Voice: Males grunt or croak. Females quack.

Habitat: Nests on marshes; winters on lakes, bays, and estuaries.

Nesting: 7–10 greenish eggs in a floating mass of reeds and grass anchored to stems of marsh plants.

Range: Alaska, Mackenzie, and Manitoba south to Minnesota, Nebraska, and California. Winters from British Columbia and Massachusetts south to the Gulf Coast and to Central America.

Although they breed mainly in the West, each fall large numbers migrate eastward to winter on the Great Lakes and along the Atlantic Coast. They are considered among the best-tasting ducks, and many thousands are shot annually. In recent years their numbers have declined drastically, but chiefly because of the draining of the large marshes they require to breed. Where they are still relatively numerous, their long V-shaped flocks are a striking sight as they move from one feeding ground to another. Their principal food is the aquatic plant known as wild celery (*Vallisneria*), and part of the bird's scientific name is a corruption of that word.

114, 161 **Common Merganser**
(*Mergus merganser*)
Swans, Geese, Ducks (Anatidae)

Description: 22–27″ (56–68 cm). Male has *flashing white sides, green head,* white breast, and long, thin red bill. Female has gray body and sides; brownish crested head sharply set off from white throat. Red-breasted Merganser is similar, but has gray sides, white neck-ring, and rust-colored breast.

Voice: Low rasping croak.

Habitat: Wooded rivers and ponds; in winter, also on salt bays.

Nesting: 8–12 pale buff eggs in a down-lined cavity or an abandoned hawk's nest.

Range: Southeastern Alaska, Manitoba, and Newfoundland south to northern New England, Michigan, and California. Winters south to northern Mexico and the Gulf Coast (rare). Also in Eurasia.

Although preferring to feed on lakes, they are often driven to rivers by cold weather; there they are found in flocks of 10 to 20 birds, all facing upstream and diving in pursuit of fish. Formerly, large numbers were shot in the belief that they destroyed valuable gamefish, but it is now understood that these birds are beneficial, preventing overpopulation of fish and thus allowing the survivors to attain greater size. Mergansers have fine tooth-like serrations along the sides of their bills which help in capturing slippery fish.

119, 164 Wood Duck
(*Aix sponsa*)
Swans, Geese, Ducks (Anatidae)

Description: 17–20″ (43–51 cm). A beautiful, crested, multicolored small duck. Male patterned in iridescent greens, purples, and blues with a distinctive white chin patch; red, rather long bill; long tail. Female grayish with broad white eye-ring.

Voice: Loud *wooo-eeek*. Also softer *peet* and *cheep* notes.

Habitat: Wooded rivers and ponds; wooded swamps. Visits freshwater marshes in late summer and fall.

Nesting: Up to 15 whitish eggs in a nest made of down in a natural tree cavity or nest-box sometimes 50 feet or more from the ground.

Range: British Columbia, Nova Scotia, and
Minnesota south to Florida and Texas.
Winters north to Washington in the
West and New Jersey in the East,
rarely farther north. Also breeds in
Cuba.

The Wood Duck's habit of nesting in
cavities enables it to breed in areas
lacking suitable ground cover. The
young leave the nest soon after
hatching, jumping from the nesting
cavity to the ground. Once in the
water, they travel through wooded
ponds with their mother. Snapping
turtles take a heavy toll of them.

121, 156 **Ring-necked Duck**
(*Aythya collaris*)
Swans, Geese, Ducks (Anatidae)

Description: 14–18″ (35–46 cm). Male has black
back and breast; purple-glossed, black-
appearing head; pale gray flanks;
vertical white mark on side of breast.
Female brownish, paler around the base
of the bill, and has a narrow white
eye-ring. Bill pale gray with a white
ring. The shape of the head—high and
angular—distinguishes this bird from
the scaups.
Voice: Soft purring notes, but usually silent.
Habitat: Wooded lakes, ponds, and rivers;
seldom on salt water except in the
southern states.
Nesting: 8–12 buff or olive eggs in a down-lined
cup concealed in vegetation near the
edge of a pond.
Range: Alaska, Manitoba, and Newfoundland
south to Maine, Colorado, and
California. Winters south to Mexico
and the West Indies.

This species might better be called the
"Ring-billed Duck," for its chestnut
neck-ring is usually seen only at close

range while the white ring on the bill is a prominent field mark. More partial to acid ponds and lakes in wooded regions than other diving ducks, it eats the seeds of aquatic plants as well as snails and insects.

122, 155 Tufted Duck
(*Aythya fuligula*)
Swans, Geese, Ducks (Anatidae)

Description: 17" (43 cm). A stocky, blackish duck with flashing *white flanks* and *drooping crest*. Female warm brown, paler on the flanks, with a small white patch at the base of the bill; no crest.

Voice: Various soft, growling notes; low whistles.

Habitat: Wooded lakes, streams, and marshes; in winter often in estuaries and shallow coastal bays.

Nesting: Usually 7–10 pale green eggs in a down-lined bowl of grass, concealed under a bush or tussock and usually near water.

Range: Northern Eurasia; casual in North America, chiefly along the coast in Alaska and the northeastern states.

This Old World bird is a counterpart of the Ring-necked Duck of North America. Indeed, on those rare occasions when a Tufted Duck turns up in our area, it may be seen with a small flock of Ring-necks. In Eurasia these birds gather in very large flocks, often with scaups and coots. In recent years there has been an increase in the number of sightings of this species in our area.

123, 157   Lesser Scaup
(*Aythya affinis*)
Swans, Geese, Ducks (Anatidae)

Description: 15–18″ (38–46 cm). Similar to the Greater Scaup but crown is higher, giving the head a more angular appearance. Male has its head glossed with purple, not green. Females are dark brown with a small white face patch, not easily distinguishable from the female Greater Scaup. In flight, the white stripe is shorter, whereas in the Greater Scaup the stripe extends three-fourths of the wing's length.

Voice: Seldom heard. Sharp whistles and guttural scolding notes.

Habitat: Ponds and marshes; in migration and winter it occurs on lakes, rivers, and ponds, and in the southern states on salt water.

Nesting: Usually 8–12 olive-buff eggs in a cup of down-lined grass hidden in vegetation often some distance from the edge of the water.

Range: Breeds from interior Alaska and northern Canada south to British Columbia, Montana, and Iowa, and occasionally farther east. Winters regularly from British Columbia and Massachusetts south to the Gulf of Mexico and northern South America.

Confined to the New World, it is thought to be descended from an earlier invasion of North America by the ancestor of both modern species of scaups. Here it evolved into a distinct species, to be joined later by a second arrival, the Greater Scaup, found in both hemispheres. In the northern states, where the Greater Scaup is more common in winter, the Lesser is often found in small parties on fresh water, while in the South it is seen in large flocks on lakes and salt water.

124, 158 Greater Scaup
(*Aythya marila*)
Swans, Geese, Ducks (Anatidae)

Description: 15–20″ (38–51 cm). Male has very
light gray body; blackish chest; and
black-appearing, green-glossed head.
Female is a uniform dark brown with
white patch at base of bill. Often seen
in large flocks on open water.

Voice: Usually silent; discordant croaking calls
on the breeding grounds.

Habitat: Lakes, bays, and ponds; in winter,
often on salt water.

Nesting: 8–12 olive or buff eggs in a down-lined
cup of grass concealed in a clump of
grass on land or in marsh vegetation
well out from shore.

Range: Alaska and northern Canada east to
Hudson's Bay and in Maritime
Provinces. Winters mainly along
Pacific, Gulf, and Atlantic coasts. Also
breeds in Eurasia.

It is most commonly seen in large rafts,
often composed of thousands of birds,
on big inland lakes. When these lakes
freeze over, the birds move to salt water.
Although the two scaups can be difficult
to tell apart, any very large flock of
scaups on the northeast coast in winter
may be assumed to be the Greater.
Because it dives for many small animals
and is not as much of a vegetarian as
the Redhead or the Canvasback, the
Greater Scaup is not considered as choice
a gamebird but is still shot in large
numbers annually.

128, 163 Hooded Merganser
(*Lophodytes cucullatus*)
Swans, Geese, Ducks (Anatidae)

Description: 16–19″ (40–48 cm). A small duck with
a slender, pointed bill. Male has *white,
fan-shaped, black-bordered crest;* dark
blackish body; dull rusty flanks; white

breast with two black stripes down the
side. Female is dull gray-brown with
head and crest warmer brown. Both
sexes show a white wing patch
in flight.

Voice: Hoarse grunts and chatters.
Habitat: Wooded ponds, lakes, and rivers;
sometimes in tidal channels in winter.
Nesting: 8–12 white eggs in a down-lined cup in
a natural tree cavity, or sometimes in a
fallen hollow log.
Range: Alaska, Manitoba, and Nova Scotia
south to Tennessee, Nebraska, and
Oregon; occasionally in southeastern
states. Winters from British Columbia,
Nebraska, and New England south to
Mexico and the Gulf Coast.

The smallest of our mergansers, they
are most often seen along rivers and in
estuaries during the fall and winter.
They are usually found in flocks of up
to a dozen, and when startled are
among the fastest flying of our ducks.
They feed chiefly on small fish, which
they pursue in long, rapid, underwater
dives, but also take frogs and aquatic
insects.

---

170 **Canada Goose**
(*Branta canadensis*)
Swans, Geese, Ducks (Anatidae)

Description: Small races 22–26″ (56–66 cm); large
races 35–45″ (89–114 cm). Brownish
body with black head and long black
neck; conspicuous *white cheek patch*. The
smaller Brant lacks the white cheek
patch.
Voice: Rich, musical honking.
Habitat: Lakes, bays, rivers, and marshes. Often
feeds in open grassland and stubble
fields.
Nesting: 4–8 whitish eggs in a large mass of
grass and moss lined with down.
Usually on the ground near water, but
sometimes in an abandoned osprey or
eagle nest.

Range: Alaska and Baffin Island south to
Massachusetts, North Carolina, and
California. Winters south to northern
Mexico and the Gulf Coast.
Widespread as a semidomesticated bird
in city parks and reservoirs.

When people speak of "wild geese" it is
generally this species they have in
mind. Familiar in every state and
province; a common sight is their
V-shaped flocks in migration. There is
much geographical variation in size;
some birds are scarcely larger than
Mallards, others are at least twice that
size. Tolerant of man, some even nest
in city parks and suburbs and are
especially noticeable in late summer
and early fall, when they gather on golf
courses and large lawns to molt, often
with one or two acting as sentinels.
When danger approaches they
sometimes crouch low with neck
extended, depending on their coloration
for protection.

174 Whistling Swan
(Olor columbianus)
Swans, Geese, Ducks (Anatidae)

Description: 48–55" (122–140 cm). The only swan
likely to be seen in most of the East.
Large, all white; black bill usually with
small yellow spot at base of upper
mandible. Holds neck straight up,
unlike the Mute Swan which bends its
neck in a graceful curve.

Voice: Mellow, rich bugling call, usually
heard from a flock of migrating birds.
Sometimes mistaken for the call of the
Canada Goose.

Habitat: Arctic tundra; winters on marshy lakes
and bays.

Nesting: 4–6 creamy white eggs in a large mass
of grass and moss on an island or at the
edge of a marshy tundra lake.

Range: Breeds in Alaska and northern Canada east to Baffin Island. Winters in Aleutians and from Washington to Baja California and from Maryland to Texas; occasionally on the Great Lakes.

Each fall large numbers of Whistling Swans pause briefly on the Great Lakes before moving to their winter headquarters along the Atlantic Coast from Chesapeake Bay to North Carolina. Often traveling in flocks of several hundred, they present a spectacular sight. Many stop on the Niagara River and are sometimes swept over the falls to their death. Because they breed in remote and little disturbed areas, they have so far escaped the fate of the closely related Trumpeter Swan, which was reduced to near extinction by hunting and habitat destruction.

177, 179 **Least Grebe**
(*Podiceps dominicus*)
Grebes (Podicipedidae)

Description: 8–10″ (20–25 cm). Robin-sized. Grayish with orange eyes and a small, dark bill. Similar to Pied-billed Grebe but smaller, with a more slender bill.

Voice: Loud *clang*.

Habitat: Quiet, thickly vegetated ponds and slow-moving streams.

Nesting: 3–6 white eggs which become stained with brown, laid in a floating or anchored nest of reeds, rushes, and rotten leaves.

Range: Southern Texas and West Indies to South America.

Smallest North American grebe. Like most grebes, when leaving the nest the adults cover the eggs with decayed vegetation to protect them from excessive heat of the sun and from predators. Least Grebes rarely leave the immediate vicinity of their breeding grounds. They feed mostly on various aquatic insects, and occasionally on small crustaceans such as crayfish. In southern Texas they are often found on ranch ponds.

185 Red-necked Grebe
(*Podiceps grisegena*)
Grebes (Podicipedidae)

Description: 18–20″ (46–51 cm). Largest grebe in eastern North America. A slender water bird with *long rufous neck; whitish cheeks;* dark cap; long, pointed *yellow bill.* Grayish body. Similar in winter, but neck gray. The long yellow bill separates this species from all other North American grebes. In flight it can be distinguished from loons by its smaller size and white wing patches.

Voice: Nasal honk. Also a loon-like wail.

Habitat: Ponds and lakes in summer; bays and estuaries in winter.

Nesting: 3–5 whitish, stained eggs in a floating mass of dead reeds and grass in reedy lakes.

Range: Northern Canada and Alaska southeast to southern Minnesota; more rarely to Quebec and New Hampshire. Winters south to Long Island, rarely to Florida. Also breeds in Eurasia.

Highly aquatic, grebes can swim with only their head above water, concealing themselves in low pond vegetation. The young, striped in black and white, are often seen riding on the parent's back. Like loons, grebes are expert divers, propelling themselves with their lobed feet as they pursue fish, crustaceans, and aquatic insects.

188, 190   **Common Loon**
(*Gavia immer*)
Loons (Gaviidae)

Description: 28–36" (71–91 cm). Goose-sized.
Heavy, long-bodied water bird with
thick pointed bill held horizontally. In
summer, head and neck black with
white collar; back black with white
spots. In winter, crown, hind neck, and
upperparts grayish; throat and
underparts white. When swimming it
rides low in the water.

Voice: Wild maniacal laugh, also a mournful
yodeled *oo-AH-ho* with middle note
higher, and a loud ringing *kee-a-ree,
kee-a-ree* with middle note lower. Often
calls at night.

Habitat: Forested lakes and rivers; oceans and
bays in winter.

Nesting: 2 olive-brown, lightly spotted eggs in a
substantial mass of vegetation near edge
of water, usually on an island.

Range: Breeds from Aleutian Islands, Alaska,
and Northern Canada south to New
Hampshire, Montana, and California.
Winters south to the Gulf Coast. Also
breeds in Iceland.

It is known for its call, a far-carrying
wail heard on its northern breeding
grounds and occasionally during
migration. Loons are expert divers and
have been caught in nets as much as
200 feet below the surface. Their
principal food is fish, but they also eat
shellfish, frogs, and aquatic insects.
Their feet are located far back on the
body, which aids them in diving; they
travel on land with difficulty,
propelling themselves forward on their
breasts.

197, 215 Spotted Sandpiper
(*Actitis macularia*)
Sandpipers (Scolopacidae)

Description: 7½″ (19 cm). Robin-sized. In breeding
plumage olive-brown above, *many black
spots below;* lacks spotting in fall and
winter.

Voice: Clear *peet-weet;* also a soft trill.

Habitat: Almost anyplace with water nearby,
both in open country and in wooded
areas.

Nesting: 4 buff, brown-spotted eggs in a nest
lined with grass or moss in a slight
depression on the ground.

Range: Northern Alaska and Canada to
southern United States. Winters
from southern United States to South
America.

This is one of the best-known of
American shorebirds. Its habit of
endlessly bobbing the rear part of its
body up and down has earned it the
vernacular name "teeter-tail." When
flushed from the margin of a pond or
stream it is easily identified by its
distinctive flight—short bursts of
rapidly vibrating wingbeats alternating
with brief glides. Most of our
shorebirds breed in the Far North; this
is one of the few that nests in the
United States.

302 Swallow-tailed Kite
(*Elanoides forficatus*)
Hawks, Eagles (Accipitridae)

Description: 22–24″ (56–61 cm). W. 50″ (1.3 m).
A graceful bird of prey, with long,
pointed wings and deeply forked tail.
Head and underparts white, back wings
and tail black.

Voice: Shrill squeals or whistles. Also a soft
twittering.

Habitat: Swamps, marshes, river bottoms, and
glades in open forests.

Nesting: 2–4 creamy white eggs, boldly spotted
with dark brown in a stick nest often
lined with moss, and usually set in a
tall tree.

Range: Breeds mainly on or near the coast from
South Carolina to Florida, formerly to
Texas; local farther inland in the Gulf
states, rare farther north. South to
southern South America.

The Swallow-tail's flight as it rides air
currents or swoops rapidly after its prey
is graceful, buoyant, and effortless. It
spends much of the daylight hours on
the wing, rarely perching on some dead
tree branch. It feeds extensively on
lizards and snakes. Much of its food is
eaten while aloft, including dragonflies
which it snatches out of the air. Like a
swallow, it skims the water to drink
and bathe.

305, 307 Bald Eagle
(*Haliaeetus leucocephalus*)
Hawks, Eagles (Accipitridae)

Description: 30–31" (76–79 cm). W. 72–90" (1.8–
2.3 m). A large blackish eagle with
white head, white tail, and a long, heavy
yellow bill. Young birds lack the white
head and tail and resemble adult
Golden Eagles, but have pale wing
linings and a more massive bill.
Voice: Squeaky cackling.
Habitat: Lakes, rivers, marshes, and seacoasts.
Nesting: 2 or 3 white eggs in a huge,
conspicuous mass of sticks in the top of
a tall tree or, less frequently, on top of
a cliff.
Range: Formerly bred throughout most of
North America, but now restricted as a
breeding bird to Aleutians, Alaska,
parts of northern and eastern Canada,
northern United States, and Florida. In
winter, along almost any body of water,
especially the larger rivers in the
interior of the continent.

Eating dead fish stranded on beaches and riverbanks has caused many Bald Eagles to absorb large amounts of pesticides, which interfere with the birds' calcium metabolism and result in thin-shelled and often infertile eggs. Once a familiar sight along rivers and coasts, our national bird is today known mainly as an occasional migrant; adults now usually outnumber young birds. Unless these pesticides can be removed from the birds' environment, we may face the loss of one of North America's most magnificent birds.

306 Osprey
(*Pandion haliaetus*)
Ospreys (Pandionidae)

Description: 21–24″ (53–61 cm). W. 54–72″ (1.4–1.8 m). A large, long-winged "fish hawk." Brown above and white below; white head with dark brown line through eye and on side of face. Wing shows distinct bend at the "wrist."

Voice: Loud, musical chirping.

Habitat: Lakes, rivers, and seacoasts.

Nesting: 2–4 white or buff, brown-spotted eggs in a bulky mass of sticks and debris placed in a tree, on rocks, flat ground, or telephone poles.

Range: Breeds from Alaska and Newfoundland south to Florida and the Gulf Coast. Winters regularly from the Gulf Coast and California south to Argentina. Also breeds in Eurasia, North Africa, the East Indies, and Australia.

This hawk is well adapted for capturing fish, which comprise its entire diet. The soles of Ospreys' feet are equipped with sharp, spiny projections that give the bird a firm grip on its slippery prey. It hovers until a fish nears the surface, then plunges feet-first into the water, grasping the fish in its talons.

315 **Peregrine Falcon**
(*Falco peregrinus*)
Falcons (Falconidae)

Description: 15–21″ (38–53 cm). W. 40″ (1 m).
Crow-sized. Adults slate-gray above
and pale below, with fine bars and spots
of black; narrow tail; *long pointed wings;*
conspicuous *black "mustaches."* Young
birds darker below and browner.

Voice: Rasping *kack-kack-kack.* Also a long
ascending wail, *WEEchew-WEEchew.*

Habitat: Open country, especially along rivers,
also near lakes, and the coast. Migrates
chiefly along the coast.

Nesting: 2–4 cream-colored, brown-spotted eggs
in a scrape with little lining, placed on
a cliff or in an abandoned eagle's nest.

Range: Formerly bred from Alaska and
Greenland south to Georgia and Baja
California, but now restricted to the
northern parts of its range in the East.
Winters north to British Columbia and
Massachusetts. Also breeds in southern
South America and in Eurasia, Africa,
and Australia.

Spectacular on the wing, in former
times they were a favorite choice for the
sport of falconry, plunging from
tremendous heights at speeds estimated
at 180 miles per hour to capture flying
birds. The Peregrine has been
drastically reduced in numbers by
pesticides (it is said that eating a single
badly contaminated duck can cause a
Peregrine to become infertile) and has
completely disappeared from all but the
most northern parts of its breeding
range. These falcons are quite tolerant
of man and formerly nested on
windowsills and ledges of buildings in
our largest cities, where they preyed on
pigeons.

331 Tree Swallow
(*Iridoprocne bicolor*)
Swallows (Hirundinidae)

Description: 5–6¼" (13–16 cm). Sparrow-sized. The only swallow in the East with metallic blue or blue-green upperparts and clear white underparts. Young birds are dull brown above but may be distinguished from Bank and Rough-winged swallows by their clear, whiter underparts.

Voice: Cheerful series of liquid twitters.

Habitat: Lake shores, flooded meadows, marshes, and streams.

Nesting: 4–6 white eggs in a feather-lined cup of grass placed in a hole in a tree or in a nest-box.

Range: Alaska, northern Manitoba, and Newfoundland south to Maryland, Nebraska, Colorado, and California. Winters north to the Carolinas, the Gulf Coast, and southern California; occasionally to New York and Massachusetts.

This bird's habit of feeding on bayberries enables it to winter farther north than other swallows. Although most on the East Coast winter in the Carolinas, a few may be found on Long Island or Cape Cod. It is the first of our swallows to reappear in the spring. It sometimes breeds in unusual situations: several pairs once nested on a ferry boat that shuttled across the St. Lawrence River, foraging on both the American and Canadian sides. Tree Swallows often enjoy playing with a feather, which they drop and then retrieve as it floats in the air. They gather in enormous flocks along the coast in fall, where they circle in big eddies like leaves caught in a whirlwind.

333 Rough-winged Swallow
(*Stelgidopteryx ruficollis*)
Swallows (Hirundinidae)

Description: 5–5¾" (13–14 cm). Sparrow-sized. Brown back with dusky throat and upper breast. The similar Bank Swallow has pure white underparts with the breast crossed by a narrow brown band.

Voice: Buzzy notes much like Bank Swallow's, but deeper and more rasping.

Habitat: Streams and rivers, especially in the vicinity of steep banks and man-made structures providing nest sites.

Nesting: 5–7 white eggs in a shallow saucer of grass and debris placed in a cliff crevice, drainpipe, or at the end of a tunnel dug by the birds in a sandbank.

Range: British Columbia, Michigan, and New Brunswick south to northern Argentina. Winters from Gulf Coast southward.

The name "Rough-winged" comes from tiny hooks on the outer primary, which give the feather a rough feel. The function of these hooks, found also in a group of unrelated African swallows, is unknown. Unlike the Bank Swallow, Rough-wings do not usually dig their own nesting burrows, but use ready-made nesting sites along streams. Thus they do not nest in large colonies like the Bank Swallow, although occasionally a few pairs may be found close together.

334 Bank Swallow
(*Riparia riparia*)
Swallows (Hirundinidae)

Description: 4¾–5½" (12–14 cm). Sparrow-sized—our smallest swallow. Brown above, dull white below; *breast crossed by a distinct brown band;* tail notched. Rough-winged Swallow is warmer brown, with dusky throat and breast without distinct brown band.

Voice: Series of buzzy notes, *bzt-bzt-bzt;* also a twitter.

Habitat: Rivers and streams, especially near sandbanks; more widespread during migration.

Nesting: 4 or 5 white eggs in a loosely built cup of grass at the end of a 2- or 3-foot tunnel in a vertical bank, which the bird excavates with feet and bill. Nests in colonies.

Range: Breeds from Alaska and Labrador south to Virginia, Texas, and California. Winters in South America. Also occurs in Eurasia.

Bank Swallows originally nested only in steep, sandy riverbanks, but like other swallows they have adapted to man and now nest in the sides of man-made excavations. They breed in colonies of from two or three pairs to a few thousand. Most lay their eggs at the same time and thus later forage for their young at the same time. Such parents have an advantage: swarms of flying insects are unevenly distributed and are more quickly located when many birds are searching together. The scientific name *riparia* is from the Latin word for "riverbank."

433 Belted Kingfisher
(*Megaceryle alcyon*)
Kingfishers (Alcedinidae)

Description: 13″ (33 cm). Pigeon-sized. *Bushy crest; dagger-like bill;* blue-gray above, white below. Male has a blue-gray breast band; female similar but with a *chestnut belly band.*

Voice: Loud, penetrating rattle, given on the wing and when perched.

Habitat: Rivers, lakes, and saltwater estuaries.

Nesting: 5–8 white eggs in an unlined chamber at the end of a tunnel up to eight feet long, dug in a sand or gravel bank.

Range: Breeds from Alaska and Canada and throughout United States. Winters south to Panama and the West Indies.

Kingfishers often hover like a tern over water where a fish is visible and dive vertically for the prey. They may also take crabs, crayfish, salamanders, lizards, mice, and insects. They often patrol a regular beat along a stream or lake shore, stopping at favorite exposed perches along the way.

434 Ringed Kingfisher
(*Megaceryle torquata*)
Kingfishers (Alcedinidae)

Description: 13" (33 cm). Pigeon-sized. Similar to the Belted Kingfisher but larger and with more chestnut on belly. Bushy crest and a large, dagger-shaped bill. Blue-gray above, *chestnut below with a white collar*. Female similar but has a gray band across the upper breast.
Voice: Harsh rattle louder than that of the Belted Kingfisher. Also a loud *kleck*.
Habitat: Tree-lined rivers, streams, and lakes.
Nesting: 5–7 white eggs in a burrow dug into sandbank.
Range: Extreme southern Texas to southern South America. Local on the lower Rio Grande.

Ringed Kingfishers are the largest of the three species of kingfishers in the United States, where they have been found in only two places on the lower Rio Grande in Texas: Laredo and Falcon Dam. Although very local within the United States, the Ringed Kingfisher has been observed regularly at Falcon Dam, but has not as yet bred there.

482 Green Kingfisher
(Chloroceryle americana)
Kingfishers (Alcedinidae)

Description: 8″ (20 cm). Robin-sized. Dark green
above, white below; *male has a broad
rufous breast band, female has a green
breast band.* Both sexes have a white
collar.

Voice: Instead of the rattle-like call of its
larger relatives, the Green Kingfisher
has an insect-like buzz and some low
clicking notes.

Habitat: Woodland streams and pools.

Nesting: 4–6 white eggs in a cavity at the end of
a burrow in a sandy bank.

Range: Extreme southern Texas to southern
South America.

Smallest of the three species found in
the United States, these birds may be
observed in southern Texas near forest-
fringed pools and streams of the clearest
water, where they sit for long periods
on a limb overhanging water until they
spot a minnow or other small fish. They
then plunge into the water after their
prey. At other times, when at a
considerable distance from water, they
feed on small lizards or grasshoppers.

Florida Swamps and Keys

In southern Florida there are a number
of freshwater and marine habitats that
are grouped together here because of
the distinctive species of birds they
contain. Mangroves are tropical trees
that grow in shallow salt water and
have stiltlike roots and evergreen
leaves. Vast marshes of sawgrass occur
in shallow fresh or brackish water. Keys
are low-lying coral or limestone islands
with tropical vegetation of West Indian
origin, such as gumbo-limbo,
manchineel, Jamaica dogwood,
mahogany, and palms.

9 **Wood Stork**
   "Wood Ibis"
   (*Mycteria americana*)
   Storks (Ciconiidae)

Description: 40–44" (102–112 cm). W. 66" (1.5 m).
              White with black flight feathers and
              tail. Head and neck bare, dark gray.
              Bill long, stout, and slightly curved,
              black in adults and yellow in immatures.
              Unlike herons, it flies with its neck
              extended.

     Voice: Dull croak. Usually silent except
              around nest. Young clatter endlessly.

   Habitat: On or near the coast, breeding chiefly
              in cypress swamps; also in mangroves.

   Nesting: 2 or 3 white eggs on a huge stick
              platform in colonies in trees.

     Range: Breeds in Florida; wanders to South
              Carolina and Texas, occasionally
              farther. Also in South America.

              Often wrongly called "Wood Ibis," this
              is a true stork. Its naked gray head has
              earned it the local name "flint head."
              These birds perch motionless on a bare
              branch or slowly stalk through marshes
              in search of food. They are sometimes
              seen circling high in the air on rising
              thermal air currents. They nest in
              enormous colonies numbering up to
              10,000 pairs, but in recent years their
              numbers have declined drastically due
              to land development, lumbering, and
              draining of their feeding grounds.

10 **"Great White Heron"**
    (*Ardea herodias occidentalis*)
    Herons, Bitterns (Ardeidae)

Description: 50" (127 cm). W. 70" (1.8 m). Largest
              of the American herons. White with
              yellow bill and legs; Great Egret has
              black legs.

     Voice: Hoarse croaks.

   Habitat: Shallow bays and mangrove islands in
              the Florida Keys.

Nesting: 3 pale blue-green eggs in a bulky stick nest placed in a bush or low tree, usually in mangroves.

Range: Islands in the Caribbean Sea and the Gulf of Mexico from Florida Bay to Cuba, Yucatán, and northern Venezuela.

Until recently, the "Great White Heron" was considered a distinct species. But both dark and white young have been found in a single nest, and it is now treated as a white phase of the Great Blue Heron that occurs only in Florida and the Caribbean region. A drive through the Florida Keys on the highway to Key West usually affords a view of several of these stately white birds.

12 American Flamingo
(*Phoenicopterus ruber*)
Flamingos (Phoenicopteridae)

Description: 48" (122 cm). W. 55" (1.5 m). Unmistakable. A tall, *long-legged, long-necked pink* bird with a downcurved bill. Wings have black tips and trailing edges.

Voice: Goose-like honking and cackling notes.

Habitat: Shallow coastal lagoons and mudflats.

Nesting: 1 white egg, on a low mound of mud on a mud flat. In colonies.

Range: The Bahamas, West Indies, Yucatán, northern South America and the Galapagos Islands. A casual on the U.S. coast from the Carolinas to Texas.

This species was formerly more numerous, and probably bred at one time along the coast of Florida. Flamingos are extremely sensitive to persecution, and today nest only in a few very isolated localities. The birds use their curiously shaped bills to strain small animals from the mud. Flamingo-like birds, known today only as fossils, lived in western North America 50 million years ago.

23 Limpkin
(*Aramus guarauna*)
Limpkins (Aramidae)

Description: 25–28" (64–71 cm). Goose-sized. Grayish-brown with white spots and streaks. Long, slender, downcurved bill Flight is jerky, like that of the cranes, with a rapid upstroke and a slower downstroke.

Voice: Loud, wailing *krrr-ow.*

Habitat: Wooded swamps and marshes.

Nesting: 5–8 buff eggs, with dark brown spots and blotches, laid in a shallow nest of marsh vegetation just above the water; more rarely in a stick nest in low trees or bushes.

Range: Local in southern Georgia and Florida ranging from the Okefenokee Swamp to the Everglades. South to southern South America.

This bird, related to the cranes and rails, is chiefly nocturnal. It feeds on the freshwater snail *Pomacea,* but also takes frogs, tadpoles, and aquatic insects. Its loud, strident, eerie call, a familiar night sound in the Florida marshes, sounds like a human in distress, so the Limpkin is known locally as the "crying bird."

90 White-tailed Tropicbird
(*Phaethon lepturus*)
Tropicbirds (Phaethontidae)

Description: 32" (81 cm). W. 37" (1 m). A white, pigeon-sized seabird with very long central tail feathers, bold black wing markings, and a yellowish bill. Young birds lack the long tail feathers and are finely barred with black above.

Voice: A harsh *ticket-ticket,* repeated frequently on the wing.

Habitat: Tropical oceans.

Nesting: 1 pinkish egg, spotted with brown, laid on a bare rock or in a crevice among rocks on an island.

Range: Bermuda and the Bahamas, and on islands in the tropical Atlantic, Indian, and Pacific oceans. A casual on the coast of Florida and the Carolinas.

These graceful seabirds take their food—small fish and squids—in shallow dives from the air. Their flight is pigeon-like. The birds are able to travel far out to sea, and after the breeding season many gather in the Sargasso Sea, hundreds of miles from the nearest land.

---

319 Short-tailed Hawk
(*Buteo brachyurus*)
Hawks, Eagles (Accipitridae)

Description: 13–14" (33–35 cm). W. 35" (1 m). Crow-sized. A small, chunky hawk with two phases: the light phase is dark above and white below; the dark phase is black above and below except for light bases to primaries. Both phases have *banded black-and-white tail.* Immature is tawny-buff below with dark streaks.

Voice: Cackles and warning screams, but is seldom heard except at nest.

Habitat: Chiefly cypress and mangrove swamps.

Nesting: 2 white eggs, spotted or blotched with brown, in a stick nest lined with leaves, sometimes decorated with Spanish moss, in a tree.

Range: Local in southern Florida. Throughout tropical America.

This rare bird is easily identified in either color phase, being the only hawk in the area that is pure black or pure white below. It often perches low on

poles or trees near swampy areas, and
darts out after birds. It also feeds on
rodents, lizards, and insects.

320 Everglade Kite
(Rostrhamus sociabilis)
Hawks, Eagles (Accipitridae)

Description: 16–18" (40–46 cm). W. 44" (1 m).
Crow-sized. Male dark slate color; its
white tail has a dark broad band; female
is brown, heavily streaked below with
banded tail like male's. Red (male) or
orange (female and young) legs.

Voice: Low cackle, chatter, or neigh, but
seldom heard.

Habitat: Freshwater marshes and lakes.

Nesting: 2–5 white eggs, heavily spotted and
blotched with brown, in a stick nest
placed in low bushes or on the
ground.

Range: Mainly Lake Okeechobee and
Loxahatchee in southern Florida.
Widespread in Central and South
America.

Also called the "Snail Kite," it feeds
exclusively on snails of the genus
Pomacea, found in shallow ponds and
swampy places. The kite's slender,
sharply hooked bill easily extracts the
living animal from the unbroken shell.
The Florida population has become
seriously reduced due to draining of its
habitat but there is evidence that it is
increasing.

328 White-crowned Pigeon
(Columba leucocephala)
Pigeons, Doves (Columbidae)

Description: 13" (33 cm). *Dark gray* with a
conspicuous *white crown.* Melanistic
Rock Doves have shorter tails and white
rather than blackish wing linings.

Voice: *Coo-coo-co-WOOO*, with an owl-like quality.

Habitat: Mangroves and occasionally in tropical hardwoods.

Nesting: 1 or 2 white eggs in a grass-lined stick nest in a tree or bush; often in colonies.

Range: Florida Keys and the West Indies; does not winter in Florida but migrates as far as the southern Caribbean Sea.

In the United States it breeds only in the mangrove swamps of the Florida Keys and, to a lesser extent, among the gumbo-limbo and mahogany trees of the adjacent mainland. In former years great numbers were shot for food, and they became very wary. With the passage of protective laws in 1913, they increased in numbers and nowadays are fairly tame. They are great fruit-eaters but also take insects and seeds.

395 Spotted-breasted Oriole
(*Icterus pectoralis*)
Orioles, Blackbirds (Icteridae)

Description: 8″ (20 cm). Bright orange with black throat, wings, and tail; white patches on wings; *black spots on sides of breast*.

Voice: Like that of other orioles—loud, varied, and continuous.

Habitat: Open country with scattered trees, orchards, gardens, and parks.

Nesting: 4 whitish eggs with black scrawls in a woven basket nest of palm fibers or other vegetable matter.

Range: Southern Mexico to northern Costa Rica. Introduced around Miami, Florida.

This handsome oriole, a native of Mexico, was first reported in the Miami area in 1949, where it was introduced, probably from escaped captives. It has since been found in Florida from Homestead to Fort Lauderdale and appears to be thriving.

426 **Gray Kingbird**
(*Tyrannus dominicensis*)
Tyrant Flycatchers (Tyrannidae)

Description: 9″ (23 cm). A stocky, large-headed,
pale gray flycatcher of coastal habitats.
Underparts whitish; dusky blackish
patch through eye; bill heavy; tail
notched, without white.

Voice: Buzzy *pe-CHEER-y* and a harsh note.

Habitat: Coastal, in mangrove thickets, on
telephone wires, and in small groves of
palms and oaks.

Nesting: 3 pinkish eggs blotched with brown in
a grass-lined stick nest placed in a
mangrove thicket, usually over or near
salt water.

Range: Coastal regions of South Carolina,
Georgia, Florida, the West Indies, and
smaller islands in the Caribbean.
Winters from the Greater Antilles to
Colombia, Venezuela, and the Guianas.

Like other kingbirds it is fearless, even
chasing hawks and crows. Noisy as well
as belligerent, it frequently emits harsh
notes as it sits on telephone wires or
exposed branches ready to dart after
flying insects.

436 **Scrub Jay**
(*Aphelocoma coerulescens*)
Jays, Magpies, Crows (Corvidae)

Description: 11–13″ (28–33 cm). Blue Jay-sized.
Wings and tail dull blue, back gray,
with dusky mask, and white throat set
off by a "necklace" of dull blue marks
on the breast. No crest.

Voice: Similar to the Blue Jay's—loud, harsh
and rasping; also has a sweet song of
trills and low warbles.

Habitat: In Florida confined to scrub oak.

Nesting: 3–6 buff or dull green eggs, spotted
with dark brown, in a bulky mass of
twigs concealed in a dense bush or low
tree.

Range: Breeds from Washington, Wyoming, and Colorado south to Texas and southern Mexico, with an isolated population in central Florida.

The isolated population in Florida is puzzling. Presumably a belt of scrub once extended from the western states across the South and into Florida. Today these birds are separated from their western relatives by more than 1000 miles. They feed on insects, seeds, and nuts, obtained chiefly on the ground. Rather shy for jays, they are often difficult to find even where they are common, except when perching on telephone wires. They soon become tame, however, and learn to come to feeders. Like others of their family, they often eat the eggs and young of other birds. They also share a tendency to carry off and hide brightly colored objects.

442 Blue-gray Tanager
(*Thraupis episcopus*)
Tanagers (Thraupidae)

Description: 7" (17 cm). Larger than a House Sparrow. Pale blue, darker on wings and tail; bend of wing whitish.
Voice: Song weak and squeaky, consisting of short irregular phrases.
Habitat: Residential areas and parks with shade trees.
Nesting: 1 or 2 grayish eggs spotted with brown, in an open cup of dead leaves and grass, placed high in a broadleaved tree.
Range: Native to tropical forests of Central and South America. Introduced in Miami, Florida.

Like many tropical tanagers, these brightly colored birds travel in small flocks in search of insects and fruit. Such flocks include mated pairs regardless of

the time of year, for Blue-gray Tanager
remain mated for life.

452　Black-whiskered Vireo
(*Vireo altiloquus*)
Vireos (Vireonidae)

Description: 5½" (14 cm). Similar to the Red-eyed
Vireo (olive-green above, white below)
but with a *dusky streak below the eye,*
giving the bird its name.

Voice: Similar to the Red-eyed Vireo but mor
abrupt, and in one- to four-note
phrases, sometimes described as *whip-
Tom-KELLY*.

Habitat: Mangroves, thick scrub, and shade
trees.

Nesting: 2 or 3 white eggs with a few small,
scattered spots in a nest of grass, leaves,
and rootlets in the fork of a branch,
usually in mangroves.

Range: Breeds in southern Florida and the
West Indies. Winters in northern
South America, less commonly in the
Lesser Antilles.

They are not shy and come regularly
into gardens and shade trees in Key
West. They may also be seen in the
dense scrub and tropical hammocks in
the Upper Keys and occasionally in
coconut palms and mangroves around
Miami. They eat insects and, rarely,
berries and other soft fruits.

508　Red-whiskered Bulbul
(*Pycnonotus jocosus*)
Bulbuls (Pycnonotidae)

Description: 8" (20 cm). Grayish above, whitish
below, with a long, conspicuous *black
crest, red cheek patch* and undertail
coverts, and a black, white-tipped tail.

Voice: Chattering notes; a whistled *queekey!*

Habitat: Residential areas, parks, and gardens.

Nesting: 2–4 pinkish-white eggs, spotted with reddish brown, in a cup of dead leaves and grass, lined with fine roots and hair, in a bush or small tree.

Range: Native to Southeast Asia; introduced and established in Miami, Florida.

This species has long been adapted to living in the vicinity of towns and villages in Southeast Asia, and is now successful in suburban Miami. Bulbuls are noisy, gregarious birds, usually traveling in flocks in pursuit of insects and fruit.

---

523 Mangrove Cuckoo
(*Coccyzus minor*)
Cuckoos (Cuculidae)

Description: 12″ (30 cm). Blue Jay-sized. Brown above, *rich buff or tawny below;* black facial mask; curved bill. Long, graduated tail with black-and-white spots at tip.

Voice: Low, guttural *gaw-gaw-gaw-gaw-gaw,* almost like a soft bark or the scolding of a squirrel.

Habitat: Only in Florida mangrove swamps.

Nesting: 2 or 3 pale greenish-blue eggs in a stick nest in a low shrub.

Range: Southern Florida through the West Indies and from Mexico to northern South America.

In North America, this species is found only in the Florida Keys and on the adjacent Gulf Coast as far as Tampa Bay. It is difficult to observe, remaining hidden in dense thickets much of the time. Strictly insectivorous, it feeds on hairy caterpillars, grasshoppers, moths, larvae, and spiders.

Grasslands

Included here are natural grasslands such as plains, prairies, and barrens, and man-made grasslands such as pastures, meadows, croplands, airfields, and golf courses.

4, 8   Cattle Egret
(*Bubulcus ibis*)
Herons, Bitterns (Ardeidae)

Description: 20" (51 cm). White with orange-buff
head and back plumes during the
breeding season. Legs yellow or orange
in adults, blackish in immatures.
Stocky yellow or orange bill.

Voice: A hoarse croaking.

Habitat: Dry land in open fields where it feeds
alongside livestock, but breeds near
water with other herons.

Nesting: 3–5 pale blue eggs in a stick nest
placed in a bush or tree in a marsh.
Usually in colonies.

Range: Chiefly southern and eastern states.
Also tropics of Mexico, Central and
South America, West Indies, and the
Old World.

Originating in the Old World, the
Cattle Egret crossed the Atlantic,
probably flying from Africa to South
America, where this species was first
reported early in the present century.
The birds gradually spread northward
through the West Indies and into
Florida, then up the east coast as far
as southern Canada by the early 1960s.
As sometimes happens when a new
species invades a new territory, there
has been a population explosion, and
they are now abundant throughout the
southern part of the country and are
breeding as far north as New England.
They follow livestock, feeding on insects
flushed up from the grass.

218   Upland Sandpiper
"Upland Plover"
(*Bartramia longicauda*)
Sandpipers (Scolopacidae)

Description: 12" (30 cm). Pigeon-sized. *Long neck
and tail,* short bill, small head; overall

warm brown with a dark rump and
primaries.

Voice: Well known for its beautiful song,
whistled trills and mournful wind-like
sounds.

Habitat: Open grassland, prairies, and hayfields
in breeding season; also, while on
migration, open country generally.

Nesting: 4 pinkish-buff eggs with brown spots,
placed in a grass-lined nest in a hollow
on the ground.

Range: Alaska and central Canada to central
United States. Winters in southern
South America.

This attractive bird of open grasslands
was formerly shot in great numbers for
food and sport, until it became very
scarce. Now given complete protection,
it has increased once again. It often flies
with wings held stiffly in a downcurve,
like a Spotted Sandpiper, especially on
its nesting grounds. When alighting,
the "Grass Plover," as it was known to
hunters, holds its wings over its back
before folding them down in a resting
position. Until recently this bird has
been called the "Upland Plover."

224 Buff-breasted Sandpiper
(*Tryngites subruficollis*)
Sandpipers (Scolopacidae)

Description: 8" (20 cm). Robin-sized. *Rich buff
underparts and yellow legs;* short, straight
bill.

Voice: Low trilled *preet;* also *tic.*

Habitat: Short-grass fields, meadows, and
prairies. Breeds in dry tundra.

Nesting: 4 pale buff, brown-blotched eggs in a
grass-lined nest on the Arctic tundra.

Range: Arctic Alaska and northwestern
Canada. Scarce fall migrant on the east
coast. Winters on Argentine pampas.

This species looks like a small buff
edition of the Upland Sandpiper, at

times its grassland associate. It is very tame and when approached merely runs through the short grass instead of flying off. Like the American Golden Plover, it undertakes an amazing migration in both spring and fall. After the nesting season in the far Northwest, it migrates southward on a broad front, ending up on the Argentine pampas to spend the winter. On the return passage in spring its movements are much more confined, carrying it chiefly up the Mississippi Valley and to the West, but ultimately back to the arctic shores of Alaska and Canada.

235, 238 Killdeer
(*Charadrius vociferus*)
Plovers (Charadriidae)

Description: 9–11″ (23–28 cm). Robin-sized. Brown above and white below, with *two black bands* on the breast and a blackish bill. In flight, tail appears bright rufous. Often bobs its head.

Voice: Clear *kill-DEEE,* repeated endlessly.

Habitat: Open country generally—plowed fields, golf courses, and short-grass prairies.

Nesting: 4 pale buff, spotted eggs in a slight depression or scrape sparsely lined with grass on bare ground.

Range: Breeds from British Columbia, Mackenzie, and Newfoundland south to the West Indies, Mexico, and Peru. Winters regularly from New Jersey and Ohio southward.

This is probably our most familiar shorebird. Not only is it abundant and conspicuous, but its loud call compels attention. When the nest is approached, the adult feigns injury, hobbling along with wings dragging as if badly wounded. This behavior often succeeds in luring a predator away from the eggs or young; the bird then "recovers" and flies off calling loudly.

through the Great Plains to Oklahoma; also on the coastal prairies of Texas.

Once found from the Atlantic Coast west to Wyoming, the Greater Prairie Chicken has been exterminated from much of this vast range through the destruction of the undisturbed prairies on which it breeds. The eastern subspecies, known as the Heath Hen (*Tympanuchus cupido cupido*) became extinct; the form inhabiting the prairies along the Gulf Coast, Attwater's Prairie Chicken (*T. c. attwateri*), may follow its eastern relative into extinction in a few years. Where they still survive, Greater Prairie Chickens perform striking courtship dances on communal display grounds: the males strut about and stamp their feet with "horns" erected and yellow sacs of skin inflated on the sides of the neck, meanwhile uttering a deep cooing call that may carry a mile. They leap and whirl in the air and threaten each other by short runs with tail raised, head down, and feather tufts erected.

---

262 Lesser Prairie Chicken
(*Tympanuchus pallidicinctus*)
Grouse (Tetraonidae)

Description: 16″ (40 cm). A smaller and paler edition of the Greater Prairie Chicken. In the male, the air sacs on the neck are reddish, rather than yellowish.

Voice: Various cackling and clucking notes; the male "booms" during courtship.

Habitat: Sandy prairies and plains, especially where there is a growth of shrubby oak.

Nesting: 11 to 13 creamy or buff-colored eggs in a grass-lined depression, usually under a low bush or shrub.

Range: Resident in southern Colorado and Kansas, south locally in western Oklahoma, Texas, and eastern New Mexico.

As in the Greater Prairie Chicken, males of this species gather and engage in communal courtship displays in which the birds dance about with the colorful air sacs on their necks inflated and uttering low cooing or "booming" notes. This species replaces the Greater Prairie Chicken in more arid grasslands; some authorities consider the two to be members of a single species.

267 Gray Partridge
(Perdix perdix)
Quail, Partridges, Pheasants
(Phasianidae)

Description: 12–14″ (30–35 cm). A small, stocky, chicken-like bird, largely gray with a black "U"-shaped mark on the underparts and a *rust-colored tail*.

Voice: Hoarse *kee-ah*. When flushed, a rapid cackle.

Habitat: Grainfields, agricultural grasslands.

Nesting: 10–20 olive eggs in a shallow depression lined with grass and concealed in vegetation.

Range: Introduced and locally established in Nova Scotia, New Brunswick, northern New York, Ontario, Ohio, Indiana, southern Michigan, Iowa, Minnesota, and across the northern part of the United States to British Columbia. Introduction in the East has been generally unsuccessful. Native to Eurasia.

Also called "Hungarian Partridge," this species is well adapted to areas of intensive agriculture, where no native gamebird can exist. It forms coveys outside the breeding season, like the Bobwhite, but does not defend a territory. In the spring the flocks break up into pairs. While the male takes no part in incubating the eggs, he does help care for the young, which leave the nest soon after hatching. The Gray

Partridge's high reproductive rate
enables it to withstand hunting,
predators, and cold snowy northern
winters, all of which take a heavy toll.

271 **Roadrunner**
(*Geococcyx californianus*)
Cuckoos (Cuculidae)

Description: 24" (61 cm). Crow-sized. A long-
legged, gray-brown *long-tailed* ground
bird with a *bushy crest.* Bright yellow
eyes at close range.
Voice: Clucks, crows, dove-like coos, dog-like
whines, and hoarse guttural notes.
Habitat: Open arid country with plenty of
thickets to serve as cover.
Nesting: 3–5 ivory-colored eggs in a flat stick
nest lined with grass, usually in thick
shrub or cactus not far aboveground.
Range: Breeds in Central California, Nevada,
Utah, Colorado, Kansas, Oklahoma,
Arkansas, and Louisiana south to
Central Mexico.

The comical-looking Roadrunner, or
"Chaparral Cock" as it is called by
cowboys, would rather run than fly.
With its twisting and turning in and
out of cactus thickets, it can easily
outdistance a man. The bird jerks its
tail from side to side or up and down;
it also elevates its bushy crest when
excited. It eats a variety of animal foods,
including small snakes, lizards, mice,
scorpions, and insects.

274 **Ring-necked Pheasant**
(*Phasianus colchicus*)
Quail, Partridges, Pheasants
(Phasianidae)

Description: 30–36" (76–91 cm). Larger than a
chicken, with a long, pointed tail.
Male has a red eye-patch, brilliant

green head, and white neck-ring; body
patterned in soft brown and iridescent
russet. Female is a mottled sandy
brown with shorter tail.

Voice: Loud crowing *cuck-cuck* accompanied by
a resonant beating of the wings. When
alarmed they fly off with a loud cackle.

Habitat: Farmlands, pastures, and grassy
woodland edges.

Nesting: 6–15 buff-olive eggs in a grass-lined
depression concealed in dense grass or
weeds

Range: Introduced from British Columbia,
Alberta, Minnesota, Ontario and the
Maritime Provinces south to New Jersey
Maryland, Oklahoma, and Central
California. Native to Asia.

The North American birds of this
species are descended from stock
brought from several different parts of
the Old World and thus are somewhat
variable. They are very tolerant of man,
often nesting on the outskirts of large
cities. Although successful in most
grassland habitats, its North American
headquarters is the central plains. After
the breakup of winter flocks, males
establish large territories and mate with
several females. At first the chicks feed
largely on insects, but soon shift to the
adult diet of berries, seeds, buds, and
leaves.

275 **Common Nighthawk**
(*Chordeiles minor*)
Nightjars (Caprimulgidae)

Description: 10″ (25 cm). W. 23″ (0.6 m). Blue
Jay-sized, usually seen in flight. Dark
with long, pointed wings and *white
patches on the outer wing.* Perches
motionless and lengthwise on branches.

Voice: Loud, nasal, buzzy *peent* or *pee-yah*.

Habitat: Aerial, but open country generally; also
cities and towns.

Nesting: 2 eggs, whitish to olive, with dark
blotches, laid on soil, rocks, logs, or
rooftop gravel.

Range: Canada to Panama and the West Indies;
winters in South America.

Its name is somewhat inappropriate,
since it is not strictly nocturnal, often
flying in sunlight, and it is not a hawk,
although it does "hawk," or catch
flying insects on the wing. On its
breeding grounds the male does a power
dive, and then, as it swerves upward,
makes a booming sound with its wings.
Its capacity to consume insects is
prodigious. Analysis of stomach
contents has shown that in a single day
one bird captured over 500 mosquitoes
and another ate 2175 flying ants.

283 Burrowing Owl
(*Athene cunicularia*)
True Owls (Strigidae)

Description: 9″ (23 cm). Pigeon-sized. Short-tailed
and long-legged; yellow eyes; no ear
tufts; *face framed in white with a blackish
collar.*

Voice: Liquid cackling; also a mellow *coo-coooo,*
repeated twice.

Habitat: Plains, deserts, fields, and airports.

Nesting: 5–7 white eggs in a long underground
burrow nest lined with grasses, roots,
and dung.

Range: Southwestern Canada, Florida, and the
West Indies to Tierra del Fuego.

This comical little bird is one of the
most diurnal of all owls. It often
perches near its hole, and when
approached too closely will bob up and
down and finally dive into its burrow
rather than take flight. The burrows
have usually been abandoned by prairie
dogs or pocket gophers, but the owls
are quite capable of digging their own.

291 Barn Owl
(*Tyto alba*)
Barn Owls (Tytonidae)

Description: 18″ (46 cm). W. 44″ (1.1 m). Crow-
sized. Buff-brown above and white
below, with *heart-shaped face* and
numerous small dark dots on white
underparts; *dark eyes,* long legs.

Voice: Its weird calls include rapid grackle-
like clicks, hissing notes, screams,
guttural grunts, and bill snapping.

Habitat: Open country, forest edge and
clearings, cultivated areas, and cities.

Nesting: 5–10 white eggs on bare wood or stone
in buildings, hollow trees, caves, or
even ground burrows.

Range: Nearly worldwide; in America from
southernmost Canada to Tierra del
Fuego.

This nocturnal ghost of a bird frequents
such places as belfries, deserted
buildings, and hollow trees. It hunts its
food—almost entirely rodents—in
garbage dumps, neglected cemeteries,
rundown farms, and similar waste lots
of large cities. Contrary to popular
belief, owls see well by day but their
large eyes give them especially good
night vision. Recent experiments have
shown, however, that Barn Owls
depend on keen hearing to locate prey.
These owls appear to practice birth
control: when food is scarce they lay
fewer eggs or do not breed at all.

292 Snowy Owl
(*Nyctea scandiaca*)
True Owls (Strigidae)

Description: 24″ (61 cm). W. 55″ (1.4 m). A big
and round-headed owl, from *pure white*
to white with dark spotting. Female is
larger and darker than the male.

Voice: Usually silent; a hoarse croak and a

shrill whistle are heard on the breeding grounds.

Habitat: Open country: tundra, dunes, marshes, fields, and plains.

Nesting: 5–8 white eggs on open tundra with a lining of feathers, mosses, and lichens.

Range: Circumpolar. Breeds in America, in Aleutians, arctic Alaska, and Canada; winters irregularly south to California, Texas, Missouri, and the Carolinas.

This great white owl is a beautiful sight as it perches upright on a fence post or flies over a marsh. Strictly a bird of open country, it is practically never seen in a tree; it sits on the ground, a rooftop, or other exposed resting place. In the Far North where it breeds, it depends largely on the lemming supply for food. Lemmings undergo periodic population changes (due to population explosion and subsequent epidemics), and when their numbers decrease the owls must migrate southward to avoid starvation. In our latitudes the owls prey on rabbits and other game, or even on dead fish on ocean beaches. In large refuse dumps they prey on Norway rats.

295 Rough-legged Hawk
(*Buteo lagopus*)
Hawks, Eagles (Accipitridae)

Description: 19–24″ (48–61 cm). W. 52″ (1.3 m). A large, long-winged hawk that often hovers. Tail white at the base and dark at the tip; head and neck gray-brown, belly blackish. All-dark and intermediate forms also occur, and can usually be identified by the tail pattern.

Voice: Loud or soft whistles, often in a descending scale.

Habitat: Tundra; winters on open plains, agricultural areas, and marshes.

Nesting: Usually 3 or 4 pale green eggs spotted with black in a mass of moss and sticks placed on a cliff or rocky outcropping in the tundra.

Range: Aleutians, northern Alaska and Baffin Island south to Manitoba and Newfoundland. Winters irregularly south to California and Virginia. Also breeds in Eurasia.

The number of eggs laid by the Rough-leg, like the Snowy Owl, depends on the food supply, with larger clutches occurring in years when lemmings are abundant. At a distance this hawk can be identified by its habit of hovering and by the way it perches: balancing precariously on the most slender twigs at the top of a tree.

299 Swainson's Hawk
(*Buteo swainsoni*)
Hawks, Eagles (Accipitridae)

Description: 18–22" (45–56 cm). W. 49" (1.2 m) A large hawk with longer, more pointed wings than the Red-tail. Uniform brown above, white below with brown breast; tail dark brown and indistinctly banded. Young birds similar to immature Red-tails but tend to have darker markings on the breast whereas young Red-tails are more heavily marked on flanks and belly. A rare all-dark form also occurs.

Voice: Long, plaintive, whistled *kreee*.

Habitat: Open plains, grasslands, and prairies.

Nesting: 2–4 white eggs, unmarked or lightly spotted with brown or black, in a nest comprising a large mass of sticks often placed conspicuously in an isolated tree.

Range: Alaska and Mackenzie south to northern Mexico and Texas. Winters chiefly in South America and often migrates eastward to Florida, where small numbers winter.

This species is a highly gregarious *Buteo,* often migrating in great soaring flocks containing thousands of birds. Its migrations are longer than those of the other species; most individuals go all the way to Argentina to spend the winter, making a round trip of as much as 17,000 miles. On their breeding grounds in the western plains, this hawk preys mainly on rodents and huge numbers of grasshoppers. It is named after the English naturalist William Swainson (1789–1855).

301 White-tailed Hawk
(*Buteo albicaudatus*)
Hawks, Eagles (Accipitridae)

Description: 21–23" (53–58 cm). W. 48" (1.2 m). Adult gray above, white below, with a narrow but conspicuous black band on its white tail and a rufous shoulder patch. Immature birds dark with a gray tail.

Voice: Musical *ke-ke-ke-ke-ke* or *cutta-cutta-cutta-cutta*.

Habitat: Coastal prairie, grassland, and scrub in semiarid country.

Nesting: 2 dull white or very pale blue eggs, unmarked or lightly spotted with brown, in a grass-lined stick nest in low bushes, cacti, and small trees.

Range: Extreme southern Texas to southern South America.

This handsome and conspicuous hawk is a common sight in south Texas where it is found perched along highways on telephone poles, fence posts, or dead trees. Its principal food is rabbits, but it is an opportunist, gathering in flocks with other hawks at brush fires to feed on rodents, rabbits, lizards, and insects driven out by the flames. Like other *Buteo* hawks, it rides the air currents on motionless wings, often soaring to great heights.

303 **White-tailed Kite**
(*Elanus leucurus*)
Hawks, Eagles (Accipitridae)

Description: 15–16″ (38–40 cm). W. 40″ (1 m). A
delicate, graceful, gull-like bird of
prey. *Largely white,* with a gray back,
black patch on upper and under surface
of the *pointed wings; tail white.* The back
and breast of young birds are streaked
with warm brown. Often dangles its
feet in flight.

Voice: Whistled *keep-keep-keep.* Also a longer,
plaintive *kreep.*

Habitat: Farmlands and prairies with scattered
trees or fencerows; mesquite grasslands.

Nesting: 3–5 white, brown-spotted eggs in a
well-made platform of twigs lined with
grass and placed in a tall tree, usually
near water.

Range: Southern California and southern Texas
to Chile and Argentina. Formerly
occurred also from South Carolina to
Florida. Nonmigratory.

The tame, elegant White-tailed Kite
was formerly shot in large numbers by
farmers who thought it threatened their
chickens, although the birds feed
almost entirely on insects and a few
rodents. The North American
population was reduced to a pitiful
remnant, and it was feared that the
species might become extinct here.
Recently, however, it has staged a
surprising and unexplained comeback,
and is again rather numerous in Texas
and California. An allied species in
southern Europe and Africa has also
increased in numbers, perhaps as a
result of some subtle environmental
change.

312 Caracara
(*Caracara cheriway*)
Falcons (Falconidae)

Description: 20–22″ (51–56 cm). W. 48″ (1.2 m).
Dark brown, with black cap and bare
red face; white throat, neck, base of
tail, and wing tips; black band at tip of
tail.

Voice: High, harsh cackle.

Habitat: Prairies, savannahs, and semi-arid areas
with open groves of palms, mesquites,
and cacti.

Nesting: 2 or 3 white eggs with heavy brown
spots and blotches in a nest made of
twigs, grasses, weeds, and briars lined
with leaves and mosses; set in palmetto
hammocks or live oaks, rarely on the
ground.

Range: Central and southern Florida, where it
is becoming scarce; local in the
southern portions of Texas and Arizona.
South to southern South America.

This scavenger has probably the most
varied diet of any bird of prey. It often
accompanies and dominates vultures at
fresh kills or carrion and also eats small
animals. It is primarily a ground-
inhabiting falcon of open prairies; its
long legs enable it to walk and run
with ease. It is the national emblem of
Mexico.

314 American Kestrel
"Sparrow Hawk"
(*Falco sparverius*)
Falcons (Falconidae)

Description: 9–12″ (23–30 cm). W. 21″ (0.5 m).
Jay-sized. Wings long and pointed, tail
long. May be recognized in any
plumage by its *rusty tail and back*. The
adult male has pale blue-gray wings,
rusty in the female. Often seen
hovering.

Voice: Shrill *killy-killy-killy*.

Habitat: Towns and cities, parks, farmlands, an open country.

Nesting: 4 or 5 brown-spotted white eggs place without nest or lining in a natural or man-made cavity.

Range: Alaska, the Northwest Territories, and Newfoundland south to Tierra del Fuego. Winters from British Columbia Illinois, and New England southward.

Unlike the larger falcons it has adapted to man and nests even in our largest cities, where it preys chiefly on House Sparrows. In the countryside it takes insects, small birds, and rodents, capturing its prey on the ground rather than in the air like other falcons. The female does most of the incubating and is fed by the male. As he nears the nest with food he calls; the female flies to him and receives the food away from the nest. After the eggs hatch, the male brings most of the food. The young stay with the adults for a time after fledging, and it is not uncommon to see family parties in late summer. This species was formerly called "Sparrow Hawk."

325 Ground Dove
(*Columbina passerina*)
Pigeons, Doves (Columbidae)

Description: 6½" (16 cm). Sparrow-sized. A short-tailed, brown dove with much *rufous in the wings and a heavily scaled breast.*

Voice: Soft cooing with rising inflection.

Habitat: Open areas such as fields, gardens, farmland, and roadsides.

Nesting: 2 white eggs on or close to the ground. The nest is often hidden in a tuft of grass or among weeds.

Range: Southern United States to northern South America. Not migratory.

This bird, as its name implies, spends much of its time on the ground, and is most commonly seen when flushed from a roadside or path in a brushy pasture. It is a rather retiring bird, and is somewhat locally distributed.

329 Barn Swallow
(*Hirundo rustica*)
Swallows (Hirundinidae)

Description: 5¾–7¾" (15–20 cm). Sparrow-sized. Our most familiar swallow, and the only one with a *deeply forked tail*. Upperparts dark steel-blue, underparts creamy buff, throat and forehead rusty.

Voice: Constant liquid twittering and chattering.

Habitat: Agricultural land, suburban areas, marshes, lake shores.

Nesting: 4–6 brown-spotted white eggs in a solid cup of mud reinforced with grass, lined with feathers and soft plant material, and placed on a rafter in a building or on a sheltered ledge.

Range: Aleutians west to Unalaska Island, Alaska and the Maritime Provinces to the Carolinas, Arkansas, and Mexico; winters in South America. Also in Eurasia.

The great majority of these birds now nest on or in buildings, but originally they used rocky ledges over streams and perhaps attached their nests to tree trunks in the shelter of branches (as do related species in Africa). Barn Swallows perform long migrations; some that breed in North America winter as far south as Argentina. Like other swallows, they migrate by day, often feeding as they travel. They are swift and graceful fliers, and it is estimated that they cover as much as 600 miles a day in quest of food for their young.

330 Cliff Swallow
(*Petrochelidon pyrrhonota*)
Swallows (Hirundinidae)

Description: 5–6″ (13–15 cm). Sparrow-sized. A stocky, square-tailed swallow with *pale buff rump.* Upperparts dull steel-blue, underparts buff-white; throat dark chestnut, forehead white. Cave Swallow of Texas and New Mexico is similar but smaller, with darker rump and buff throat.

Voice: Constant squeaky chattering and twittering.

Habitat: Open country near buildings or cliffs; lake shores and marshes in migration.

Nesting: 4–6 white eggs in a gourd-shaped structure of mud lined with feathers and placed on a sheltered cliff face or under eaves (in New England they are called Eave Swallows). In colonies.

Range: Alaska, Ontario, and Nova Scotia south to Virginia, Missouri, and Central America. Winters in South America.

As its name implies, this swallow originally nested on cliffs. The introduction of House Sparrows was a disaster for these birds, since the sparrows usurp their nests and often cause the swallows to abandon a colony. Long, cold, rainy spells while the young are in the nest cause widespread mortality since the adults are unable to obtain enough insects.

351 Red-headed Woodpecker
(*Melanerpes erythrocephalus*)
Woodpeckers (Picidae)

Description: 10″ (25 cm). Jay-sized. Strikingly colored: *entire head red,* wings and tail bluish-black, white below, *large white wing patch on each wing* and a white rump, conspicuous in flight. Immature resembles the adult except for its gray head.

Voice: Various chirps, cackles, and squawks. Most often a loud *churr-churr* and *yarrow-yarrow-yarrow.*

Habitat: Open country, farms, rural roads, open park-like woodland, and golf courses.

Nesting: 5 white eggs placed without nest lining in a cavity in a tree, telephone pole, or fence post.

Range: Saskatchewan, Manitoba, and Quebec south to Florida, the Gulf Coast, and New Mexico. Scarce in northeastern states. Winters in southern South America.

These woodpeckers are fond of open agricultural country with groves of dead and dying trees, particularly orchards. They often fly-catch, swooping low across a highway or along the shoulder of a road after flying insects. Red-headed Woodpeckers are driven off by aggressive Starlings, which occupy the nest holes, and by the removal of dead trees. Like the California Woodpecker, they store nuts and acorns, hiding them in holes and crevices. One was observed putting acorns into a hole in a post that was open at the other end; it never discovered where its acorns went.

365 Palm Warbler
(*Dendroica palmarum*)
Wood Warblers (Parulidae)

Description: 5½" (14 cm). An olive-drab, streaked, ground-feeding warbler with bright olive rump, bright yellow undertail coverts, and a *distinctive habit of wagging its tail.* The underparts vary from yellow to dull whitish, depending on age and geography; adults in spring have a *rufous cap.*

Voice: Weak, dry trill like that of a Chipping Sparrow but slower.

Habitat: In summer, bogs in the North; during migration, open places, especially weedy fields and borders of marshes.

Nesting: 4 or 5 white, brown-speckled eggs in
a grass nest with shreds of bark lined
with feathers and rootlets, placed on the
ground in a grass clump, often at the
base of a small tree or bush.

Range: Central Canada to the extreme northern
portions of the United States. Winters
from southern United States to the
West Indies and Honduras.

The Palm Warbler is one of the first
warblers to arrive in the spring, and at
this season is commonly found feeding
quietly on the ground, sometimes with
flocks of sparrows. It is unusual among
warblers of the genus *Dendroica* in
nesting on the ground; the only other
species that does this is the rare
Kirtland's Warbler.

385, 386 American Goldfinch
(*Carduelis tristis*)
Grosbeaks, Buntings, Finches,
Sparrows (Fringillidae)

Description: 4½–5" (11–14 cm). Smaller than a
sparrow. Breeding male *bright yellow*
with a white rump, *black forehead, white
edges on black wings and tail,* and yellow
at bend of wing. Female and winter
male duller and grayer with black wings,
tail, and white wing bars. Travels in
flocks; undulating flight.

Voice: Bright *per-*chick-*o-ree,* also rendered as
potato-chips, delivered in flight and
coinciding with each undulation.

Habitat: Brushy thickets, weedy grasslands, and
nearby trees.

Nesting: 4 or 5 pale blue eggs in a well-made
cup of grass, bark strips, and plant
down placed in the upright fork of a
small sapling or a shrub.

Range: Southeastern British Columbia and
Newfoundland south to Georgia,
Arkansas, central Oklahoma, southern
Colorado, central Utah, and Baja
California; widespread in the Northeast.

Winters south to the Gulf Coast and southern Mexico.

This familiar and common species is often called the "Wild Canary." Since their main food is seeds, nesting does not begin until midsummer or late summer, when weed seeds are available. Thus goldfinches remain in flocks until well past the time when other species have formed pairs and are nesting. Because they nest so late, only a single brood is raised each season. In the winter they gather in large flocks, often with other finches such as redpolls and siskins.

391 Western Meadowlark
(*Sturnella neglecta*)
Orioles, Blackbirds (Icteridae)

Description: 8½–11″ (21–28 cm). Robin-sized. Streaked brown above, bright yellow below, with a bold black "V" on the breast. Very similar to Eastern Meadowlark, but *upperparts paler, and yellow of throat extending onto cheeks.* Best told by voice.

Voice: Rich, flute-like jumble of gurgling notes, usually descending the scale; very different from the Eastern Meadowlark's series of simple, plaintive whistles.

Habitat: Meadows, plains, and prairies.

Nesting: 3–7 white eggs with dark brown and purple spots in a domed cup of grass and weed stems concealed in grass or weeds.

Range: British Columbia, Manitoba, northern Michigan, and northwestern Ohio south to Louisiana, central Texas, and northern Mexico. Has spread eastward in recent years. Winters north to Nebraska and Utah.

The clearing of eastern North American forests has caused this species to extend

its range eastward beyond the Great
Lakes, where it has occasionally
interbred with the Eastern Meadowlark
They are so similar that it was not until
1844 that Audubon noticed the
difference and named the western bird
neglecta because it had been overlooked
for so long. The song of the Western
Meadowlark is often heard on
Hollywood sound tracks even when the
movie setting is far from the bird's
range.

---

392 Eastern Meadowlark
(*Sturnella magna*)
Orioles, Blackbirds (Icteridae)

Description: 9–11" (23–28 cm). Robin-sized. A
stocky brown-streaked bird with *white-
edged tail; throat and breast bright yellow,
breast crossed by a black "V."* Western
Meadowlark is very similar, but paler
above and the yellow of its throat
extends onto cheeks. Best distinguished
by voice.

Voice: Clear, mellow whistle, *see-you, see-yeeeer;*
a loud rattling alarm note.

Habitat: Meadows, pastures, and prairies; in
migration, in open country generally.

Nesting: 3-7 white eggs spotted with brown and
dull lavender in a partly domed
structure of grass concealed in a
depression in a meadow.

Range: Breeds from southeastern Ontario, Nova
Scotia, Minnesota, southwestern South
Dakota, New Mexico, and Arizona
through Central America to northern
South America. Winters as far north as
New England and Nebraska.

One of the best-known birds of
American farmlands, its cheerful song,
usually delivered from a conspicuous
perch, is familiar in most rural areas.
Meadowlarks are often polygamous;
more than one female may be found
nesting in the territory of a single male.

Because they often breed in hayfields, the nests may be destroyed by mowing; unless the season is well advanced, they will normally nest again. In migration and winter they band together in groups of up to a dozen birds and can be found in almost any open, grassy area.

418 Scissor-tailed Flycatcher
(*Muscivora forficata*)
Tyrant Flycatchers (Tyrannidae)

Description: 14" (35 cm), of which more than half is a very *long and deeply forked black-and-white tail;* adult has *bright salmon-pink sides and belly;* head, upper back, and breast pale grayish-white.

Voice: Harsh *kee-kee-kee-kee.* Also a chattering and twittering like that of the Kingbird.

Habitat: Open country along roadsides and on ranches with scattered trees and bushes; also fence wires and posts.

Nesting: 5 creamy, brown-spotted eggs in a bulky stick nest lined with soft fibrous material and placed in an isolated tree.

Range: South-central United States north to Missouri and Nebraska. Winters from Mexico to Panama and on the Florida Keys.

These conspicuous flycatchers attract the attention of the most casual passerby. They are especially numerous in southern Texas, and one may see many in a day's drive by watching fence posts and wires along the road. Scissor-tails are as noisy and aggressive as kingbirds and will chase birds much larger than themselves. In spring they put on a wonderful aerial courtship display. With their long scissor-like tail they can maneuver and "sky-dance" gracefully. Nearly all of their food is captured on the wing; included in their diet are many insects harmful to agriculture.

421 **Northern Shrike**
(*Lanius excubitor*)
Shrikes (Laniidae)

Description: 9–10½" (23–26 cm). Robin-sized. Pale
gray above, white below, with faint
barring on underparts and a bold black
mask *ending at bill.* Black tail with white
edges. Stout, hooked bill. Usually seen
perched in the top of a tree in the open.

Voice: Mixture of warbles and harsh tones
with a Robin-like quality.

Habitat: Open woodlands and brushy swamps in
summer; open grasslands with fence
posts and scattered trees in winter.

Nesting: 4–6 pale gray eggs spotted with dark
gray and brown. Nest a large mass of
twigs, lichens, moss, and feathers,
usually in a dense conifer.

Range: Alaska and the Labrador Peninsula to
Quebec, Saskatchewan, and northern
British Columbia. Winters south to
Virginia, Texas, and northern
California.

Unusual among songbirds, shrikes prey
on small birds and rodents, catching
them with the bill and sometimes
impaling them on thorns or barbed wire
for storage. Like other northern birds
that depend on rodent populations, the
Northern Shrike's movements are
cyclical, becoming more adundant in
the South when northern rodent
populations are low. At times they hunt
from an open perch, where they sit
motionless until prey appears; at other
times they hover in the air ready to
pounce on anything that moves.

422 **Loggerhead Shrike**
(*Lanius ludovicianus*)
Shrikes (Laniidae)

Description: 8–10" (20–25 cm). Robin-sized.
Slightly smaller than a Northern

Shrike, pale gray above, white below,
with black face mask *extending over the
bill;* dark crown.

Voice: Variety of harsh and musical notes and
trills. A thrasher-like series of double
phrases.

Habitat: Grasslands, orchards, and open areas,
with scattered trees; open grassy
woodlands; deserts in the West.

Nesting: 4–6 white eggs, spotted with gray and
brown, in a bulky mass of twigs and
grass lined with plant down and
feathers, set in a thorny shrub or tree.

Range: Breeds from southern British Columbia,
central Alberta, central Saskatchewan,
southern Manitoba, southern Ontario,
southern Quebec, and Maritime
Provinces to southern Florida, the Gulf
Coast, and Mexico. Winters north to
Virginia and northern California.

In the southern half of North America
this species is the counterpart of the
Northern Shrike of boreal regions of
Alaska and Canada. In behavior and
choice of habitat the two species are
essentially similar although the
Loggerhead preys on insects more than
its northern relative. Its flight is
undulating with alternate rapid
fluttering and gliding. Since it has no
talons, it impales its prey—usually a
small bird, mouse, or insect—on a thorn
or barbed wire fence to facilitate tearing
it apart then or at a later time; hence its
other name, "Butcher Bird."

423 **Eastern Kingbird**
(*Tyrannus tyrannus*)
Tyrant Flycatchers (Tyrannidae)

Description: 8½" (21 cm). Dark gray above, blackish
on head, white below; *black tail with
white tip;* usually-concealed red
crown patch.

Voice: Harsh and strident notes, often

ascending, like *killy-killy-killy,* and others that sound like squeaky chattering.

Habitat: Open country; farms, orchards, roadsides, and lake and river shores.

Nesting: 3 or 4 creamy white eggs in a stick nest lined with grass, rootlets, and hair placed in a tree or bush.

Range: Central Canada to southern United States. Winters from Peru to Bolivia.

These noisy, conspicuous birds are named for their aggressive behavior, often driving away birds much larger than themselves, such as crows and hawks, especially near their nests. In late summer and early fall they often flock, and large numbers pursue flying insects; they also feed on wild berries, which they deftly pluck while on the wing.

---

440   **Eastern Bluebird**
(*Sialia sialis*)
Thrushes (Turdidae)

Description: 7″ (17 cm). Sexes similar; the male *bright blue above with a reddish-brown breast and white belly;* the female is duller.

Voice: Its call, when flying overhead, is an unmistakable liquid and musical *turee* or *queedle.* Song is a soft melodious warble.

Habitat: Open farmlands with scattered trees.

Nesting: 4–6 pale blue eggs in a loose cup of grasses and plant stems in natural tree cavities, old woodpecker holes, fence posts, and bird boxes.

Range: East of the Rockies from southern Canada to the Gulf of Mexico and as far as the mountains of central Mexico.

This beautiful bird is a favorite of many people and is eagerly awaited in the spring after a long, cold winter. In places where Bluebird nest-boxes are erected and Starlings and House Sparrows are controlled, up to six pairs of bluebirds will nest on as many acres. In the past 25 years bluebirds have become uncommon in the East for reasons not altogether clear. Competition for nest sites may be a critical factor.

441 Mountain Bluebird
(*Sialia currucoides*)
Thrushes (Turdidae)

Description: 7″ (18 cm). Male pure sky blue above, paler blue below, with a white abdomen; female similar but duller and grayer.

Voice: Soft warbling notes.

Habitat: Breeds in high mountain meadows with scattered trees and bushes; in winter descends to lower elevations, where it occurs on plains and grasslands.

Nesting: 5 or 6 pale blue eggs, in a nest of grass and plant fibers in a natural cavity or bird box.

Range: Southern Alaska, Mackenzie, and Manitoba south to western Nebraska, New Mexico, Arizona, and southern California; winters from British Columbia and Montana south through the western United States to central Mexico.

This species has longer wings and a more graceful, swallow-like flight than the Eastern Bluebird. In eastern North America, it is known mainly as a winter visitor to the western plains. These birds usually travel in small parties, and search for food by hovering in the air and dropping down to pick up insects on the ground.

467 Western Kingbird
(Tyrannus verticalis)
Tyrant Flycatchers (Tyrannidae)

Description: 9" (23 cm). Robin-sized. Pale gray
above, yellow below with white throat;
black tail edged with white.

Voice: Noisy chattering and twittering; also a
sharp *whit.*

Habitat: Open country; ranches, roadsides,
streams, and ponds with trees.

Nesting: 4 creamy white eggs in a stick nest
lined with plant fibers and placed in a
tree or bush.

Range: British Columbia, Manitoba, and
Minnesota, south to Kansas, Oklahoma,
and northern Mexico. Winters mainly
in Central America.

Like the Horned Lark, the Western
Kingbird has benefited from the
cutting of forests; the species has moved
eastward in recent decades. During fall
migration a few are always seen along
the Atlantic Coast. In the Southwest,
especially in arid regions, there are two
other kingbirds, Cassin's and Tropical,
that look like the Western; however,
the Western is distinguished by white
feathers on the sides of the black tail.

510 Wheatear
(Oenanthe oenanthe)
Thrushes (Turdidae)

Description: 5½–6" (14–15 cm). A very rare,
sparrow-sized bird of open ground.
Warm brown above, buff-pink below;
bold white rump and sides of tail contrast
with black center and tip of tail, which
form an inverted "T."

Voice: Harsh *chak-chak!;* song a jumble of
warbling notes.

Habitat: Barren pastures and beaches in winter;
nests in rocky tundra.

Nesting: 5–7 pale green eggs in a fur-lined cup
of grass concealed under a rock, in a

rabbit burrow, or in a crevice in a wall.

Range: Alaska, Greenland, and northern Canada, appearing very rarely in northern U.S. Also in Eurasia and North Africa.

This Old World species has recently colonized North America from two directions, Siberian birds entering Alaska and European birds crossing to Greenland. Each fall these birds retrace their routes, wintering in Africa where many of the 17 other species of wheatears are found. Occasionally one turns up in populated parts of North America in spring and fall. The scientific name *Oenanthe* is from the Ancient Greek meaning "wine-flower," alluding to the fact that these birds return to Greece in the spring just as the vineyards blossom.

515, 570 Brewer's Blackbird
(*Euphagus cyanocephalus*)
Orioles, Blackbirds (Icteridae)

Description: 8–10″ (20–25 cm). Robin-sized. Male is solid black with purplish-blue iridescent head and yellow eyes. Female is gray with dark eyes. Similar to Rusty Blackbird, but male Rusty has green reflections on head; female Rusty has yellow eyes and jerks its head as it walks.

Voice: Gurgles, squawks, and whistles.

Habitat: Prairies, fields, and farm yards.

Nesting: 3–5 gray eggs with dark brown spots in a nest of coarse grass and twigs reinforced with mud and lined with fine grass and hair, placed on the ground or in a tree. Forms loose colonies of up to 30 pairs.

Range: British Columbia and Manitoba east to the Great Lakes and south to Indiana, Texas, and northern Mexico. Winters north to Tennessee and southern British Columbia.

This blackbird, named for 19th century ornithologist Dr. Thomas M. Brewer of Boston, is best known as a winter visitor to stockyards and farms, where it feeds on spilled grain. It also takes insects that are stirred up by livestock and plows. It nests in hayfields, but its young are usually fledged before the hay is harvested. During breeding season it has an elaborate display that includes fluffing out the feathers, wing quivering, cocking the tail, and pointing the bill upward.

517, 574 Bronzed Cowbird
"Red-eyed Cowbird"
(Molothrus aeneus)
Orioles, Blackbirds (Icteridae)

Description: 8½" (21 cm). Sexes similar; bronze-black with bluish-black wings and tail. Prominent red eye can be seen at close range. Brown-headed Cowbird smaller with a distinctive brown head.

Voice: Wheezy and guttural whistling notes and various squeaks and squeals.

Habitat: Pastures, roadside thickets, ranches, open country generally; also parks and orchards.

Nesting: 1–3 blue-green eggs laid in other birds' nests, particularly nests of orioles, tanagers, flycatchers, buntings, and grosbeaks, more rarely thrashers and thrushes.

Range: Southern portions of Arizona, New Mexico, and south central Texas through Mexico and Central America to western Panama.

Until recently called "Red-eyed Cowbird." During courtship both sexes, especially the males, erect their neck feathers into a ruff. The males bow and jump up and down, whistling unmusical squeaky calls. Like their close relatives, the Brown-headed Cowbirds, these birds follow livestock, especially cattle, snapping up insects flushed from the grass. They alight on the backs and necks of livestock to feed on ticks. Cowbirds also feed extensively on seeds and grain. During the colder months these birds form enormous flocks and move around the countryside with other species of blackbirds.

527 Lark Sparrow
(*Chondestes grammacus*)
Grosbeaks, Buntings, Finches, Sparrows (Fringillidae)

Description: 5½–6½" (14–16 cm). Head boldly patterned with black, chestnut, and white; streaked above; white below with a black spot in the center of the breast; tail black with white edges.

Voice: Alternating buzzes and melodious trills.

Habitat: Grassland with scattered bushes and trees; open country generally in winter.

Nesting: 3–5 white eggs, heavily spotted with dark brown and black, in a well-made cup of grass and plant stems on the ground or in a bush.

Range: British Columbia, Saskatchewan, northern Minnesota, and southern Ontario to Alabama, Louisiana, and northern Mexico. Winters from the Gulf Coast and California south to El Salvador. It has long been recorded along the eastern seaboard in fall.

The easiest way to find Lark Sparrows is to drive through grasslands and watch for the birds to fly up into trees along the road. The nests of Mockingbirds have been found with the eggs of both species in them, but it is not clear whether the sparrows have simply taken over an abandoned nest or have driven away the original occupants; since Mockingbirds are very aggressive, the latter seems unlikely.

531 **Tree Sparrow**
(*Spizella arborea*)
Grosbeaks, Buntings, Finches,
Sparrows (Fringillidae)

Description: 5½–6½" (14–16 cm). Gray head with
rufous crown and ear-stripe; streaked
brown above; plain gray below with
dark spot in center of breast. Similar to
Field Sparrow but larger and without
white eye-ring or pink bill.

Voice: One or two clear notes followed by a
sweet, rapid warble. Winter feeding call
a silvery *tsee-ler.*

Habitat: Arctic willow and birch thickets, fields,
weedy woodland edges, and roadside
thickets in winter.

Nesting: 4 or 5 pale blue eggs speckled with
brown in a bulky, well-insulated cup of
bark strips and weed stems lined with
feathers and hair, concealed in low
tundra vegetation.

Range: Alaska, northern Saskatchewan, northern
Manitoba, and northern Quebec south to
Newfoundland, central Quebec, and
British Columbia. Winters regularly
south to the Carolinas, Arkansas, and
California.

This northern species is a winter
visitor. Unlike northern finches such as
siskins and crossbills, its number seems
to depend on weather, not on the food
supply—the birds are less numerous in
mild winters. They roam the snow-
covered landscape in flocks, uttering
tinkling calls and often visiting feeders.

532 **Field Sparrow**
(*Spizella pusilla*)
Grosbeaks, Buntings, Finches,
Sparrows (Fringillidae)

Description: 5¼" (13 cm). The combination of the
bright pink bill, rufous cap, white eye-ring,
and unstreaked buff breast distinguishes
it from other sparrows.

Voice: Series of soft, plaintive notes, all on the
same pitch, accelerating to a trill at the
end.

Habitat: Abandoned fields and pastures grown
up to weeds, scattered bushes, and
small saplings.

Nesting: 4 pale green, brown-spotted eggs in a
woven cup-shaped nest of grass lined
with rootlets or fine grass and set on or
near the ground.

Range: Breeds from northern North Dakota,
central Minnesota, northern Wisconsin
and central New England south to
Georgia, Mississippi, Louisiana, and
central Texas. Winters south to the
Gulf of Mexico and northeastern
Mexico.

When farms and pastures become
overgrown with weeds and bushes,
birds such as Field Sparrows and Indigo
Buntings move in and nest. Although
shyer than its close relative the Chipping
Sparrow—and thus more difficult to
observe—it may be studied at leisure
when it sings its sweet plaintive song
from a conspicuous perch atop a bush or
fence post. During fall migration it may
be seen among flocks of mixed sparrows.

535 Clay-colored Sparrow
(*Spizella pallida*)
Grosbeaks, Buntings, Finches,
Sparrows (Fringillidae)

Description: 5–5½″ (13–14 cm). A small sparrow
with streaked crown and upperparts and
clear gray breast; similar to an immature
Chipping Sparrow but brighter, with
rump buff-brownish instead of lead
gray, sides of neck gray, and buff cheek
patch bordered above and below with
black. Grasshopper Sparrow has buff
underparts.

Voice: Series of four or five toneless, insect-like
buzzes.

Habitat: Brushy grasslands and prairies.

Nesting: 3–5 pale blue eggs spotted with dark
           brown in a bulky cup of hair-lined grass
           placed in a bush or clump of weeds up
           to six feet above the ground.

Range: North-central Canada and Illinois south
           to Nebraska and Montana; occasionally
           east to western New York. Winters
           regularly north to southern Texas and
           New Mexico.

This western relative of the Chipping
Sparrow has been gradually extending
its range eastward and now breeds in
the eastern Great Lakes region. Each
spring and fall a few individuals, most
of them immatures, appear on the
eastern seaboard, where they can be
difficult to distinguish from immature
Chipping Sparrows. Such strays often
associate with flocks of Chipping
Sparrows.

536   Grasshopper Sparrow
(*Ammodramus savannarum*)
Grosbeaks, Buntings, Finches,
Sparrows (Fringillidae)

Description: 4½–5″ (11–13 cm). A small, chunky
               grassland sparrow with a *clear buff breast*
               and dark rufous, scaly upperparts; has
               pale central stripe on crown; tail short
               and pointed.

Voice: A high-pitched, insect-like *kip-kip-kip,
               zeeee,* usually uttered from the top of a
               weedstalk.

Habitat: Open grassy and weedy meadows,
               pastures, and plains.

Nesting: 4 or 5 white eggs speckled with red-
               brown in a cup of grass, often domed,
               lined with rootlets and hair.

Range: British Columbia, Manitoba, and New
               Hampshire south to Florida, the West
               Indies, and Mexico. Winters north to
               North Carolina, Texas, and California.

This elusive sparrow—named for its
buzzy song—is sensitive to subtle

changes in its habitat. As soon as a weedy field grows up or trees have filled in abandoned pastures, it no longer uses them as breeding sites. In other parts of the country it chooses different habitats, such as palmetto grasslands in Florida. Less of a seed-eater than our other grass sparrows, it feeds largely on insects.

537 Henslow's Sparrow
(*Passerherbulus henslowii*)
Grosbeaks, Buntings, Finches,
Sparrows (Fringillidae)

Description: 5″ (13 cm). Dull olive-green head, red-brown back and necklace of streaks on the breast.

Voice: Explosive, two-note sneeze, *tsi-lick.*

Habitat: Local in moist or dry grassland with scattered weeds and small shrubs.

Nesting: 4 whitish, brown-spotted eggs in a woven grass nest on the ground, usually in a grass clump.

Range: Northeastern United States south to east-central, wintering in the Gulf and south Atlantic states.

This sparrow is secretive and mouse-like, skulking low in the grass. It relies on running rather than flying, and is seldom observed unless perched atop some weed stalk uttering its insect-like "song." These birds are sometimes found in loose colonies of up to a dozen pairs, but one to three pairs are more common. Curiously, it may be present in a certain locality and absent from a seemingly similar habitat not far away. It was named for John Henslow, prominent early 19th century English botanist.

Baird's Sparrow
(*Ammodramus bairdii*)
Grosbeaks, Buntings, Finches,
Sparrows (Fringillidae)

Description: 5–5½" (13–14 cm). A pale, streaked
sparrow, whitish below, breast crossed
by a band of narrow black streaks;
bright ocher crown stripe.

Voice: Three short notes followed by a musical
trill on a lower pitch.

Habitat: Dry upland prairies.

Nesting: 3–5 white eggs blotched and scrawled
with dark brown in a cup of weed stems
and grass concealed in grass or weeds on
the ground.

Range: Saskatchewan and Manitoba south to
Minnesota and Montana. Winters in
Texas, Arizona, and northern Mexico.

These elegant grass sparrows were first
described in 1844 by Audubon, who
named it after Spencer F. Baird, 19th
century ornithologist and Secretary of
the Smithsonian Institution. The total
population is small, and once they leave
the breeding grounds they are difficult
to find. Even on their breeding
grounds, one must search hard for the
habitat that suits them. Here a few
singing males can be found, usually
perched on the tip of weed stalks.

Cassin's Sparrow
(*Aimophila cassinii*)
Grosbeaks, Buntings, Finches,
Sparrows (Fringillidae)

Description: 5" (13 cm). A drab, nondescript
sparrow with finely streaked crown and
back, plain buff-white underparts, and
gray rump and tail.

Voice: Musical trill preceded and followed by
one or more clear notes, usually given
in flight.

Habitat: Sparsely vegetated country; barren
rocky areas with scattered cacti and

yuccas, and short grass. It uses such plants, as well as fence posts and wires, as song perches.

Nesting: 4 white eggs in a deep cup of plant fiber and grass lined with hair and set on the ground in a grass clump or at the base of a bush or a cactus.

Range: From Colorado and Kansas to northern Mexico.

This secretive species, like nearly all grass-inhabiting birds, is difficult to study. It is named for John Cassin, an early 19th century ornithologist at the Philadelphia Academy of Natural Sciences.

---

538 Le Conte's Sparrow
(*Passerherbulus caudacutus*)
Grosbeaks, Buntings, Finches, Sparrows (Fringillidae)

Description: 5″ (13 cm). Similar to the Sharp-tailed Sparrow of the Great Plains, but crown stripe is white instead of gray; *wide reddish collar* on nape and upper back.

Voice: Two very thin, insect-like hisses.

Habitat: Moist grassland and boggy meadows; also dry fields in winter.

Nesting: 4 whitish, brown-spotted eggs in a grass cup lined with hair and set on the ground, usually in a grass clump.

Range: South-central Canada to north-central United States. Winters in the central and southern states.

This elusive bird keeps to the thick grass like all grass-loving sparrows except when it mounts an exposed perch to sing. It is almost impossible to flush, for it prefers running to flying. Common in the prairie regions of the Midwest, it inhabits the drier grass borders of rush-grown marshes. It was named for Major John Le Conte of Georgia, an early American naturalist (1818–1891).

545 Dickcissel
(*Spiza americana*)
Grosbeaks, Buntings, Finches,
Sparrows (Fringillidae)

Description: 6" (15 cm). Male like *miniature
Meadowlark* (yellow breast with black
"V") but has a heavy bill and a *chestnut
wing patch.* Female much like female
House Sparrow, but with narrow
streaks along the sides, and yellowish
throat and breast.

Voice: Song sounds like *dick-dick-cissel,* the
first two notes being sharp sounds
followed by a buzzy, almost hissed
cissel, repeated over and over again from
a conspicuous perch on a fence, bush,
or weed.

Habitat: Open country in grain or hay fields and
in weed patches.

Nesting: 4 or 5 pale blue eggs in a cup of plant
stems and grass set on or near the
ground, often in alfalfa and clover
fields.

Range: Chiefly in the north-central states south
to the Gulf states. Winters from
Mexico to northern South America.

Formerly common in farming regions of
the eastern states, especially on the
Atlantic coastal plain, it disappeared
from that region by the middle of the
last century and is now most numerous
in the Midwest. It appears in small
numbers on the east coast during the
fall migration and rarely but regularly
in winter at feeders, often with House
Sparrows.

546 Water Pipit
(*Anthus spinoletta*)
Pipits (Motacillidae)

Description: 6–7" (15–17 cm). Sparrow-sized. A
slender brown bird of open country.
Often wags its tail and usually walks
rather than hops. Crown and upperparts

a cup of grass lined with fur and
feathers and concealed among rocks or
in tundra vegetation.

Range: Aleutians, northern Alaska and
Greenland south to northern Quebec
and central Alaska. Winters regularly
to Pennsylvania and Oregon.

This circumpolar bird, often called
"Snowflake," breeds farther north than
almost any other land bird. In severe
winters large flocks descend to our
northern states, where they favor the
most barren places. They can be found
at beach parking lots in the dead of
winter searching for weed seeds.

548 Savannah Sparrow
including "Ipswich Sparrow"
(*Passerculus sandwichensis*)
Grosbeaks, Buntings, Finches,
Sparrows (Fringillidae)

Description: 4½–6″ (11–15 cm). Pale and streaked,
with a bright yellow eyebrow and flesh-
colored legs. Tail notched; other
grassland sparrows have shorter, more
pointed tails.
Voice: High-pitched, buzzy *tsip-tsip-tsip-se-e-e-
srr.*
Habitat: Fields, prairies, salt marshes, and
grassy dunes.
Nesting: 4–6 pale blue-green eggs, variably
spotted and speckled with dark brown,
in a cup of grass lined with finer plant
material and hair.
Range: Aleutians, Alaska, Mackenzie, and
Labrador south to New Jersey,
Missouri, and northern Mexico.
Winters regularly north to
Massachusetts and southeastern Alaska.

This most abundant and familiar of the
grass sparrows shows a great deal of
color variation over its wide range. One
larger and paler form that breeds at
Sable Island, Nova Scotia, was until

recently considered a separate species, the "Ipswich Sparrow." These birds are able runners; once discovered, they drop into the grass and dart away. In the fall they migrate southward in huge numbers and may then be found almost anywhere—even in city parks.

549, 566 Lark Bunting
(*Calamospiza melanocorys*)
Grosbeaks, Buntings, Finches,
Sparrows (Fringillidae)

Description: 6–7½" (15–19 cm). Sparrow-sized. Male black with conspicuous *white wing patches,* most evident in flight. Female duller and streaked with brown, but also shows much white in wings. Usually seen in flocks.

Voice: Long, varied series of trills. Call a soft *hoo-ee.*

Habitat: Open plains and fields.

Nesting: 4–6 pale blue eggs, usually unmarked, in a loose cup of twigs and grass often lined with hair and placed on the ground under a clump of weeds or grass.

Range: Breeds from British Columbia, Manitoba, and Minnesota south to Texas and New Mexico. Winters from southern Texas and Arizona to central Mexico.

Usually seen in large flocks feeding along roadsides. On the breeding grounds they are quite gregarious, several pairs crowding into a few acres of suitable habitat. Since there are few elevated song perches in their grassland breeding area, males advertise their presence with a conspicuous song flight. Often one can see several singing males in the air at one time, providing watchers an easy way to locate a nesting colony. Like many seed-eating birds, they supplement their summer diet with insects.

550 Vesper Sparrow
(*Pooecetes gramineus*)
Grosbeaks, Buntings, Finches,
Sparrows (Fringillidae)

Description: 5–6½" (13–16 cm). A grayish, streaked
sparrow with *white outer tail feathers,
narrow white eye-ring,* and a small patch
of chestnut on the bend of the wing.

Voice: Slow series of four clear musical notes,
the last two higher, ending in a
descending series of trills—sometimes
rendered as *come-come-where-where-all-
together-down-the-hill.*

Habitat: Fields, pastures, and roadsides in
farming country.

Nesting: 4–6 white eggs heavily spotted with
brown in a well-made cup of grass and
rootlets concealed in grass on the
ground.

Range: British Columbia, Ontario, and Nova
Scotia south to the Carolinas, Texas,
Colorado and California. Winters from
New England to the Gulf Coast and
Mexico.

The rich, musical song of this sparrow
is a most distinctive sound on rolling
farmlands. Long known as the "Bay-
winged Bunting," the bird was given
the pleasing if somewhat inappropriate
name Vesper Sparrow by the naturalist
John Burroughs, who thought the song
sounded more melodious in the evening.
The bird is usually found on the ground
but often mounts to an exposed perch
to deliver its song.

551 Lapland Longspur
(*Calcarius lapponicus*)
Grosbeaks, Buntings, Finches,
Sparrows (Fringillidae)

Description: 6–7" (15–17 cm). Sparrow-sized. *The
only longspur in most of the East.* Breeding
male has black face, crown, and upper
breast; chestnut nape; streaked

above and white below with streaked
flanks. Female and winter male dull
and without bold pattern; best identifie
by largely black tail with white
outermost tail feathers. Smith's
Longspur has a similar tail but is alway
buff above and below and usually show
a small white wing patch.

Voice: Rattling call. Flight song is sweet and
bubbling.

Habitat: Arctic tundra; winters in open
windswept fields and on grassy coastal
dunes. Often found on parking lots
along the coast in winter.

Nesting: 4 or 5 pale olive-green eggs heavily
spotted with brown and purple in a
grass-lined hollow in the ground and
concealed under a clump of grass or a
dwarf birch.

Range: Aleutians, northern Alaska, the Arctic
islands, and Greenland to northern
Quebec and southern Alaska. Winters
regularly to New York and California.
Also in northern Eurasia.

This species is the only one of four
longspurs that is found in both
hemispheres. Like other longspurs, it is
almost invisible on the ground; often a
whole flock will dart into the air at an
observer's feet, only to disappear again
when they land on bare ground a few
hundred yards away.

552 **Chestnut-collared Longspur**
(*Calcarius ornatus*)
Grosbeaks, Buntings, Finches,
Sparrows (Fringillidae)

Description: 5½–6½" (14–16 cm). Sparrow-sized.
Similar to the Lapland Longspur, but
breeding male has *wholly black
underparts* and some white on its face.
Tail of female and winter male similar
to that of Lapland Longspur but with
more white at sides.

Voice: Soft, sweet, and tumbling, somewhat

like the Western Meadowlark.
Habitat: Dry elevated prairies and short-grass
plains.
Nesting: 3–5 pale green eggs spotted with
brown and lavender in a grass-lined
hollow under a clump of grass.
Range: Alberta and Manitoba south to
Minnesota and Wyoming. Winters
from Colorado and Kansas south to
Texas and northern Mexico.

The upland prairies favored for nesting
have been extensively planted in wheat,
so these longspurs are much less
numerous than formerly. They need
only a small area, however, and often
several pairs will crowd into a patch of
land or even the narrow strips of
unplowed grassland along highways.
Here the males can be seen singing
from the tops of fence posts, rocks, or
tall weed stalks.

553 McCown's Longspur
(*Calcarius mccownii*)
Grosbeaks, Buntings, Finches,
Sparrows (Fringillidae)

Description: 5¾–6" (14–16 cm). Sparrow-sized.
Breeding male streaked above with
black crown, whitish face, and black
mustache; gray below with a bold black
band across breast. Female and winter
male duller and more streaked; best
identified by tail pattern, which is
largely white with central pair of tail
feathers black and with narrow black
band at tip.
Voice: Dry rattle; also a clear sweet warble
given during a fluttering flight with
wings raised high over back.
Habitat: Arid plains.
Nesting: 3 or 4 pale green eggs spotted with
dark brown and black in a hollow
scrape lined with fine grass and hair on
open ground.
Range: Alberta, western Manitoba, and

southwestern Manitoba south to the Dakotas, Wyoming, and Colorado. Winters from Nebraska and Colorado south to northern Mexico.

This longspur nests in higher and more arid short-grass plains than does the Chestnut-collared Longspur, and so has been less affected by plowing of the prairie. They so dislike moisture that in wet seasons they may abandon areas where they normally are abundant. In summer they feed chiefly on grasshoppers, but in fall and winter, when they gather in large flocks with other longspurs and with Horned Larks, they prefer seeds. In winter plumage they can be difficult to distinguish from the other longspurs, but close up they are easily identified by their stouter bill.

554 Smith's Longspur
(*Calcarius pictus*)
Grosbeaks, Buntings, Finches, Sparrows (Fringillidae)

Description: 5¾–6½″ (15–16 cm). Sparrow-sized. Breeding male streaked dark brown and buff above, clear warm buff below; bold black-and-white head pattern. Small white wing patch most evident in flight; tail black, with white outer feathers. Females and winter males duller and without head pattern, but always much buffier than other longspurs.

Voice: Dry rattle, like running a finger along the teeth of a comb.

Habitat: Arctic tundra and forest edge; winters on open grassy plains.

Nesting: 3–5 pale brown eggs spotted with darker brown, in a grass-walled hollow lined with plant down and feathers and concealed under a clump of grass or a dwarf willow.

Range: Northern Alaska across northern

Canada to Hudson Bay. Winters from Nebraska south to Texas.

Longspur identification is difficult in the Midwest, where all four species winter, but this species, clad in warm buff the year around, can be told at a glance. At times they are found in huge flocks moving over the dry winter grasslands in search of seeds, uttering a distinctive clinking call. On the Arctic tundra they seem to prefer drier, more elevated areas than does the Lapland Longspur.

555, 567 Bobolink
(*Dolichonyx oryzivorus*)
Orioles, Blackbirds (Icteridae)

Description: 6–8″ (15–20 cm). Larger than a House Sparrow. Breeding male largely black with *white rump* and back, *dull yellow nape.* Female and winter male rich buff-yellow, streaked on back and crown. *Short, finch-like bill.* Female Red-winged Blackbird is darker, less buffy, and has a longer bill.

Voice: Flight song is a series of joyous, bubbling, tumbling, gurgling phrases with each note on a different pitch. Call a soft *pink,* often heard on migration.

Habitat: Prairies and meadows; marshes during migration.

Nesting: 4–7 eggs spotted with red-brown and purple; in a poorly made but well-concealed cup of grass, stems, and rootlets placed on the ground in a field.

Range: Breeds from British Columbia, Manitoba, and Newfoundland south to Pennsylvania, Colorado, and northern California. Winters in southern South America.

The Bobolink was probably confined to the central grasslands originally, but with the settling of the Northeast it quickly spread into New England.

Now, with farms abandoned and the land returning to forest, the species is declining. Each fall, migrant Bobolink used to gather in large numbers in southern rice fields, where their habit eating grain earned them the name "Ricebird."

---

556 **Horned Lark**
(*Eremophila alpestris*)
Larks (Alaudidae)

Description: 7–8″ (17–20 cm). Larger than a sparrow. Brown, with *black stripe below eye, black crescent on breast, and black "horns"* (not always seen). Walks rather than hops. In flight, tail seen as black with white edges. Similar-looking pipits have brown tails and lack the fac pattern.

Voice: *Ti-ti.* Song delivered in flight is a high pitched series of tinkling notes.

Habitat: Plains, fields, airports, and beaches.

Nesting: 3–5 brown-spotted gray eggs in a hollow in the ground lined with fine grass.

Range: Arctic south to North Carolina, Missouri, coastal Texas, and northern South America. Also in Eurasia and North Africa.

The only true lark in the New World, this is one of our earliest nesting birds. Even in the northern states, nests may be found in February, when the first se of eggs is often destroyed by severe snowstorms. As many as three broods are raised each year. The species favors the most barren habitats; as soon as thick grass begins to grow in an area, the birds abandon it. In the fall they roam over the open countryside in large flocks, often in company with pipits, longspurs, and Snow Buntings.

577 Smooth-billed Ani
(Crotophaga ani)
Cuckoos (Cuculidae)

Description: 14″ (35 cm). Jay-sized. Black, with a very long tail half the length of the bird. Huge bill with arched ridge.

Voice: Slurred double note with a rising inflection that has a whining, metallic quality; quite different from that of the Groove-billed Ani.

Habitat: Open agricultural country, often near cattle or other livestock; also found in scrub and thickets.

Nesting: 3–5 blue-green (often stained) eggs in a bulky stick nest in dense vegetation. Probably polygamous.

Range: Southern Florida; also from the West Indies and Mexico to South America.

These birds have some peculiar traits. Usually several females lay eggs in a single nest, deposited in layers separated more or less by leaves or grass. Up to 30 eggs have been found in one nest. Those at the bottom do not hatch. The females share incubation, often two or more simultaneously. Anis prefer open, cultivated country. They often alight on the backs of cattle to remove ticks.

582 White-necked Raven
(Corvus cryptoleucus)
Jay, Magpies, Crows (Corvidae)

Description: 19–21″ (48–53 cm). Crow-sized. Similar to the Common Raven but somewhat smaller. White bases to feathers of neck and breast seldom seen. Best told by voice.

Voice: Harsh *kraak,* higher-pitched than the Common Raven's.

Habitat: Arid grasslands and mesquite; plains and deserts.

Nesting: 5–7 dull green eggs spotted and streaked with brown and purple. Nest a loose mass of thorny sticks lined with grass, moss, and bark strips and placed in an exposed tree or on a telephone pole.

Range: Central Texas, New Mexico, and Arizona south into Mexico. Winters north to the United States border.

It replaces the Common Raven at lower elevations, and in our part of its range is the only raven likely to be seen. More gregarious than its larger northern relative, many are often found at garbage dumps. The birds gather in noisy and conspicuous roosts. During the breeding season, however, they are not social, pairs nesting in widely spaced territories.

City Parks and Suburban Areas

Areas much modified by man,
including lawns, gardens, parks, well-
planted residential areas, as well as
vacant lots, industrial areas, and urban
districts. The birds treated here are all
very tolerant of such disturbed habitats.
During migration, these areas may be
visited briefly by birds of a variety of
habitats; ducks and geese may stop off
on ponds and reservoirs, and warblers,
vireos, orioles, flycatchers, and sparrows
may frequent trees and shrubbery. In
winter, finches, chickadees, nuthatches,
and woodpeckers may turn up at
feeders, and owls may be found in
groves of pines or cedars.

322 **Mourning Dove**
(*Zenaida macroura*)
Pigeons, Doves (Columbidae)

Description: 12″ (30 cm). Soft, sandy buff with a
long, pointed tail bordered with white.
Voice: Low, mournful (hence its name) *coo-ah*
coo, coo, coo.
Habitat: Open fields, parks, and lawns with
many trees and shrubs.
Nesting: 2 white eggs in a loosely made nest of
sticks and twigs in low bushes and tall
trees, more rarely on the ground.
Range: Southern Alaska, British Columbia,
Saskatchewan, Ontario, Quebec, and
New Brunswick to Panama and the
West Indies. Winters north to northern
United States.

This abundant bird has benefited from
man's cutting the forest and burning of
the grass. It is common in rural areas in
all parts of the United States, as well as
city parks and, in winter, suburban
feeders. In some states it is hunted as a
gamebird while in others it is protected
as a "songbird." Its species name
macroura is Greek for "long-tailed."
The young are fed regurgitated,
partially digested food known as pigeon
milk.

323 **Ringed Turtle Dove**
(*Streptopelia risoria*)
Pigeons, Doves (Columbidae)

Description: 12″ (30 cm). A slender, pale sandy dove
with a narrow black collar on the
hindneck and a rounded, not pointed,
tail. Mourning Dove similar but darker
with pointed tail and no collar.
Voice: Soft mellow *kooo-krooo,* rising and then
falling in pitch.
Habitat: City parks, suburban areas, usually
where trees are present.
Nesting: 2 white eggs in a flimsy saucer of twigs
and grass on a window ledge or in a
dovecote.

Range: Introduced and established in the
vicinity of Miami and Tampa, Florida,
and in many other cities in the world.

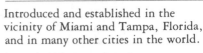

This dove has been domesticated for so
long that no one is sure which wild
species is its ancestor, although it is
thought to be an African species.
During its centuries in captivity it has
become adapted to living with man,
and is unsuccessful in rural areas. Even
today, its pleasing call makes it a
favorite cage bird.

327 Rock Dove
(*Columba livia*)
Pigeons, Doves (Columbidae)

Description: 13½" (34 cm). Chunky, with a short,
rounded tail. Generally bluish-gray
with two narrow black wing bands and
a broad black terminal tail band; *white
rump*.
Voice: Soft, guttural cooing.
Habitat: City parks, suburban gardens, and
farmland.
Nesting: 2 white eggs in a crude nest lined with
sticks and debris placed on cliffs,
buildings, and bridges.
Range: Native and resident in much of the
temperate and subtropical regions of
the Old World north of the Equator.
Introduced into many other parts of the
world and now widely established
through much of North America.

Everyone knows the Rock Dove or
domestic pigeon as a city bird,
subsisting on handouts, or nesting in
the country in pigeon cotes on farms.
Few have seen them nesting in their
ancestral home—cliff ledges or high
among the rocks. Over centuries, many
varieties and color strains have been
developed in captivity through selective
breeding. Since they have been accused

of carrying human diseases, there have been several attempts to eradicate them from our cities; but they are so prolific that little progress has been made toward this end.

332, 336   **Purple Martin**
(*Progne subis*)
Swallows (Hirundinidae)

Description: 7–8½" (18–21 cm). Bluebird-sized. Our largest swallow. Adult male dark steel-blue. Female and immature male duller above, pale gray below. Overhead similar in shape to Starling but flight more buoyant and gliding.

Voice: Liquid, gurgling warble. Also a penetrating *tee-tee-tee*.

Habitat: Open woodland, residential areas, and agricultural land.

Nesting: 4 or 5 white eggs in a mass of grass and other plant material placed in a natural cavity—sometimes a hole in a tree but more often in a "martin house" with many separate compartments, where the birds nest in a colony.

Range: Breeds from British Columbia, Manitoba, and Nova Scotia south to the West Indies and central Mexico. Winters in South America.

The custom of erecting a martin house to attract these beneficial birds was practiced by the early settlers and, before them, by the southern Indian tribes, who hung clusters of hollow gourds in trees near their gardens. In other areas the species nested in tall dead trees riddled with woodpecker holes, but these original colonies never reached the size—as many as 200 pairs—of colonies found in large martin houses today.

335 Chimney Swift
(*Chaetura pelagica*)
Swifts (Apodidae)

Description: 5½" (14 cm). Sparrow-sized. Stubby,
brownish-gray body (appearing black in
flight) with very short tail; long, narrow,
curved wings.

Voice: Loud, chattering twitters.

Habitat: Breeds and roosts in chimneys; feeds
entirely on the wing.

Nesting: 4 or 5 white eggs in a nest made of
twigs cemented together with the bird's
saliva and fastened to the inner wall of a
chimney or, rarely, in a cave or hollow
tree.

Range: Eastern North America, breeding from
southeastern Saskatchewan, southern
Manitoba, central Ontario, southern
Quebec, Nova Scotia, south to the Gulf
states. Winters in the upper Amazon
basin.

Members of this family are among the
fastest fliers in the bird world. Swifts
spend all of their daylight hours on the
wing and only come to rest at evening.
They feed exclusively on flying insects.
They drink water and bathe by dipping
into the water of a pond or river as they
fly over it. Since they never perch, they
gather twigs in flight, snapping them
off with their bill or feet as they pass.
Sometimes a twig fails to break and the
bird is tossed backward, only to return
again. They gather in communal roosts
in air shafts or large chimneys, often
whirling in a huge circle as they funnel
down for the night. Their winter range
was unknown until recently when a few
banded swifts were recovered from the
Amazon Valley in Peru.

348   Common Flicker
including "Yellow-shafted Flicker"
and "Red-shafted Flicker"
(*Colaptes auratus*)
Woodpeckers (Picidae)

Description: 12″ (30 cm). A large brownish
woodpecker. *Brown back* with dark bars
and spots; *whitish below with black spots,
black crescent* on breast; *white rump* in
flight. Eastern birds have *red patch on
nape* (male has a black "mustache") and
yellow wing linings. Western birds lack
nape patch (males have red "mustache"
and salmon wing linings).

Voice: Loud, repeated *flicker* or *wicka-wicka-
wicka.* Also a loud *kleeer.*

Habitat: Open country with trees; parks and
rural estates.

Nesting: 6–8 white eggs in a tree cavity, power
pole, or bird house.

Range: Alaska, Manitoba, and Newfoundland
south to southern Florida, the Gulf
Coast, and southern Mexico. Also in
the West Indies.

Flickers are the only brown-backed
woodpeckers in the East. They are the
only woodpeckers in North America
that commonly feed on the ground,
searching for ants and beetle larvae on
lawns or even sidewalks. During
courtship and to proclaim their
territory, flickers hammer on dead
limbs or tin roofs. On the Great Plains
the "yellow-shafted" and "red-shafted"
forms meet; they interbreed, hybridize,
and are considered one species.

393, 394   Northern Oriole
including "Baltimore Oriole" and
"Bullock's Oriole"
(*Icterus galbula*)
Orioles, Blackbirds (Icteridae)

Description: 7–8½″ (18–21 cm). Eastern male,
formerly "Baltimore Oriole," has black

head, back, wings, and tail; orange breast, rump, and shoulder patch. Eastern female olive-brown with dull yellow-orange underparts and two dull white wing bars. Western male, formerly "Bullock's Oriole," is similar to eastern male but has orange cheeks and eyebrow and large white wing patch. Western female has whitish underparts.

Voice: Clear and flute-like whistled single or double notes in short, distinct phrases with much individual variation.

Habitat: Deciduous woodland and shade trees. Before its decline, the American elm was a favorite nesting site for the eastern bird.

Nesting: 4–6 grayish eggs spotted and scrawled with dark brown and black. Nest a well-woven pendant bag of plant fibers, bark, and string suspended from the tip of a branch.

Range: Breeds from British Columbia, Saskatchewan, and Nova Scotia south to Georgia, Louisiana, and northern Mexico. Winters from southern Mexico southward.

Until recently the western populations of this bird ("Bullock's Oriole") were thought to be a separate species from the eastern populations which were called the "Baltimore Oriole." When trees were planted on the Great Plains, the two forms extended their ranges and met. Despite the differences in their appearance, it was found that they interbreed freely, and most birds in the central plains are hybrids. Orioles readily accept short pieces of yarn for nesting material and apparently show no color preference.

400 **American Robin**
"Robin"
(*Turdus migratorius*)
Thrushes (Turdidae)

Description: 9–11″ (23–28 cm). Gray above, brick-red below. Head and tail black in males, dull gray in females. Young birds are spotted below.

Voice: Song is a series of rich caroling notes, rising and falling in pitch: *Cheer-up, cheerily, Cheer-up, cheerily.*

Habitat: Towns, gardens, open woodland, and agricultural land.

Nesting: 3–5 blue-green eggs in a well-made cup of mud reinforced with grass and twigs, lined with softer grasses and placed in a tree or on a ledge or windowsill; they usually have two broods a season.

Range: Alaska, Manitoba, and Newfoundland south to the Carolinas, Arkansas, and Guatemala; occasionally breeds along the Gulf Coast. Winters north to Newfoundland, southern Ontario, and British Columbia.

Robins originally nested in forests; where they still do so they are much shyer than the Robins of the dooryard. They breed only rarely in the Deep South, where they prefer large shade trees on lawns. Although usually considered a harbinger of spring, Robins often winter in the northern states, where they frequent cedar bogs and swamps and are not usually noticed by a casual observer, except when they gather in large roosts, often containing thousands of birds. As with many birds, their normal mortality rate is about 80 percent a year.

Habitat: Thickets and brush, residential areas and gardens.

Nesting: 4 or 5 glossy blue-green eggs in a bulky mass of twigs, stems, and leaves lined with finer plant material and concealed in a dense bush or in a tangle of vines.

Range: British Columbia, Manitoba, and Nova Scotia south to Florida, Texas, and Washington. Winters from the Gulf Coast and the Carolinas to Panama.

Formerly known as the "Catbird," its name has now been changed officially to Gray Catbird because there is an all-black species, the Black Catbird, in southern Mexico. It often announces its presence by a harsh, cat-like whine issuing from a dense tangle; the bird responds to an imitation of this call, popping suddenly into view for a better look. Catbirds are largely insectivorous, and their pleasing song has made them welcome in suburban gardens.

429 **Dark-eyed Junco**
including "White-winged Junco,"
"Slate-colored Junco," and
"Oregon Junco"
(*Junco hyemalis*)
Grosbeaks, Buntings, Finches,
Sparrows (Fringillidae)

Description: 5–6½" (13–16 cm). Sparrow-sized. Variable, but generally slate-gray or gray-brown above, with white abdomen sharply demarcated from gray of breast. Shows white along sides of tail in flight. Pink bill. Some birds have buff flanks.

Voice: Trill like the Chipping Sparrow but slower and with a more musical, tinkling quality. Also a soft twittering.

Habitat: Coniferous or mixed forests; winters in fields, gardens, city parks, and roadside thickets.

Nesting: 3–5 pale green, brown-spotted eggs in a deep, well-made cup of grass, moss, and strips of bark well concealed on or near the ground in vegetation in a bank or on the forest floor.

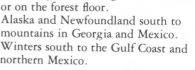

Range: Alaska and Newfoundland south to mountains in Georgia and Mexico. Winters south to the Gulf Coast and northern Mexico.

Until recently the many geographical forms of this bird were considered separate species, but since they interbreed wherever their ranges meet, they are now considered one species. The eastern form, formerly called the "Slate-colored Junco," is the only one usually encountered in the eastern states. Occasionally, however, black-headed, rusty-flanked western birds, "Oregon Juncos," may also be seen, and the "White-winged Junco" from the Black Hills in South Dakota is an accidental winter visitor. Juncos are among the commonest of our winter birds, often visiting feeders.

---

435   **Blue Jay**
(*Cyanocitta cristata*)
Jays, Magpies, Crows (Corvidae)

Description: 12" (30 cm). *Bright blue* above with much white and black in the wing and tail; white below; black facial markings; *prominent crest.*

Voice: Raucous *jay-jay,* harsh cries, and a rich variety of other calls. One is almost identical to the scream of the Red-shouldered Hawk. Also a musical *queedle-queedle.*

Habitat: Chiefly oak forest, but now also city parks and suburban yards, especially where oak trees predominate.

Nesting: 4–6 brown-spotted greenish eggs in a coarsely built nest of sticks lined with grass and well concealed in a crotch or forked branch of a tree, often a conifer.

Range: East of the Rockies, from southern Canada to the Gulf of Mexico.

Although sometimes disliked because they chase smaller birds away from feeders, Blue Jays are among our handsomest birds. They often bury seeds and acorns, and since many are never retrieved they are, in effect, tree planters. They have a violent dislike of predators, and their raucous screaming makes it easy to locate a hawk or a roosting owl. Although seen throughout the year, they are migratory and travel in large loose flocks in both spring and fall. In the East, birds from farther north replace the local population in winter.

466 **Eastern Phoebe**
(*Sayornis phoebe*)
Tyrant Flycatchers (Tyrannidae)

Description: 7″ (17 cm). Dull olive-green without an eye-ring or wing bars. *Wags its tail*.

Voice: Clear *phoe-be,* repeated many times; the second syllable is alternately higher or lower than the first. Distinctive, short *chip*.

Habitat: Open woodland near streams; cliffs, bridges, and buildings with ledges.

Nesting: 4 or 5 white eggs in a mud-and-grass nest lined with moss and hair. The nest is attached to ledges of buildings, bridges, cliffs, wells, and quarries; also under roots of fallen trees.

Range: Breeds in Canada and the United States east of the Rockies, south to the northern limits of the Gulf states. Winters from Virginia and the Gulf Coast south to Mexico.

The Phoebe arrives early in spring and departs late in fall, sometimes even staying through the winter in the northern states. In the absence of insects its winter food is berries. Phoebes are extraordinarily tame at the nest. It was probably the first bird ever banded: Audubon marked one with a

silver wire on the leg in 1840 and
recorded its return the following year.

479 **Ruby-throated Hummingbird**
(*Archilochus colubris*)
Hummingbirds (Trochilidae)

Description: 3½″ (9 cm). Tiny. Metallic green
above, white below; male has a *brilliant
red throat.* Needle-like bill.

Voice: Mouse-like twittering squeak. In flight
they make humming sounds with their
wings, which accounts for their name.

Habitat: Suburban gardens, parks, and
woodlands.

Nesting: 2 white eggs the size of large peas in a
woven nest of plant down held together
with spider silk. The nest, about 2
inches in diameter, is covered with
lichens and is saddled to the branch of a
tree, usually in a forest clearing.

Range: The only hummingbird breeding east of
the Mississippi River. Breeds from
southern Canada to the Gulf Coast.
Winters chiefly from Mexico to Panama
and north to the immediate Gulf states.

These smallest of all birds are
particularly attracted to tubular red
flowers such as salvia and trumpet
creeper, as well as bee balm, petunia,
jewelweed, and thistle. Hummers are
also attracted to artificial feeders—red
glass tubes filled with a mixture of
honey and sugar water. With their
remarkable powers of flight they are the
only birds that can fly backwards as
well as hover in one spot like an insect.
They are constantly in motion,
perching on twigs or wires only briefly
to rest and to survey their
surroundings, or when they are at the
nest. During courtship the female sits
quietly on a perch while the male
displays in a pendulum dance,
swinging in a wide arc and buzzing
loudly with each dip.

480 Rufous Hummingbird
(*Selasphorus rufus*)
Hummingbirds (Trochilidae)

Description: 3½–4" (9–10 cm). Male has bright
rufous upperparts and flanks and an
iridescent orange-red throat. Female
green above, with a rufous tinge on
rump and flanks, and with much rufous
in the tail. Female Ruby-throated
Hummingbird is similar but lacks
rufous on rump and flanks.

Voice: An abrupt, high-pitched *zeee;* various
thin, squealing notes.

Habitat: Mountain meadows, forest edges; in
migration and winter often in gardens
with hummingbird feeding stations.

Nesting: 2 white eggs in a lichen-covered cup of
plant down and spider web, attached to
a horizontal branch.

Range: Southeastern Alaska, British Columbia,
southwestern Alberta, and western
Montana south to Washington, Oregon,
Idaho and northern California. Winters
mainly in Mexico. Occurs in small
numbers along the Gulf Coast during
migration and winter, and casually in
the Carolinas.

This species is known in eastern North
America mainly as a scarce migrant and
winter visitor to Louisiana and Texas.
While in that area it feeds chiefly on
the flowers of hibiscus and salvia, which
often bloom all winter long. A few
birds generally spend the winter, but
may disappear abruptly when the first
severe cold spell arrives; it is not known
whether these birds succumb to the
cold or quickly move farther south.

484 Monk Parakeet
(*Myiopsitta monachus*)
Parrots (Psittacidae)

Description: 11" (28 cm). Bright green above and
gray below with scalloping on the

throat; primaries dark blue; tail long
and pointed.

Voice: Loud, harsh, screeching *eeeh-eeeh*.

Habitat: City parks, suburban yards, and semi-
open country.

Range: Introduced locally in the United States
Native to southern South America.

Nesting: 5 or 6 white eggs in a huge, bulky
stick nest placed in a tree or on top of
a power pole, or attached to a building
wall. The nest is domed and has
entrances to the egg chambers on the
sides and bottom.

This noisy but attractive parrot was first
reported wild in the late 1960s,
presumably having escaped from a
shipment at New York's Kennedy
Airport. Since that time it has spread to
surrounding regions. Its huge stick
nests, used both for breeding and
roosting, are conspicuous and may
contain from one to as many as six pairs
of birds. Because of its fondness for
fruits and grain, the Monk Parakeet is
now feared as a potential pest and is
being controlled by destruction of its
nests.

486 House Wren
(*Troglodytes aedon*)
Wrens (Troglodytidae)

Description: 4½–5¼″ (11–13 cm). A tiny bird with
a short tail that is often held cocked
over the back. Dusky brown above,
paler below, with no distinctive
markings. Similar Winter Wren is
smaller, darker, with a shorter tail and
a pale eyebrow.

Voice: A gurgling, bubbling, exuberant song,
first rising, then falling.

Habitat: Residential areas, city parks, farmlands,
and woodland edges.

Nesting: 5–8 white eggs, thickly speckled with
brown, in a cup lined with feathers and
other soft material contained within a

flycatchers. These social birds have the amusing habit of passing berries or even apple blossoms from one bird to the next down a long row sitting on a branch, until one bird eats the food.

516, 571 Brown-headed Cowbird
(*Molothrus ater*)
Orioles, Blackbirds (Icteridae)

Description: 6–8″ (15–20 cm). Male black with glossy brown head; female plain gray. Both have a finch-like bill.

Voice: Squeaky gurgle. Call is *check* or a rattle.

Habitat: Agricultural land, fields, woodland edges, and suburban areas.

Nesting: 4 or 5 white eggs, lightly speckled with brown, laid one at a time in the nests of other songbirds.

Range: British Columbia, central Saskatchewan, central Ontario, Quebec, and Newfoundland south to Virginia, Louisiana, and northern Mexico. Winters regularly north to Maryland, Texas, and California.

This species and the Bronzed Cowbird are the only North American songbirds that are brood parasites, laying their eggs in the nests of other birds and leaving them to the care of foster parents. Unlike parasitic Old World cuckoos, which lay eggs closely resembling those of a host species, cowbirds lay eggs in the nests of over 200 other species, most smaller than themselves. Some host species eject the unwanted egg, others lay down a new nest lining over it, but most rear the young cowbird as one of their own. It has been suggested that cowbirds became parasitic because they followed roving herds of bison and had no time to stop to nest. The young cowbird grows quickly at the expense of the young of the host, taking most of the food or pushing them out of the nest.

524 Eurasian Tree Sparrow
(*Passer montanus*)
Weaver Finches (Ploceidae)

Description: 6" (15 cm). Streaked brown above, dull white below. *Crown chocolate brown,* throat black, *cheek white with prominent black spot.* Sexes alike. The male House Sparrow is similar, but has a gray crown and lacks the black spot on the cheek.

Voice: Loud chirping, similar to that of the House Sparrow.

Habitat: City parks, suburbs, and farmland.

Nesting: 5 brown-spotted buff eggs in a tree cavity, bird box, or hole in a wall.

Range: Introduced around St. Louis, Missouri, in 1870. Native to Europe and much of Asia.

This introduced species differs from its relative, the House Sparrow, in that the sexes are alike. It is much less aggressive and quarrelsome; and it is more gregarious, often assembling in larger flocks. Altogether, it is a more attractive bird, both in appearance and behavior. These weavers sometimes visit grainfields and feed on corn, oats, and wheat, but they also consume many injurious weed seeds and, to a lesser extent, insects.

525, 526 House Sparrow
(*Passer domesticus*)
Weaver Finches (Ploceidae)

Description: 5–6½" (13–16 cm). Male has *black throat,* white cheeks, and chestnut nape; gray crown and rump. Female and young are streaked dull brown above, dingy white below, with pale eyebrow.

Voice: Shrill, monotonous, noisy chirping.

Habitat: Cities, towns, and agricultural areas.

Nesting: 5 or 6 white eggs lightly speckled with brown in a loose mass of grass, feathers, strips of paper, string, and similar

debris placed in a man-made or natural
cavity. Two to three broods a season.
Sometimes builds a globular nest in a
tree.

Range: Introduced and now found throughout
temperate North America. Native to
Eurasia and North Africa, and
introduced on all continents and on
many islands.

Wherever this species occurs it is
intimately associated with man, as its
scientific name *domesticus* suggests. The
entire North American population is
descended from a few birds released in
Central Park, New York City, in 1850.
These birds found an unoccupied
niche—the many towns and farms of
the settled parts of the country—and
quickly multiplied. As so often
happens, introduced species can become
a problem, and the House Sparrow is
no exception. Because they compete for
food and nest sites, some native species
have suffered. Although they consume
insects and weed seeds, they may do
considerable damage to crops.

530 Chipping Sparrow
(*Spizella passerina*)
Grosbeaks, Buntings, Finches,
Sparrows (Fringillidae)

Description: 5–5½" (13–14 cm). A small sparrow.
Upperparts are brown streaked with
black; underparts, sides of face, and
rump are gray; *chestnut crown; white
eyebrow* with thin black line through
eye. Young birds have streaked crown,
buff eyebrow, and duller underparts.

Voice: Thin musical trill, all on one note like
a sewing machine.

Habitat: Grassy woodland edges, gardens, city
parks, brushy pastures, and lawns.

Nesting: 3–5 pale blue eggs lightly spotted with
brown in a solid cup of grass and stems,
almost always lined with hair, placed in

shrubbery or in a tangle of vines.
Range: Breeds from the Yukon, Manitoba, and
Newfoundland south to Florida,
Nicaragua, and Baja California. Winters
from California, Tennessee, and
Maryland southward.

The bird's habit of lining its nest with
hair has earned it the name "Hairbird."
They formerly utilized horsehair, but
with the decline in the use of horses
they take any hair available and will
even pluck strands from the coat of a
sleeping dog. Originally an inhabitant
of natural clearings and brushy forest
borders, they are now found in gardens
and suburban areas and have become a
familiar songbird. During most of the
year they feed on the ground, but in
the breeding season males always sing
from an elevated perch. Their food
consists mainly of seeds, but in summer
the adults and the young feed on
insects.

542 Song Sparrow
(*Melospiza melodia*)
Grosbeaks, Buntings, Finches,
Sparrows (Fringillidae)

Description: 5–7" (13–17 cm). A common sparrow
with heavily streaked underparts and a
*large central spot on breast. Pumps its tail
in flight.*
Voice: 3 short notes followed by a varied trill,
sometimes interpreted as *Madge-Madge-
Madge, put-on-your-tea-kettle-ettle-ettle.*
Habitat: Thickets, pastures, undergrowth in
gardens, and city parks.
Nesting: 3–5 pale green, brown-spotted eggs in
a well-made cup of grass and leaves,
often lined with hair, concealed in
weeds on the ground or in a low bush.
Range: Aleutians, Alaska and Newfoundland
south to the Carolinas, North Dakota,
and Mexico. Winters from southern
Canada to the Gulf Coast and Mexico.

Probably the best known of our native
sparrows, it is found almost everywhere
in North America. Over its vast range
the species shows a great deal of
geographical variation. In Alaska and
the Aleutian Islands the birds are large,
dark, and long-billed; it is hard to
believe they are the same species as the
familiar bird of our lawns and parks.

565 Starling
(*Sturnus vulgaris*)
Starlings (Sturnidae)

Description: 7½–8½" (19–21 cm). Smaller than a
Robin. A short-tailed, chunky,
iridescent black bird; long, pointed
bill, yellow in summer and dark in
winter. Plumage flecked with white in
winter.

Voice: A series of discordant, musical,
squeaky, and rasping notes; often
imitates other birds. Call a descending
whee-ee.

Habitat: Cities, suburban areas, farmlands, and
ranches.

Nesting: 4–6 pale blue eggs in a mass of twigs,
grass, and trash lined with finer plant
material and feathers placed in a tree or
building cavity.

Range: Introduced. Occurs from Alaska and
Quebec south to the Gulf Coast and
northern Mexico. Native to Eurasia,
and introduced also in South Africa,
Australia, New Zealand, and on certain
oceanic islands.

Conditioned by centuries of living in
settled areas in Europe, it easily
adapted to American cities when 100
birds were liberated in Central Park,
New York City, in 1890. Since then it
has spread over most of the continent.
Its large roosts are often located on
buildings and may contain tens of
thousands of birds. These congregations
create much noise, foul the area, and

have proved difficult to drive away.
Starlings are aggressive birds and
compete with native species for nest
cavities and food. There has been much
debate regarding their economic value,
but their consumption of insects seems
to tip the balance in their favor.

572, 573   **Common Grackle**
(*Quiscalus quiscula*)
Orioles, Blackbirds (Icteridae)

Description: 12″ (30 cm). Blue Jay-sized. *Long
wedge-shaped tail* displaying a
longitudinal ridge or keel when in
flight. Appears all black at a distance
but is actually highly iridescent, with
colors varying from blue to purple to
green to bronze, depending on the
light. Bright yellow eyes.

Voice: Clucks. High-pitched, rising screech
like a rusty hinge.

Habitat: Lawns, parks, fields, open woodland.

Nesting: 5 pale blue eggs with black scrawls in a
bulky stick nest lined with grass,
placed anywhere from low in a bush to
high in a tree. Partly in colonies,
breeding most often in tall evergreens.

Range: Southern Canada to the Gulf states east
of the Rockies.

These familiar birds arrive from the
South early in spring and depart late in
fall. In some northern areas they
congregate by the thousands during
migration as well as in winter roosts.
Their diet is extremely varied,
including insects, crayfish, frogs, mice,
nestling birds, and eggs as well as
grains and wild fruits. At feeders they
are especially attracted to cracked corn.
They are most numerous near dwellings
and are even found raiding litter
baskets at public beaches.